New Honzons   10/13   £16.99

PLANE TRUTH

D0589624

Plane Truth

Aviation's Real Impact
on People
and the Environment

Rose Bridger

PlutoPress
www.plutobooks.com

First published 2013 by Pluto Press
345 Archway Road, London N6 5AA

www.plutobooks.com

Distributed in the United States of America exclusively by
Palgrave Macmillan, a division of St. Martin's Press LLC,
175 Fifth Avenue, New York, NY 10010

British Library Cataloguing in Publication Data
A catalogue record for this book is available from the British Library

ISBN 978 0 7453 3033 4 Hardback
ISBN 978 0 7453 3032 7 Paperback
ISBN 978 1 8496 4960 5 PDF eBook
ISBN 978 1 8496 4962 9 Kindle eBook
ISBN 978 1 8496 4961 2 EPUB eBook

Library of Congress Cataloging in Publication Data applied for

This book is printed on paper suitable for recycling and made from fully
managed and sustained forest sources. Logging, pulping and manufacturing
processes are expected to conform to the environmental standards of the
country of origin.

10 9 8 7 6 5 4 3 2 1

Typeset from disk by Curran Publishing Services Ltd, Norwich, England
Simultaneously printed digitally by CPI Antony Rowe, Chippenham, UK
and Edwards Bros in the United States of America

Contents

Acronyms

AAI	Airports Authority of India
ACI	Airports Council International
AEF	Aviation Environment Federation
AFRAA	African Airlines Association
AIP	Airport Improvement Program/Aviation Integrity Project
ASN	Aviation Safety Network
ATM	air traffic management
BA	British Airways
BOD	biological oxygen demand
CAPA	Centre for Aviation
COD	chemical oxygen demand
CTL	coal-to-liquid
CWN	Clean Water Network of Florida
EADS	European Aeronautic Defence and Space Company
EAS	Essential Air Service
EHDA	Ethiopian Horticulture Development Agency
EHPEA	Ethiopian Horticultural Producers and Exporters Association
EPA	Environmental Protection Agency
EU	European Union
EU-ETS	EU Emissions Trading Scheme
FAA	Federal Aviation Administration
FoE	Friends of the Earth
GDP	gross domestic product
GTL	gas-to-liquid
HACAN	Heathrow Association for the Control of Aircraft Noise
IATA	International Air Transport Association
ICAO	International Civil Aviation Organization
IPCC	Intergovernmental Panel on Climate Change
JRC	Joint Research Centre
kWh	kilowatt hours

LNG	liquefied natural gas
MIT	Massachusetts Institute of Technology
MRAP	mine-resistant ambush-protected (vehicle)
NARA	Northwest Advanced Renewables Alliance
NATO	North Atlantic Treaty Organization
NDC	National Disaster Committee
NGO	non-government organisation
NRDC	Natural Resources Defense Council
OMP	O'Hare Modernization Program
PPP	public–private partnership
RPK	revenue passenger kilometres
RTK	revenue tonne kilometres
RSPB	Royal Society for the Protection of Birds
SCADA	System Control and Data Acquisition
SDPH	State Department of Public Health
SIPRI	Stockholm International Peace Research Institute
STAND	Shut This Airport Nightmare Down
TEU	twenty foot equivalent units
TIACA	The International Air Cargo Association
ULD	unit load device
UN	United Nations
UNEP	UN Environment Programme
UNICEF	UN Children's Fund
US	United States
USAF	US Air Force
USDA	US Department of Agriculture
WHO	World Health Organization
WTO	World Trade Organization

Glossary

Airside Airport area involved in aircraft take-off and landing, past security checkpoints

Apron Airport area where planes are parked, loaded, unloaded and refuelled

Cabin The area in aircaft where the passengers are seated

Fuel farm An airport's aviation fuel storage and distribution facility

Fuselage The main body of an aircfaft, excluding the tail and wings

Landside The airport area before the security checks to board aircraft

Payload The total passenger or cargo capacity of an aircraft

RPK The number of passengers multiplied by the number of kilometres flown

RTK The number of tonnes of cargo multiplied by the number of kilometres flown

Shipping Transportation of goods by any mode

Shipment Goods transported together as a single consignment, by any mode

Taxiway Airport roadways, connecting runways to ramps, hangars and terminals

A Note on the Text

I have followed the industry terminology of referring to air cargo as 'volume' rather than 'weight'. Technically it is actually the weight, i.e. tonnage, that is being referred to.

All non-US currency is converted to US dollars, calculated using the exchange rate on the date the reference was published.

Acknowledgements

I am grateful to the following for insights and information: Anzir Boodoo, Sarah Clayton, Robbie Gillett, Stephen Grey, Martin Grimshaw, Tim Johnson, Miriam Kennet, Tom Lines, Stanley Mamu, Brian Ross, Brendon Sewill, John Stewart, Geoff Tansey, Denis Walker, Derek Wall and Linda Young. Thank you to all at Pluto Press, especially Roger Van Zwanenberg, David Castle and Melanie Patrick. Thank you to Susan Curran for wonderful copy editing. And special thanks to my husband Jonathan for support, inspiration and taking me on long walks to maintain my sanity.

Rose Bridger
June 2013

Introduction

If you look at satellite images of the world's cities, the pale grey shape of an airport is likely to be the most prominent human-made feature. Looking closer, major airports have a grid-like appearance. Linear runways are surrounded by grey buildings, access roads and patches of grass. Most of the airport site is invisible from the ground. Passengers are confined to the accessible areas of terminals, seeing little but shops, food outlets and advertising. When I began writing about aviation it was obvious that visiting airports would not be enlightening. So I didn't go anywhere. Instead, I used the internet to research operations and expansion plans all over the world.

The growth of aviation, over the course of little more than a century, has been remarkable. On 17 December 1903, the first aeroplane, designed and built by two brothers, Orville and Wilbur Wright, flew for twelve seconds, covering 250 metres, over the Cape Hatteras sands in North Carolina.[1] By 2011, the number of air passengers reached 5.44 billion[2] and the global fleet of commercial aircraft numbered 19,890. Airport expansion plans are informed by forecasts made by Boeing and Airbus, the two firms supplying most of the global fleet. Both firms predict that passenger numbers and the global aircraft fleet will double over the next 20 years.[3]

The speed of flight brings many advantages. Journeys across the world, taking just a few hours by plane, are rarely undertaken by surface transport. Multiple legs by some combination of road, rail and boat take days or weeks. Air transport enhances global connectivity, bringing the tremendous benefit of increasing communication, and building understanding, between people of different cultures. For all the sophistication of electronic communication, we still feel a strong need to meet face to face, to share the same space. No form of representation can replace actually being present in a beautiful landscape or a lively city.

Yet aviation expansion is one of the most divisive issues of our time. The primary reason for opposition is the high environmental cost. Localised environmental damage, near airport sites, is not felt by flyers, but by people on the ground. New airports and runways inevitably entail displacement of people, and the loss of wildlife habitats and farmland. Neighbouring communities are subjected to high levels of air pollution and noise. In democratic countries, where people have a say in planning decisions, and the right to freedom of expression and protest, proposals for a new runway or a new airport are often met by a vigorous anti-expansion campaign. Protest is not confined to local concerns. Aviation, fossil-fuel dependent and energy intensive, is a fast-growing source of greenhouse gases, which cause climate change, a global environmental crisis threatening our survival. In general, emissions per passenger are higher than for surface travel.

The same is true for air cargo, carried in the belly-hold of passenger flights and in dedicated freighters, an industry that attracts little publicity. A modal shift to surface transport would significantly reduce carbon emissions, but expansion of freight terminals is underway, and Boeing predicts that air cargo growth will follow a similar trajectory to passenger numbers, doubling over 20 years.[4] Consumer goods, such as electronic products and fashion garments, are air freighted so that arrival in stores coincides with marketing campaigns. Whole aircraft are filled up with livestock and wild animals. Perishable produce – fruit, vegetables, fish and flowers – is the main export from poor southern countries. Air cargo also plays an important role in industry, from resource extraction to manufacturing.

There is no technofix on the horizon that will reconcile aviation expansion with reduction in greenhouse gas emissions. New aircraft are only marginally more fuel-efficient. Biofuels are the only viable alternative to fossil-fuel-derived kerosene. The enormous amounts of energy used to grow and process crops mean

2

that biofuel greenhouse gas emissions are higher than from fossil fuels. Dreams of miracle biofuel crops have come to nothing. The crops used for aviation biofuel either consist of, or displace, food crops, contributing to rising food prices and hunger.

As the environmental damage of aviation becomes more widely recognised, proponents of expansion emphasise economic benefits from passengers' expenditure and trade in goods. But the economic impacts are not straightforward. Aviation places a heavy burden on taxpayers. The majority of airport construction is government funded. Tax exemptions on fuel for international flights underpin airlines' economic viability. Sales of duty-free goods at airports and in flight drain tax revenue from national exchequers. Aircraft manufacturing by Boeing and Airbus is heavily subsidised. Since the economic downturn, governments in all world regions have intervened to prop up ailing national airlines with financial support packages.

Invariably, airport expansion is announced with the promise of high levels of employment, but evidence is mounting that the level of job creation is overstated. Airports are highly mechanised, creating more jobs for robots than for people. Host communities do not necessarily reap income from tourism. Short-haul flights, which could be replaced by surface transport, are increasing, as are domestic flights, which do not bring the advantages of international connectivity. Airports' evolution into destinations in their own right – with a proliferation of shops, restaurants, hotels and entertainment complexes – erodes the economic boon to the surrounding region. 'Non-aeronautical revenue' from these facilities is used to cross-subsidise expansion and reduce charges to airlines. Airports capture more of travellers' expenditure, and the facilities draw trade from the local market. The economic effect is the very opposite of boosting businesses in the catchment area, which is held up as the main rationale for airport expansion.

This book looks critically at all these issues. Chapter 1 examines aviation growth and greenhouse gas emissions. The eastward shift of economic power is reflected in the scale of airport expansion in Beijing and Dubai. Emissions from flying raise issues of inequity. But flight remains the preserve of a small minority, who are, in global terms, affluent. A global elite leaves an even heavier carbon footprint from luxury flights, in first and business class and on private jets. The aviation industry has a track record of avoiding regulations enforcing emissions reduction, and overstates the potential of reductions from traffic management and aircraft fuel efficiency.

Aviation biofuels are covered in Chapter 2. Jatropha, an inedible crop, was planted all over Africa and Asia, but failed to thrive on infertile land. A drive to fill US military aircraft with biofuel made from camelina, a nutritious oilseed crop, threatens to sacrifice food supplies at the altar of increasing domestic energy supply. Growing algae, on water, avoids land use issues, but only minute volumes of algal biofuel have been produced.

Chapter 3 explores the many ways in which airports blight communities. High levels of noise inflicted on people living under flightpaths are more than a nuisance; they cause serious health problems. Air pollutants emitted by aircraft are linked to respiratory illnesses and cancer. Uncontrolled runoff of de-icing fluid into waterways has a devastating effect on aquatic life. Airports built on floodplains in Chennai, Mumbai and Bangkok have exacerbated flooding in neighbouring communities. Leaks from fuel tanks and pipelines cause long-term contamination of groundwater. Aviation fuel is highly flammable, and there have been fires and explosions at depots and refineries.

Chapter 4 examines aviation's impacts on wildlife and farmland. Bird strikes (collisions between aircraft and birds) can endanger flights. When attempts to frighten birds away from airports fail, they are killed. Culls have increased, new methods have been devised to keep birds away from airports. Building 'greenfield' airports, on undeveloped land, obliterates wildlife habitats and agricultural land. All over India, there is tumultuous protest against acquisition of farmland for greenfield airports.

None of the environmental damage caused by aviation is

apparent to passengers. Chapter 5 addresses the industry's efforts to present a green image. Passenger terminals are showcases for energy efficiency and recycling. A growing number are topped with solar panels and windmills. But the energy supplied is only sufficient for a small proportion of the requirements of airport buildings, and negligible compared with the energy provided by the jet fuel pumped into aircraft. Airlines and airports run environmental awareness campaigns, lecturing passengers on how to green their lifestyles. None of this has any bearing on the flights, by far the most environmentally damaging aspect of operations.

Air cargo is considered in Chapter 6, within the context of multimodal transportation of goods, and the far larger volumes transported by ship. Types of goods that are transported by air are all of high value, with the exception of perishable food and flowers. Ethiopia's flower, fruit and vegetable exports are growing rapidly, but earnings have not reached the millions who depend on emergency food aid.

Aviation's role in the industrial system is explored in Chapter 7. Air cargo supports the globalisation of manufacturing with delivery of components to sites dispersed around the globe. The world's largest aircraft deliver heavyweight and outsized industrial equipment. The oil industry's dependence on aviation is increasing as exploration and extraction moves into ever more challenging terrain, deeper under the oceans and further north towards the arctic.

Chapter 8 begins with aviation's role in supporting resource extraction in Africa. Delivery of mining equipment has been intertwined with supply of illicit weapons. Of all regions, Africa has the highest accident rate, and the death toll includes people living alongside runways. Mining, served by perilous airstrips in steep mountains, fuels conflict in the Democratic Republic of Congo. The chapter concludes with the pivotal role of aviation in wars waged by states, from reconnaissance missions in early hot air balloon flights to the US rendition programme, flying people to secret prisons where they are tortured.

Chapter 9 tackles US government subsidies for aviation. Stimulus funding granted to airports, in the aftermath of the financial crisis and subsequent economic downturn, was mainly spent on concrete. Construction of the Northwest Florida Beaches Airport, in forested wetlands, was government funded. In the state of Illinois, government funding poured in for expansion of Chicago O'Hare, land purchase for a proposed greenfield airport in Peotone, and a series of failed ventures at MidAmerica Airport, a white elephant in the midst of farmland.

Chapter 10 analyses the economic drawbacks of aviation, including the burden on taxpayers, the elimination of airport jobs, and airports' appropriation of income from the flow of passengers through non-aeronautical activities. Airports' non-aeronautical revenue from commercial development on real estate, beyond the airport boundary, is examined in Chapter 11. The global phenomenon of the 'aerotropolis' – airports surrounded by urbanisation – is predicated on airport ownership of, and revenue from, the land upon which development takes place. Land that is not built on can be turned to income generation, from food and biofuel crops. Autocratic governments in Asia designate large greenfield sites for aerotropolis development. A number of US airports are cashing in on oil wells and the shale gas boom.

Continued growth in passenger numbers and cargo volumes, in spite of the economic downturn, is explored in Chapter 12. I identify three key factors: rising non-aeronautical revenues, airlines' resilience in the face of rising fuel prices, and government provision of airport capacity expansion on the basis that it drives economic growth. But the evidence that aviation expansion increases economic growth is unconvincing, and it is the wrong metric for assessing the benefits to the host community and wider society.

The economic case for aviation expansion is dubious. The environmental damage caused by aviation is undeniable. Transition to a sustainable transportation system, curbing aviation growth, is vital. I hope this book helps to achieve it.

1

The Future of Flight

The World's Busiest Airports

For many years, rivalry between airports to rank as the busiest in the world, handling the highest number of passengers, was a two-horse race between North America's two main hubs, Chicago O'Hare and Atlanta. O'Hare topped the list from its opening in 1962, but Atlanta began to catch up in the 1980s, and the two airports were in close competition until 1998, when Atlanta edged ahead. Atlanta has been the world's busiest passenger airport every year since, extending its lead over O'Hare. In 2011, it handled more than 92 million passengers.[1]

Atlanta Airport is to the south of the city. Seen from above, the grey rectangle, delineated east-to-west by five parallel runways, dwarfs other urban features. O'Hare maintained the position of the world's second busiest passenger airport until 2009, when it was overtaken by Heathrow. But Heathrow has maintained its position as the world's busiest international airport, handling over 64 million international passengers in 2011.[2] Atlanta is predominantly a domestic airport, handling flights between US destinations; 171 of its 199 gates are used for domestic traffic.[3]

A successful campaign against a third runway curtailed further growth at Heathrow, but expansion plans lie dormant rather than dead. In 2012, British prime minster David Cameron broke a pre-election 'no ifs, no buts' pledge not to allow a third runway, setting up a commission to rule on the issue of Heathrow expansion.[4] One of the options under consideration is a plan to increase the number of runways to four, entailing encroachment of the airport footprint over land to the west of the established site.[5]

In 2010, Beijing Airport handled nearly 74 million passengers, overtaking Heathrow to take second place behind Atlanta. Beijing widened its lead over Heathrow in both 2011 and 2012.[6] John D. Kasarda, a business professor at the University of Carolina and a prominent advocate of aviation expansion, contrasted the rapid construction of Beijing's third terminal with the stalled growth and protracted uncertainty over Heathrow. Beijing's new terminal was built from 'from raw ground' in the same time frame as the planning enquiry for Heathrow's Terminal 5. Kasarda acknowledges the role of autocratic government in the speed and scale of the expansion, specifically the aviation ministry with its doctrine 'Democracy sacrifices efficiency'. Fifteen villages were flattened and 10,000 residents were displaced with no compensation. There was no debate over plans for Beijing's second airport; not even the location was disclosed.[7]

Aviation expansion in Dubai is even more ambitious. Dubai Airport is on course to match Atlanta's passenger numbers by 2018.[8] In one phase of the expansion programme, for Concourse 2 and Terminal 3, Dubai Airport was reputedly the largest construction site in the world. Preparation of foundations for the site involved the excavation of 10 million cubic metres of earth.[9] After the laying of the first basement slab, in November 2003, 2.4 million cubic metres of concrete and 450,000 tonnes of steel were used over the course of 693 days. Fifty-five tower cranes and 65 concrete truck mixers were in simultaneous use.[10] Terminal 3 opened in October 2008, as the economic downturn began. It has been built for exclusive use by Emirates Airlines, the largest airline in the Middle East and Dubai's flag carrier, designated and wholly owned by the government. By the end of 2012, Dubai Airport had increased its passenger numbers by more than 28 per cent, to more than 52 million.[11]

If Dubai's new airport, called Al Maktoum, is completed and

operates at full capacity, with five parallel runways, it will outrank the city's older airport, and Atlanta, as the busiest passenger airport in the world. It is named after Emir Sheikh Rashid bin Saeed Al Maktoum, who ruled Dubai for 32 years until his death in 1990, Over 35 years ago, he allocated 140 sq. km for the new airport with a city, Dubai World Central, to be built around it.[12] Al Maktoum Airport aims to handle 160 million passengers per year, and to become the world's biggest cargo airport, handling 12 million tonnes per year.[13] This would be almost triple the volumes currently handled by Hong Kong, which overtook Memphis as the world's busiest cargo airport in 2010.[14]

Two thousand tonnes of steel were used to build Al Maktoum's 'fuel farm', the fuel storage and distribution facility. Three cylindrical tanks can hold 9.5 million litres of jet fuel.[15] This volume of liquid is comparable to the 10 million litres of water in the aquarium in Dubai Mall, one of the largest in the world, hosting 33,000 sea creatures, seen through the world's largest acrylic viewing panel.[16] The fuel farm's fire-fighting facility can hold 6 million litres of water.[17] Operations at Al Maktoum began on 21 June 2010 with the arrival of an Emirates Airlines Boeing 777 freighter, a cargo aircraft with a capacity of 105 tonnes.[18]

In 2008, a symbol of Dubai's aviation dominance arrived in London, on a roundabout at the road entrance to Heathrow, near the tunnel running under the north runway. About 25 million people per year travel past the roundabout, making it a prime advertising site.[19] A mesh of fences appeared, followed by hoardings with an advertising campaign for Emirates Airlines' Airbus A380 service. The first class service offers the ultimate luxury: private suites, lie-flat beds, massaging chairs, spacious bathrooms, two shower spas, a bar, lounge and flat-screen televisions with a choice of 1,200 channels. Behind the hoardings, the site was reinforced with 600 tonnes of concrete. On 24 July 2008, a model Emirates Airbus A380 was unveiled.[20]

Emirates' model A380 is a third of the size of the real plane, which is the world's largest passenger plane. It has a wingspan of nearly 80 metres and is almost as long from nose to tail. The name of the airline is written in gold-coloured paint in English and Arabic along the fuselage and there is a stylised, wavy version of the black, red and green lines of the UAE flag on the tail.[21] The model was made in Rancho Cucamonga, California, trucked to Ontario then flown to Heathrow in ten components, on board the world's largest plane, a Russian freighter, the Antonov-225.[22] The components were too heavy to offload from the Antonov-225 with the usual winch crane, so a mechanised ramp was flown in from Germany.[23]

The Supersonic Dead End

Before the model Airbus A380 appeared at the entrance to Heathrow, a 40 per cent scale model of a British Airways (BA) Concorde plane occupied the site. Concorde was the famous supersonic aircraft, capable of flying faster than the speed of sound, long and narrow with a distinctive pointed, drooping nose. When Concorde made its first flight in 1969, it symbolised the future of air travel. The British and French governments bankrolled its development, and in 1976 it began commercial service. Dignitaries, celebrities and company executives hurtled over the Atlantic Ocean, between Heathrow, Paris, New York and Washington, enjoying plush seating, gourmet meals and champagne. Concorde flew almost twice as high as a subsonic plane at 20,000 metres above sea level and over twice as fast. A flight from London to New York took just three and a half hours. The plinth supporting the model Concorde at the entrance to Heathrow boasted 'Arrive before you leave' as, with New York time being five hours behind London time, travellers appeared to gain an hour and a half.

Yet Concorde was a commercial failure, consigned to history in little over 30 years. No commercial purchasers emerged for the planes, so they were given to BA and Air France at zero cost. This distortion of the balance sheet underpinned these airlines' claims that Concorde operated with a profit.[24] Concorde's high fuel consumption raised its operating costs. It needed to be heavier than a subsonic plane in order to be strong enough to withstand the high speed and altitude. The aircraft burned about 17 litres of fuel per passenger per 100 km, six and a half times more than a Boeing 747 model of the same period.[25]

Unprecedented speed and luxury failed to attract the predicted number of passengers. There was capacity for 100 passengers, but the proportion of seats filled, referred to in the industry as the 'load factor', was frequently as low as 50 per cent.[26] Concorde was even less popular with communities living under flightpaths. As the plane accelerated, it broke the sound barrier and emitted an unmistakable thunder-like sound, called a sonic boom.

Concorde's developers anticipated that there would be 1,500 supersonic aircraft in service by the year 2000.[27] But just 20 Concorde planes were built, and only 14 entered commercial service. As the engines aged they were beset with technical problems. For each hour of flight, a Concorde was 20 times more likely to have an engine problem than a Boeing 747. Over the years, there were many incidences of tyres bursting, damaging the engines and fuel tanks.[28]

On 25 July 2000, a Concorde taking off from Charles de Gaulle Airport in Paris hit a piece of debris on the runway. This burst one of the plane's tyres, and shards of rubber from the tyre ruptured a fuel tank. The plane caught fire and crashed into a hotel. Everyone on board was killed: 100 passengers and nine crew, along with four people on the ground. Investigation by the French courts concluded that the cause of the accident was a small piece of metal on the runway, which had fallen off a Continental Airlines plane that took off minutes before the Concorde.[29]

The accident hastened Concorde's demise. In 2003 the entire fleet was retired from service. Yet the grounded Concorde planes fascinate aviation enthusiasts, taking pride of place in airport viewing parks and aviation museums in France, the United Kingdom and the United States. The model Concorde that

preceded the model Airbus A380 at Heathrow was dismantled and transported to the Brooklands Museum of aviation
and transport in Surrey just south of London, where it was
reassembled for display at the entrance.[30]

Concorde turned out to be a technological dead end. Since
the planes were grounded, supersonic flight has been confined
to military and experimental purposes. Aerion, a US firm, is
manufacturing supersonic luxury private jets for eight to twelve
passengers, as luxurious and spacious as the most expensive
subsonic private jets, with room to walk around, lie-flat beds,
sofas and a shower.[31] High fuel consumption remains an intrac-
table problem, so the new jets are expected to appeal to the
wealthiest niche market, able to afford the high operating cost.
Design changes that might muffle the sonic boom include slender
fuselages, a drag-reducing wing and a telescopic rod attached to
the nose of the plane to disrupt sound waves. If noise reduction
is insufficient to comply with regulations, the new jets might only
fly at supersonic speeds over the ocean.[32]

As supersonic flight shunted into the sidelines, the subsonic
jet age continued and another giant plane, the Boeing 747, came
to dominate the skies. The first test flight took place in 1969,
the same year as Concorde's first flight. Commercial service
began in 1970, and the 747 became the workhorse of long-haul,
high-capacity flight, renowned worldwide as the 'Jumbo Jet'.
By 2009, Boeing 747s had made 17 million flights and flown
nearly 78 billion km, equivalent to travelling to the moon and
back 100,000 times.[33] Boeing 747 freighters, with a payload of up
to 105 tonnes, provide more than half of the world's dedicated
freighter capacity.[34] Boeing 747s are still being manufactured, and
are assembled in the same factory in Everett, Washington. The
747 was the world's largest passenger jet until April 2005, when
the Airbus A380 made its maiden flight.

The A380 is outsized by the Antonov-225, the Russian
freighter which transported Emirates Airlines' model A380 to
Heathrow. It has a wingspan of just over 8 m, a distinctive

appearance with two tailfins, and six engines. At its highest point, the tail, it stands over 18 m tall, about the height of a six-storey building. The Antonov-225 was built to carry Russia's Buran space shuttle on top, but as the Soviet Union collapsed, so did its space programme. The Buran programme was cancelled in 1988. After a single flight carrying the shuttle, the Antonov-225 was modified to carry outsized cargo. It has a maximum payload, or cargo capacity, of 250 tonnes, and in 2001 set a world cargo record, lifting four Ukrainian tanks, weighing 253 tonnes, to an altitude of over 2 km.[35] The Antonov-225's inaugural commercial flight, in 2002, carried 216,000 ready meals from Germany to Oman for the US military.[36]

Ever since, the giant plane has supported military and humanitarian operations and carried mundane payloads of heavyweight industrial equipment. Memphis Airport claimed a record for the highest number of Antonov-225 flights for a single project. In June 2007, four gas turbines, part of an emergency power station, were flown from Memphis to Kuwait City. Each turbine, weighing 133 tonnes, required a separate flight and filled up the belly of the plane with 10 cm of space to spare at the top of the cargo deck. The rest of the power station was transported on six barges, an ocean liner, Boeing 747s and an Antonov-124.[37]

The Antonov-124 is the world's second largest cargo plane, with a wingspan of 73 m. Unlike the single Antonov-225, a fleet has built up; by 2008 there were 28 in commercial service, plus another 25 utilised by the Russian Air Force.[38] In the future Antonov-124s might have a role in Russia's space programme, flying objects to high altitude and launching them from the rear doors.[39] Meanwhile, the fleet supports space programmes in a workaday capacity, carrying equipment for satellites and the International Space Station.[40]

Satellites have orbited the earth since the launch of the Soviet Sputnik in 1957. This triggered the space race between the United States and the Soviet Union, but our ambitions for space travel have been thwarted. Expeditions to the moon fizzled out and manned expeditions to explore the solar system remain a distant prospect. Astronomical satellites helped make discoveries like quasars and planets in other solar systems, but the emphasis of space programmes turned inwards, to communication and observation of our home planet. Communication satellites relay television, radio and telephone signals. The Global Positioning System (GPS) network of satellites can pinpoint the location and movement of any object on or near the surface of the earth. A bewildering range of applications includes tracking aircraft, map-making, navigation for cars, trucks and ships, monitoring the flow of fuel along pipelines, following the movements of livestock and pets and tracking the migratory patterns of wild animals.

Earth observation satellites have brought unprecedented understanding of ecosystems. Increasingly, these satellites monitor human-made environmental problems: thinning of the ozone layer, deforestation, urban sprawl, soil erosion, depletion of groundwater and acidification of the oceans. Climate change is the most urgent environmental problem. Satellites monitor shrinking polar ice caps, retreating glaciers, the increased severity of storms, floods and droughts and the devastating impact on ecosystems.

Aviation and the Global Greenhouse

Greenhouse gases cause climate change, and fossil fuels – oil, gas and coal – are the main source of emissions. Industrialisation is built on the remarkable properties of fossil fuels. The energy provided by a barrel of oil is equivalent to the physical labour of five agricultural labourers working non-stop twelve hours per day for five years.[41] Accessing remaining fossil fuel deposits has taken precedence over making a transition to renewable alternatives: solar, wind, tidal, wave and geothermal power. The endgame is extreme oil, a process of diminishing returns. More energy is used to extract deposits lying deeper beneath the earth's surface and closer to polar regions. Lower-grade deposits are exploited, chiefly tar sands and shale gas embedded in sedimentary rock.

Aviation is a fast-growing source of greenhouse gas emissions. Global emissions from aviation grew 11.2 per cent between 2005 and 2010.[42] In addition to carbon dioxide, the main greenhouse gas, several other pollutants emitted by planes – methane, nitrogen oxides, sulphate, soot and ozone precursors – have a warming effect. Linear condensation trails, 'contrails', which planes leave in the sky, compound the warming effect. The water vapour can form cirrus clouds, wispy formations in the higher levels of atmosphere, which trap heat. In 2009, the Intergovernmental Panel on Climate Change (IPCC), the world's highest authority on the issue, calculated aviation's contribution to climate change caused by greenhouse gas emissions at 4.9 per cent.[43]

In general, transportation by air emits more greenhouse gases than a comparable surface journey by road, rail or ship. However, close analysis reveals a more complex picture. Writer and activist George Monbiot compared different modes of transport based on emissions per passenger. For every kilometre a passenger travels by air, in a fully loaded plane, the carbon emissions are comparable to a car carrying three or four passengers. Taking a single flight racks up more emissions than a long period of driving a car. A London to New York return flight emits 1.2 tonnes of carbon dioxide per passenger, comparable to driving a car for a year. Journeys on some types of passenger ships result in higher emissions than flying, due to the sheer weight of what is on board the vessels. Car ferries are laden with passengers' vehicles. Cruise ships are effectively floating holiday resorts, carrying everything from cinemas and casinos to swimming pools.

Regular trains have lower carbon emissions than planes, but emissions increase when speed exceeds 200 km per hour. Emissions per passenger from train travel at ultra-high speed, 350 km per hour, are comparable to an Airbus A321. Ultra-high-speed rail is not, as widely advocated, an environmentally friendly replacement for short-haul flights. A modal shift from air to high-speed rail will only reduce emissions if trains are powered by electricity, supplied by power stations using renewables, or fossil fuels with effective capture and storage of carbon dioxide emissions. Yet new coal and gas power stations are being built without carbon capture and storage.[44] This leaves us in a quandary over the future of high-speed, long-distance journeys. Emissions reduction necessitates not just modal shift, but an overall reduction in travel.

The speed of flight makes it the ultimate convenience, so demand management must overcome vociferous opposition from the wealthy and powerful people who fly the most. Frequent flyers are able to structure their lives around being where they want to be, when they want to be there. But flying is likely to be the dominant factor in an individual's 'carbon footprint', cancelling out the benefits of frugality in other areas and efforts such as home insulation, recycling and using public transport. Anirvan Chatterjee and Barnali Ghosh identified flying as the culprit behind their high carbon footprint, describing it as 'totally undoing every other green effort we were making'. They spent a year travelling around the globe without flying. Their experience of journeys that are a matter of hours by air, but take days or weeks on trains, ferries and container ships, is documented on the 'Year of No Flying' website.[45] It is a refreshing antidote to endless reams of travel writing about idyllic destinations, paying little regard to the environmental damage caused by the journey. Chatterjee went on to be a key member of Aviation Justice, the US campaign for a more just and sustainable aviation system.[46]

Frequent Flyers

Flying is, in the main, the preserve of people who are, in global terms, comparatively wealthy. Airbus's 2009 statistics show a strong correlation between countries' gross domestic product (GDP) and their population's propensity to fly. Citizens of

16

several African countries took between 0.01 and 0.1 trips per capita. At the higher end of the spectrum, citizens of a host of wealthy countries took between one and ten trips per capita. The correlation between low gross GDP and low propensity to fly is less applicable to island nations. The Bahamas, Maldives, St Lucia and the Seychelles are among the island nations in the lowest quartile of the GDP index whose populations fly more than wealthier countries.[47] The population of these islands is in the hundreds of thousands rather than millions, so they can be regarded as outliers. Citizens of wealthy, industrialised countries undertake the vast majority of air travel.

Presenting its 2010 statistics, Airbus described the rising number of flights in emerging economies, most notably China, India, Brazil and Russia, as evidence of an 'effective and continuing democratisation of aviation'.[48] But the number of flights taken by people in different social classes is likely to reflect inequalities within the country. A report by Sally Cairns and Carey Newson showed that aviation growth in the United Kingdom was mostly due to better off people flying more. Between 2000 and 2004, at five major airports – Manchester, Gatwick, Heathrow, Stansted and Luton – the number of international leisure trips by the lowest two household income bands fell. The number of trips taken by households in the higher income bands increased, most markedly in the highest band. This was just one of several findings that refuted the aviation industry's argument that expansion is socially inclusive. Cairns and Newson concluded: 'Available data show that air travel is still primarily undertaken by richer sections of society.'[49]

Monbiot's research provided further evidence that aviation expansion reinforces rather than reduces inequality. His analysis revealed that the majority of budget airline flights originating from the United Kingdom, costing a little as a few dollars, were taken by the wealthy. Low-cost flights did not make flying more accessible to poorer people; they could not afford the accommodation and other expenses incurred on foreign holidays. People in the two lowest social classes bought only 6 per cent of tickets.

One survey showed that UK citizens with second homes abroad took an average of six return flights per year.[50]

A study of highly mobile travellers, by Stefan Gössling, Jean-Paul Ceron, Ghislain Dubois and Michael C. Hall, found that 'a very minor share of humanity accounts for a large part of the overall kilometres travelled and the consequent impacts'. Only a small proportion of the world's people ever step on a plane. In 2006, it was estimated that, per annum, only about 2–3 per cent of the global population take an international flight. A case study of 4,510 French citizens showed that individuals categorised as frequent travellers, within the country and abroad, used aircraft at a rate 558 per cent higher than the average. Their carbon emissions from travel were about four times higher than people who travelled less frequently and over shorter distances.

Gössling and colleagues researched the small minority of 'hypermobile' travellers. One employee of Hewlett-Packard in Denmark made 43 international trips in a single year, and the singer in a Swedish pop band spoke of 'sitting on aircraft 260 days per year'. A study of 252 international tourists visiting Zanzibar in Tanzania in 2002–03 identified a subgroup who each covered 90,000 km a year, more than twice the distance around the globe. The ten most frequent travellers had covered twice this distance. The disproportionately high level of carbon emissions from hypermobile travellers should be tackled as a climate policy issue. However, these people are predominantly members of 'political, economic and cultural elites', who are unlikely to instigate measures to restrain their globetrotting habits.[51]

Luxury air travel is more environmentally damaging than economy flights. More spacious seating in first and business class means that fewer passengers can be accommodated, resulting in higher carbon emissions per passenger. Airbus claimed that the A380 would emit 17 per cent less carbon than the Boeing 747, on the basis that the aircraft would have 525 seats. Yet when Singapore Airlines made the first A380 flight in October 2007, the plane only contained 471 seats. Emirates and Qantas fitted out A380s for use on long-haul routes with 489 and 450 seats respectively.[52]

Carbon emissions from travelling by private jet are in different league. A report by the Institute for Policy Studies and campaigning NGO Essential Action estimated that a Cessna Citation X jet, flying from Los Angeles to New York, emits 16,134 kg of carbon dioxide. A commercial airliner travelling the same journey emits 701 kg per passenger. If a Citation X flies at full capacity, carrying eight people from Los Angeles to New York, the emissions per passenger are eight times higher than travelling on a commercial airline. Private jets are frequently used by a single person, in which case the emissions are 23 times higher.[53] The economic downturn did not curb growing use of the largest private planes, used by wealthy executives of big companies. Deliveries went up 13 per cent in 2009 and 2010.[54] Private jet fuel consumption is even more profligate than the spaciousness and luxury on board suggests. About a third of flights are empty legs, picking up and dropping off owners and customers and returning to base to avoid airport parking fees.[55]

Transportation of cargo does not involve grading to provide different levels of comfort and luxury. Space is optimised in order to cram in as much cargo as possible, so comparing emissions from different modes – trucks, trains, ships and planes – is less complex than for transportation of passengers. Calculations by the UK government showed that per tonne km (the number of tonnes of cargo multiplied by the number of kilometres transported) emissions of carbon dioxide from air freight are 4.6 times greater than road transport, 29 times greater than rail, and between 30 and 150 times greater than shipping. Fuel efficiency increases with the size of the ship.[56] Modal shift of transportation of goods, from air to surface transport, would bring a considerable reduction in emissions, with the proviso that high-speed rail does not bring the carbon savings of regular rail services. The reduction in emissions from the aviation sector would be substantial. Professor Peter Morrell of Cranfield University estimated that air cargo accounts for about 25 per cent of global aviation fuel use.[57]

Regulatory Avoidance

Aviation has a track record of avoiding regulation to enforce reduction in carbon emissions. The industry received preferential treatment in the 1997 Kyoto Protocol, an international agreement setting targets to reduce greenhouse gas emissions. Emissions from international aviation, along with shipping, were excluded. Responsibility for reducing aviation's emissions lies with the International Civil Aviation Organization (ICAO), an agency of the United Nations established by the 1944 Chicago Convention to coordinate international air transportation and standardise operating procedures. ICAO endorsed the inclusion of aviation in national or regional schemes requiring airlines to limit greenhouse gas emissions in 2004, but has failed to translate this commitment into practice. The EU Emissions Trading Scheme (EU-ETS), an emissions cap applied to energy-intensive industries such as power stations, refineries, iron steel and cement, food and drink and vehicle manufacture, came into force in 2005. In 2007 ICAO decided against requiring airlines to participate in the scheme. The European Federation for Transport and Environment's verdict was that ICAO had prevented action towards emissions reductions in the aviation sector for more than a decade.[58]

Aviation was due to be brought into the EU-ETS at the beginning of 2012, forcing all airlines flying to and from the European Union to purchase allowances for their carbon emissions. Research by the Aviation Environment Federation (AEF), a UK non-profit organisation, revealed that the proposed terms for aviation's entry were lenient. Other sectors must reduce emissions by at least 20 per cent by 2020 compared with 1990. Aviation's emissions were to be capped at 97 per cent of average emissions between 2004 and 2006 for 2012, with a small reduction in the cap, to 95 per cent, from 2013. Furthermore, while other sectors are forced to buy a growing proportion of permits at auction, airlines would receive most of their permits for free. AEF also pointed out that carbon emissions from aviation might not, in actuality, be reduced under the provisions of the EU-ETS. If sectors fail to reduce their emissions, they can buy permits from other industrial sectors or from elsewhere in the world.[59]

As the date for inclusion in the EU-ETS approached, airlines in several non-European countries intensified lobbying efforts in order to avoid compliance. By September 2011 26 nations, including China, India, Russia and the United States, had signed a declaration opposing the EU-ETS. In February 2012, representatives of these nations met in Moscow to discuss joint action against the scheme.[60] In response, the European Union suspended introduction of the EU-ETS to flights to and from Europe for a one-year period, until November 2013, and ICAO agreed to establish a high-level advisory group to craft an international emissions reduction programme.[61] Time will tell if this is a genuine commitment from ICAO, or continuation of obfuscation and delaying tactics.

As the aviation industry avoided legally binding commitments to reduce emissions, it announced its own targets. In the build-up to the December 2009 UN climate summit in Copenhagen, the International Air Transport Association (IATA), the trade association for airlines, issued a statement headlined 'Halving emissions by 2050 – aviation brings its targets to Copenhagen'. It contained the following statement:

> Airlines, airports, air navigation service providers and manufacturers are calling for a global approach to reducing aviation emissions and are united in a commitment: to improve fuel efficiency by an average of 1.5% per year to 2020; to stabilize carbon emissions from 2020 with carbon-neutral growth; and to a net reduction in carbon emissions of 50% by 2050 compared to 2005.[62]

In the face of the urgency of climate change, the aviation industry makes no commitment to reduce emissions until after 2020. Instead, it pledges improvements in fuel efficiency over this timeframe. In their 2009 book *Climate Change and Aviation*, Stefan Gössling and Paul Upham point out that estimated future efficiency gains, of around 1–1.5 per cent per year, are set to be outpaced by aviation's annual growth of 5–6 per cent, resulting in a continued increase in absolute emissions. Gössling and Upham also challenge projections made on the basis that the rate of efficiency gains can be maintained: 'Most of the energy efficiency gains in aviation history were achieved in the early periods of aircraft development. Efficiency gains by new aircraft are likely to be comparably lower.'[63]

The aviation industry's target for emissions reduction between 2020 and 2050 is aspirational; achieving it depends on future technological advances. A communiqué, issued by a global 'Aviation and Environment Summit' to the December 2010 UN climate summit in Cancun, reiterated the targets announced by IATA in 2009. It stated that 'The three areas of industry development that carry the greatest potential for emissions reduction are new technologies, air traffic management improvements and the use of sustainable aviation biofuels.'[64]

Emissions reduction from the use of biofuels, explored in the next chapter, is unproven, and the industry only expects biofuels to provide a small proportion of jet fuel consumption. Improvements in the accuracy of air traffic management (ATM) enable planes to fly more efficiently. The main ergonomic measures are 'continuous descent' – a smoother landing path instead of the usual step-by-step approach – minimising 'holding stacks' of aircraft flying in circles waiting to land, and reducing the distance between planes at take-off and landing. A 2010 study by researchers at Oxford University estimated that ATM improvements could reduce carbon dioxide emissions from aviation by up to 8 per cent.[65] Increased emissions from aviation growth at the current rate, doubling every 20-year period, is set to dwarf emissions reduction from ATM.

The Future Fleet

The aviation industry's communiqué to Cancun highlights new aircraft as 'the most effective tool for lowering CO_2 emissions'.[66]

This may well be true, but there is no indication that innovations in aircraft design will be sufficient to bring about a substantial reduction in emissions. Barring some unforeseen technological breakthrough, new aircraft will only be marginally more fuel-efficient than the current fleet. If aviation's entrenched growth path continues, emissions reduction from slightly more fuel-efficient aircraft will be counterbalanced many times over by enlargement of the fleet. Boeing predicted that the size of the commercial aircraft fleet will double over 20 years, from 19,890 planes in 2011 to 39,780 in 2031.[67]

Announcement of Boeing's mid-sized 787, or 'Dreamliner', in 2005, with the promise of 20 per cent fuel savings compared to similar-sized jets, led to a rush of orders from 56 airlines, making it the fastest-selling jet in history. Lightweight plastic composites replace aluminium as far as possible, and the plane relies on battery-powered electronics instead of heavyweight hydraulics to operate systems.[68] But production was plagued with technical glitches and protracted labour disputes. Industry commentators dubbed the 787 the '7 late 7' and 'Dream-on-liner'. In November 2010, test flights over Seattle came to a halt after a fire forced an emergency landing.[69] The inaugural 787 flight, from Tokyo to Hong Kong on 26 October 2011, was three years behind the original schedule.[70]

By the end of 2012, 50 787s were in service, flown by All Nippon Airways, Japan Airlines, United Airlines, Chile's LAN, Air India, LOT Polish Airlines, Qatar Airways and Ethiopian Airlines. But the entire flagship fleet was grounded in January 2013, because of concerns over a battery fault. On 7 January 2013 there was an electrical fire on board a Japan Airlines 787 parked at Boston Logan. Eight days later an All Nippon 787 made an emergency landing at Takamatsu in western Japan. Passengers and crew were evacuated using inflatable chutes. There was a burning smell in the cockpit, and investigators discovered that the battery was swollen and burnt, with a charcoal-like appearance.

Concerns that the high-energy lithium-ion batteries might overheat, causing heat damage to surrounding structures, releasing flammable electrolytes and posing a fire risk, have dogged the 787 since its inception. The US Federal Aviation Authority (FAA) only certified use of the batteries after Boeing introduced elaborate safeguards.[71] All 787s were grounded, and deliveries halted, for investigation by Boeing and regulatory agencies. Modifications including a new containment enclosure and venting system for the battery were approved, and Ethiopian was the first airline to return a 787 to service, at the end of April 2013.[72] The cause of the battery fires was not identified, and two had occurred within 50,000 hours, a significantly shorter period than the maximum of one such incident in 10 million flight hours required by the special conditions the FAA attached to certification. Nevertheless, Boeing and the FAA concluded that there was no risk of a catastrophic fire.[73]

With the difficulties in bringing 787s into service, it is understandable that aircraft design is conservative, averse to the cost and risk of radical changes. Design ideas showing potential for substantial improvements in fuel efficiency have been deprived of investment. These include innovations that might minimise 'drag', the friction between the plane and air, such as tens of thousands of small holes along the top of an aircraft's wings, or a conical extension on the rear of the fuselage. A strut from the belly to the fuselage could reduce the weight of the wings by up to two-thirds. Wing-shaped aircraft are more streamlined, making them more fuel efficient, but have only been taken up by the US military.[74]

The only radically different aircraft taking to the skies are airships. Airships predate aeroplanes but fell out of use after the Hindenburg, filled with flammable hydrogen, burst into flames over New Jersey in 1937. Modern airships, filled with non-flammable helium, can be seen hovering over tourist attractions including central London, San Francisco Bay and Lake Constance in Germany, where the first Zeppelin airship flew in 1900. Airships could do more than enable people to enjoy viewing the earth from above, and play a significant role in transporting passengers and cargo. New models can reach speeds of up to 200 km per hour. While this is no match for a Boeing 747's cruising speed of about 900 km per hour, it is comparable with high-speed rail, and airships bring other advantages: they are quieter and able to land at inaccessible locations as there is no need for a runway. Although still powered by fossil fuels, airships' climate-changing impact is up to 90 per cent less than conventional aircraft. Yet we are unlikely to see significant numbers of airships over the next few decades. Neither governments nor private investors have stepped up with the hundreds of millions of dollars necessary to scale up production.[75]

Flight is uniquely dependent on oil, refined into kerosene, to provide the concentrated, portable source of energy that is required to overcome gravity and travel at speed. As yet, the only alternatives being incorporated into mainstream aviation, transporting significant numbers of passengers and volumes of cargo, are synthetic fuels made from oil and gas, and biofuels derived from plants. These fuels are used as 'drop-in' supplements to the kerosene supply.

Hydrogen fuel is not a viable alternative to kerosene, as it is made using fossil fuels and producing it is energy intensive. Moreover, hydrogen fuel is four times bulkier than oil, so fuel tanks need to be larger, seriously compromising the aerodynamics of prototype aircraft.[76] Several small hydrogen-burning 'cryoplanes' carry sensors and communications equipment for earth observation, monitoring borders, weather services and military surveillance. Boeing's Phantom Eye, fitted with two Ford pick-up truck engines modified to burn hydrogen, carries 200 kg of sensors and communications equipment, and can stay aloft for four days.[77]

The first flight of a solar-powered plane, the Solar Impulse, took place over Switzerland in April 2010. This did not herald a breakthrough from dependence on fossil fuels. The plane's design illustrates the difficulty of harnessing a sufficiently concentrated supply of energy for flight from the sun's rays. The entire wingspan, similar to a Boeing 747 at nearly 64 m, is covered in 12,000 solar cells, but the aircraft seats one person and weighs just 1.6 tonnes, less than a saloon car.[78] In May 2011 the Solar Impulse made its first international flight, from Switzerland to Belgium, travelling at 40 km per hour, the speed of a car trundling along in second gear.[79] In February 2013 Solar Impulse began a coast-to-coast flight from San Francisco to New York. The aircraft is expected to make three or four stopovers en route. It is a sad indictment of the limitations of solar-powered flight that, in order to begin the journey across the United States, the Solar Impulse had to be carried from Switzerland across the Atlantic. It was transported on board a Boeing 747 freighter.[80]

The UK-built Zephyr is even lighter than the Solar Impulse, weighing just over 50 kg. Solar arrays made from amorphous silicone the thickness of a sheet of paper cover the 22.5 m wingspan. Zephyr's future will be in unmanned earth observation and military communications. In July 2010, the plane flew over an Arizona army range for two weeks, achieving a world record for the longest unmanned flight.[81]

The mainstream media paint an unrealistic picture of solar aircraft. Each flight is reported as a futuristic miracle, promising a new age of flight, divorced from the context of growth of the conventional oil-dependent fleet and the heavier planes that are entering service. Boeing's 747-8 freighter has a maximum payload of 140 tonnes. A demonstration flight over California in August 2010 set a weight record for all Boeing's aircraft. The total weight of the plane, loaded with steel plates, was 456 tonnes.[82] This is 256 times heavier than the Solar Impulse, and more than 9,000 times heavier than the Zephyr. A fully loaded Airbus A380 is even heavier than a Boeing 747-8. Its maximum take-off weight is 569 tonnes. An upgraded Airbus A380, with a maximum take-off weight of 573 tonnes, is in development.[83]

2

Feeding the Fuel Tanks

Alternative Fuels

Aviation's attempts to diversify its fuel supply, to reduce dependence on oil first turned to coal and gas. Coal-to-liquid (CTL) and gas-to-liquid (GTL) kerosene are already in use. South Africa developed CTL fuel in the 1970s, utilising its coal reserves in response to trade sanctions imposed in opposition to the apartheid regime, which restricted its oil imports.[1] Johannesburg's OR Tambo, the busiest passenger airport in South Africa, has dispensed a 50 per cent blend of CTL fuel, produced by energy and chemical firm Sasol, and conventional kerosene since 1998. In 2008, Sasol gained international fuel authorities' approval for commercial use of 100 per cent CTL fuel.[2]

Qatar Airways performed the first GTL commercial passenger flight, in 2009. An Airbus A340 flew from London Gatwick to Doha on a 50/50 blend of GTL fuel and conventional kerosene.[3] Qatar, sitting on the world's third biggest proven gas deposits, has constructed the largest GTL facility in the world 80 km to the north of Doha. It will supply the city's new airport, currently in the final phases of construction.[4] CTL and GTL fuels are a retrograde step. Processing the fuel is highly energy intensive, making the carbon dioxide emissions higher than conventional oil-derived kerosene.[5]

Diminishing reserves of all types of fossil fuels led to a search for biofuel substitutes, made from plant material, or 'biomass'. Oil and biotechnology firms, airlines, aircraft manufacturers, governments and venture capitalists have invested heavily in research and development. The industry demands 'drop in' fuels, identical to and blended with conventional kerosene, so that no adaptation of existing fuel supply infrastructure or aircraft engines is necessary. This poses a considerable challenge as kerosene is produced to stringent international standards, with a high flash point of 38°C to reduce the risk of explosion, and a low freezing point so it does not thicken at high altitude temperatures as low as -50°C.

The first biofuel test flight took place in February 2008. A Virgin Atlantic Boeing 747 flew from London to Amsterdam with 20 per cent biofuel made from coconuts and babassu nuts, a type of palm used for cooking oil, in one of four engines. This small proportion of biofuel, for a short-haul flight, used the equivalent of 150,000 coconuts. If the plane had been able to fly on 100 per cent coconut oil, the flight would have used 3 million coconuts.[6]

Biofuels made from food crops, predominantly ethanol from corn and sugarcane, and biodiesel from soya, palm and rapeseed, are already in use for power stations and road vehicles. The diversion of edible crops to biofuels reduces food supplies, contributing to rising prices and hunger. The issue came to the fore in 2008, when a steep hike in food prices pushed an additional 100 million people deeper into poverty. The crisis was multifactorial. Biofuels, drought, higher energy prices impacting on food production and financial speculation in grains all played a role. A confidential World Bank report, obtained by the *Guardian* newspaper, found that using food crops for biofuel was responsible for 75 per cent of the price increase.[7]

Governments created the market for biofuels. At least 52 countries, including all 27 EU member states, have adopted quantitative mandates for biofuel to be blended into petroleum fuels. Demand is driven by the scale of consumption in the United States, the European Union, China and Brazil.[8] Brazil is the world's biggest sugarcane producer, and most of its cars run on 'flex fuel', a blend of gasoline and sugarcane ethanol.

The main rationale for the US biofuels mandate is to reduce dependence on foreign oil and boost farm income. Most of the supply comes from ethanol derived from domestically grown corn, but imports of Brazilian sugarcane ethanol have increased.[9]

The EU biofuels mandate was introduced on the basis that biofuels emit fewer greenhouse gases than fossil fuels, but this has been widely refuted. Biofuels were founded on a fallacy: that they are 'carbon neutral' because the carbon released into the atmosphere is counterbalanced by the carbon plants absorb as they grow. There would be some merit to this argument if the world's biofuel consumption were constrained to keep pace with the rate of plant growth. But plant matter that has taken months, years, even decades to grow is burned in a matter of minutes. Furthermore, every stage of biofuel production involves fossil fuel inputs: petroleum-derived fertilisers and pesticides, mechanical harvesting and several stages of processing into fuel and transportation. Clearing and ploughing land releases carbon from soil or peat and existing vegetation. There are further emissions from 'indirect land use change': when agricultural land is turned over to energy crops, new areas of forest, peatland and grassland are cleared for food production.

All forms of biomass have a lower energy density than fossil fuels. Enormous amounts of feedstock crops are required to make biofuel, and vast areas of land are required to grow the feedstock. Rachel Smolker, co-director of Biofuelwatch, an NGO dedicated to raising awareness of the negative impacts of industrial biofuels, describes this critical drawback as a 'massive "land footprint" – very little energy from a lot of land area'. She highlights the US corn crop as an example: 'The US currently dumps on order of 40 percent of its corn crop into ethanol production, contributing a miniscule portion of our overall transport energy.'[10]

The EU biofuels mandate commits governments to sourcing 10 per cent of transport energy from renewable sources by 2020. An Oxfam briefing paper, 'The hunger grains', states that member states are 'set to meet this target almost exclusively using biofuels made from food crops'. Land used to produce biofuels for the European Union in 2008 could have produced sufficient wheat and corn to feed 127 million people for the year. Modelling by the European Commission's Joint Research Centre (JRC) indicates that use of biodiesel to meet the 10 per cent by 2020 target would consume almost a fifth of global vegetable oil production. The European Union relies heavily on imported crops for biofuels, and 2008 figures for the proportion supplied by imports, 42 per cent of biodiesel and 24 per cent of ethanol, are likely to be underestimates. Vast tracts of land in Africa, Asia and Latin America have been acquired for biofuel crops, often as a result of land deals made without the consent of affected communities. Biofuel production in Indonesia, Ghana and Mozambique has strong links with EU markets.[11]

In October 2012 the European Union edged towards considering a cap on biofuels made from food crops, when an internal report acknowledged the pressure on global food markets and greenhouse gas emissions from indirect land use change.[12] The possibility of a policy shift did not influence the EU Biofuels Flightpath, a programme aiming to produce 2 million tonnes of aviation biofuels per year by 2020. A $13 million project aims to create a European aviation biofuel supply chain, predominantly using camelina grown in Spain.[13] Camelina is an edible crop. The oil is rich in omega 3 essential fatty acids, which are lacking in most western diets. It is also used as cooking oil and animal feed.

Crop Failure

Mounting criticism over the use of food crops for fuel led to investigation of inedible feedstocks. The search for an inedible crop suitable for aviation biofuel honed in on jatropha, a poisonous shrub. Jatropha grows up to 3 m high and produces clusters of green pods containing between three and five oval black seeds, yielding up to 40 per cent pale yellow oil. When large-scale cultivation began in 2007, advocates insisted that jatropha would thrive on arid, infertile land, promising a solution to the conflict between fuel production and food supplies. The world's first jatropha-powered biofuel test flight took off from Auckland Airport on 30 December 2008. An Air New Zealand Boeing 747 flew over the Hauraki Gulf for two hours, with a 50 per cent blend of jatropha oil in one of the plane's four engines. The jatropha was sourced from Malawi, Mozambique, Tanzania and India, and the supplier verified that the land was not previously virgin forest or grassland and was unsuitable for the 'vast majority' of food crops.[14]

Responsible sourcing of a small batch of jatropha, for a single test flight, is commendable. Finding sufficient land to supply a sizeable portion of the world's jet fuel use is a different matter. Jatropha planting in Africa and Asia has resulted in the same story of crop failure. It failed to thrive on marginal land so was planted on farmland, displacing food crops. Even when cultivated on prime agricultural land, lavished with fertilisers, jatropha provided disappointing yields and was vulnerable to pests. Farmers who had been encouraged, or coerced, into growing jatropha made financial losses when the projected yields failed to materialise. Many more were displaced when governments handed land over to foreign firms for large plantations.

The Indian government earmarked 134,000 sq. km of land as suitable for jatropha in 2007. This included areas categorised as 'waste land', but in communal use by the poorest rural people for food, fuel and timber. Tracts of land in Chhattisgarh were cleared for jatropha plantations. The forest department brought in herds of cattle to trample on staple crops of rice and lentils. Forcible jatropha planting displaced hundreds of families from land they had nurtured for centuries. By 2009, it became evident that the crop needs fertile soil, irrigation, manure or other fertilisers, and is vulnerable to pests and disease. Farmers who were encouraged to grow jatropha did not get an income from it, and the government leased land to international firms at nominal rents.[15]

The Mozambique government's biofuels strategy was driven by attracting foreign investors, deliberately excluding civil society participation. Documentation was rarely translated into local languages and unconstitutional decrees were passed, ignoring community land rights. The vast majority of planting was on arable land, and yields were poor, even with the application of fertilisers. Plantations on land with the highest rainfall still depended on irrigation. Heavy infestations of fungi, viruses and insects could not be removed with pesticides and spread to food crops.[16]

In the Kavango region of Namibia, where agriculture benefits from higher rainfall levels than most of the country, 14,000 jatropha trees were planted. Half of the seed crop was eaten by termites and the other half remained unsold when the biofuel producer pulled out of the deal. All around the country, yields were minimal even on fertile soils. The slightest frost damaged the plants. Antelopes ate the leaves and mice ate the seeds.[17]

The Kenyan government encouraged farmers in Kibwezi, a village in a drought-prone region in the south-east of the country, to plant jatropha, but the crops shrivelled and lost their leaves and seeds.[18] In Dakatcha woodlands near Kenya's coast, a haven for biodiversity including globally important threatened bird species and home to 20,000 people growing crops including pineapples, maize and cassava, 500 sq. km were set aside for a jatropha plantation. A study commissioned by ActionAid, Birdlife International, NatureKenya and RSPB (the Royal Society for the Protection of Birds) estimated that greenhouse gas emissions from land clearance, planting, growing, harvesting, processing and transportation would be between 2.5 and six times higher than fossil fuel equivalents.[19]

Norwegian firm Scanfuel acquired 4,000 sq. km in the Ashanti region of Ghana to plant jatropha. Farmers rejected the payment offer but Scanfuel began clearing the land with heavy machinery, obliterating settlements, crops and shea trees which yield nutritious oil and can live for 300 years.[20] Jatropha crops on good-quality agricultural land in Swaziland were attacked by fungi and insects, and prone to diseases including leaf spots and root rot.[21] In Tanzania, large areas of the Namatibile coastal forest, home to endangered species including bushbabies, lions and elephants, were cleared for jatropha.[22] Jatropha planting on the Philippine island of Mindanao met with protests over the displacement of rice, corn, banana and root vegetable crops.[23]

Lufthansa introduced jatropha to the fuel mix for commercial flights for a trial period. Beginning in July 2011, an Airbus A321 flew the four times per day Hamburg–Frankfurt route using a 50 per cent blend of jatropha, camelina and unspecified animal fats in one engine. The project was subsidised by the German government to the tune of nearly $2 million. Jatropha was sourced from the Grobogan district of central Java. The Javanese government promoted jatropha as the 'new money tree', but Berry Nahdian Forqan, executive director of Friends of the Earth (FoE) Indonesia, said that farmers and workers had 'converted land from food to fuel crops, in return for ridiculously low payments'.[24] In January 2012, Lufthansa conducted the first ever biofuel trans-atlantic flight to the United States, but this marked the end of the jatropha trial, as there was an insufficient supply for routine operations.[25]

Bombs Not Food

Jatropha planting in the United States proved disastrous. Thirty-six growers in Highlands Country, Florida, signed up to plant over 140 sq. km in 2008. Congressman Tim Mahoney announced that the area was to become 'the biofuels capital of America', but plants at a test plot could not withstand the cold. By 2010, the leaves had fallen off.[26] Unsurprisingly, trial planting of camelina, native to northern Europe with a similar climate, was more successful. Camelina is an annual plant growing up to 1 m high, part of the brassica family and closely related to mustard. Small pale-yellow flowers are succeeded by pea-like green pods containing golden seeds yielding up to 40 per cent oil. Camelina's nutritional value is recognised in many European countries and in Canada, where it can be purchased in small bottles as a premium healthy product. It is similar to flax oil, hence the plant is also known as 'false flax'.

The first biofuel test flight carrying passengers as well as crew used camelina grown in Montana by a company called Sustainable Oils. A KLM Boeing 747 flew for one hour from the airline's Schiphol base on 23 November 2009, with 50 per cent camelina-derived fuel in one engine.[27] Camelina for two single-seat military aircraft flights, in spring 2010, was also supplied by Sustainable Oils. A 90 minute A-10C Thunderbolt II flight from Eglin Air Base in Florida on 25 March was the first ever to use a blend of camelina and conventional jet fuel in all the aircraft's engines.[28] The second flight took place on 22 April. An F/A-18 Hornet flew on a 50/50 blend of camelina oil and conventional kerosene at the Naval Air Warfare Center in Patuxent River, Maryland. The flight was timed to coincide with Earth Day, when events to raise environmental awareness are held all over the world, and the plane was dubbed the 'Green Hornet'.[29] The Hornet aircraft is a supersonic strike fighter, capable of striking down enemy aircraft and bombing enemy targets on the same mission. 'Green' is a notoriously elastic term, but surely it is impossible to reconcile with killing and maiming people. The US military fully intends to use biofuels in actual warfare.

Test flights demonstrated the airworthiness of camelina-based jet fuel, and spurred efforts to use the crop to feed all kinds of military vehicles. By March 2011, Sustainable Oils had been contracted to supply 1.9 million litres of camelina biofuel to the US Air Force (USAF), Navy and Army. Simultaneously, the value of camelina as a food crop, for animal feed, received formal recognition. The US Department of Agriculture (USDA) approved inclusion of camelina meal, the crushed residue after most of the oil has been extracted, in livestock and poultry feed.[30]

A few weeks later, USDA launched a camelina growing scheme to increase the supply for military and commercial aircraft, making farmers in an area covering 200 sq. km in Montana, Washington State and California eligible for reimbursement of the majority of the cost of cultivation for up to five years. USDA sidestepped the issue of using farmland for fuel, pointing out that camelina can be grown in rotation with wheat.[31] This implies that camelina will make land more productive, but farmers are already adept at crop rotation, growing different types of crops in succession to obviate the need for, or shorten, fallow periods and keep land productive.

The US military tested biofuels in an operational setting in July 2012, during the biennial Rim of the Pacific military exercise around the Hawaiian islands. Successful test flights using a 50/50 mix of camelina oil and conventional jet fuel galvanised plans for deployment of a 'Great Green Fleet', powered by alternative fuels, by 2016.[32]

In the slightly longer term, both the USAF and the US Navy have set a target for domestic biofuels to meet 50 per cent of energy consumption by 2020.[33] This raises the question of how much American farmland would have to be planted with biofuels. I made a calculation based on current energy consumption and yields predicted by the main camelina oil supplier, Sustainable Oils. The USAF consumes 9.88 billion litres of oil per year,[34] so 4.94 billion litres of biofuel would be required to meet the 50 per cent target. Sustainable Oils released three new camelina varieties in spring 2011, advertising oil yields averaging 132.6 litres per hectare.[35] If this yield were achieved, and camelina were to supply half of the USAF's energy, 372,549 sq. km of farmland would need to be planted with camelina, more than one tenth of all the farmland in the United States.[36] An even greater land area would be necessary if yields were lower; projections by a firm with a commercial interest in selling its seeds must be treated with scepticism. A peer reviewed paper published by the United States

Association for Energy Economics estimated camelina yields of half this amount, even with the requisite rainfall and fertilisers.[37] Biofuelwatch points out that camelina is an especially poor choice of feedstock as oil yields are lower than those of other biofuel crops such as palm and rapeseed.[38]

Jet fuel accounts for 54 per cent of the US military's energy consumption. Even more land would be needed for biofuel to contribute to the supply for cruisers, destroyers, trucks and other vehicles. The military is the largest energy consumer in the United States, but only accounts for less than 2 per cent of total consumption.[39] The example of the likely land take for military biofuels shows that there is insufficient land for domestically produced biofuels to supply a significant proportion of America's total energy requirements. Smolker states it clearly: 'Even if we were to devote every square inch of arable land and water to the task we would barely scratch the surface of current energy consumption.'[40]

Feeding the US military with biofuels threatens a substantial reduction in the country's capacity for food production. It is also a bad bet in the quest for energy security. Farmers can never be certain of a good harvest. With all types of crops, there is a risk that yields will be decimated by disease, pests or inclement weather, the latter severely exacerbated by climate change. The effect of extreme weather on crops is already evident in the United States. In summer 2012, crops withered in the worst drought in for 50 years and the Midwest corn belt was worst affected. Drought-stressed crops were afflicted with outbreaks of aflatoxin, a liver toxin banned from the food supply even at low concentrations.[41]

Green Crude

Algae, microscopic plants growing on water, emerged as a potential energy source in the early 1970s. Yet in spite of millions of dollars of investment and subsidies, very little fuel has actually been produced.[42] Continental Airlines conducted the first ever test flight to use algae in the fuel mix. A Boeing 737 completed a two-hour flight from Houston on 7 January 2009, with 50 per cent biofuel, supplied by San Diego-based Sapphire Energy, in one of the plane's two engines. The proportion of algae in the biofuel was just 2.5 per cent. The remaining 97.5 per cent consisted of jatropha oil. Tim Zenk, Sapphire Energy's vice president of corporate affairs, brimmed with optimism over the potential of algae energy, saying, 'Crude oil is nothing but algae from 10 million years ago during a great algae bloom that got transported underground and today we call it crude oil. ... We take that process and speed it up by 10 million years and produce green crude.'[43]

Such confidence in technological capability to replicate powerful geological processes is unwarranted. Fossil fuels are dead microorganisms that have been compressed under thick layers of rock, in intense heat, for hundreds of millions of years. The challenges of replicating these conditions, responsible for the high energy density of fossil fuels, have not been surmounted. In 2011, global production of algae only amounted to about 20,000 tonnes. Professor Jerry Brand of the University of Texas said, 'No-one knows how to grow any kind of microorganism at very large scale – multiple hectares'. Species with the combination of three key qualities – high oil content, fast reproduction and hardiness – have proved difficult to seek out and reproduce.[44]

Algae test flight programmes have been constrained by lack of volumes. Biofuel for a Japan Airlines Boeing 747 flight over the ocean to the east of Sendai, on 30 January 2009, consisted of less than 1 per cent algae, supplied by Sapphire Energy, mixed with jatropha and camelina.[45] Algae test flights in 2010 were confined to small military planes. A Royal Netherlands Air Force Apache helicopter flew with 50 per cent biofuel made from algae and used cooking oil. Airbus's parent company, European Aeronautic Defence and Space Company (EADS), conducted two test flights of a Diamond DA42, a four-seat propeller plane, with 100 per cent algae-derived biofuel in one of the two engines, at the Berlin Air show in June 2010, then a few weeks later at the Farnborough Air Show in southern England.

EADS had intended to use an Airbus plane for the Farnborough test flight, but insufficient algae based fuel was available.[46] Nevertheless, EADS hailed algae as 30 times more productive than terrestrial crops, and speculated that 6,000 sq. km of algae beds could supply 10 per cent of global aviation fuel by 2025–30.[47] Algae production on this scale remains in the realms of science fiction. In 2012, EADS formed a partnership with ENN, a Chinese bioenergy company producing a mere 10 tonnes of algal biofuel per year.[48]

Algae's prolific growth is due to its photosynthetic efficiency, harnessing sunlight to convert carbon dioxide into organic compounds. As it grows it absorbs more carbon dioxide than any other type of plant. Enthusiasts promote visions of algae farms soaking up industrial emissions, helping solve the climate crisis. But the first-ever comprehensive life-cycle assessment of the environmental impacts of algae biofuel, led by Andres Clarens, civil and environmental engineering professor at the University of Virginia, encompassed many production methods and concluded that the greenhouse emissions were higher than for biofuel derived from corn and canola, a variety of rapeseed. Fossil fuel use included prodigious amounts of fertilisers and processing machinery including centrifuges to separate the algae from water.[49] Sapphire Energy, the algae producer that supplied the Continental Airlines and Japan Airlines test flights, has stated that energy is one of its main costs. Algae is skimmed from the surface of circular vats with a giant rotating arm, put through two filters and a two-storey centrifuge then trucked to a refinery.[50]

The USAF tested algae fuel for the first time on 20 June 2011. A Seahawk helicopter flew on 50 per cent algal fuel supplied by Solazyme, a San Francisco-based biofuel producer.[51] Six months later, Solazyme supplied algal biofuel for a United Airlines Boeing 737 flight from Houston to Chicago. Algae made up

40 per cent of the fuel mix, and Solazyme was contracted to supply United Airlines with nearly 76 million litres of algal fuel per year. If this order is fulfilled, it will amount to just 1 per cent of the airline's fuel consumption.[52] The name of the fuel producer, Solazyme, has connotations of solar energy. But the algae were grown in the dark, and fed with industrial sugars.[53] Producing the algae depends on nutrients from a terrestrial crop, so it raises the same energy input and land use concerns as other biofuels.[54] Solazyme is building a commercial-scale algae fuel factory, next to a sugarcane mill in Sao Paolo, thanks to a $120 million loan from the Brazilian Development Bank.[55]

Cooking Oil and Cellulose

During 2011, Finnair, KLM, Thomson Airways, Air France and Alaska Airlines conducted commercial flights partially powered by used cooking oil.[56] FoE immediately identified the main pitfall of the latest new fuel source, the sheer volumes required. Thomson Airways' biofuel trial flight burned 100 litres of fuel per passenger. FoE calculated that it would take 100 years for the average person to save up this amount of used cooking oil, and slammed the flight as a 'hollow PR stunt'.[57]

A series of 75 Alaska Airlines flights, from Seattle to Washington and Portland, used fuel containing 20 per cent used cooking oil. Billy Glover, Boeing's vice president of environment and aviation policy, claimed that the used cooking oil fuel resulted in half the carbon emissions of conventional jet fuel, based on analysis that discounted the emissions from food production, before the cooking oil was processed into jet fuel.[58] Processing the used cooking oil into jet fuel cannot be disassociated from the full life-cycle. Incorporating used cooking oil into the jet fuel supply would create a market for it, helping to perpetuate wasteful food processing which uses, then discards, large amounts of edible oil.

A report by Lukas Ross of the Oakland Institute found that if all the used cooking oil in the United States were to be used for jet fuel, in excess of 700 million litres in 2010, this would only be sufficient to keep the country's planes aloft for three days. Furthermore, unravelling the full supply chain reveals that adopting used cooking oil as biofuel does impact on food supplies. In 2000, three-quarters of US cooking oil was used for animal feed. By 2012, one-third of this oil had been diverted to biofuel production. Farmers replaced it with alternative sources of livestock feed, such as corn and palm oil.[59]

A number of initiatives aim to produce jet fuel from wood, including a plant at Stockholm's Arlanda Airport,[60] a Finnair scheme using locally sourced woodchips[61] and a Virgin Australia demonstration plant using Australian-grown eucalyptus.[62] Wood is already burned for heat and to generate electricity. Liquid fuel made from wood, and other fibrous biomass such as grasses, husks, stems and leaves – known as 'cellulosic biofuel' – has only been produced in small quantities. In the United States, more than $1.5 billion of grants and loans have been poured into companies promising technological breakthroughs, to little avail. A 2011 report by the National Academy of Sciences concluded that 'currently, no commercially viable biorefineries exist for converting cellulosic biomass to fuel'.[63]

Colorado-based Gevo failed to produce cellulosic biofuel in spite of millions of dollars of government funding, then turned to making speciality chemicals and fuel from corn.[64] LanzaTech, a firm specialising in carbon capture and alternative fuels, has produced jet fuel from gases emitted by heavy industry and lignin, an inedible part of the cell walls of plants arising as a by-product of cellulosic ethanol production.[65] Utilisation of lignin marks a technological advance, but wider applicability depends upon scale production of cellulosic ethanol.

The Northwest Advanced Renewables Alliance (NARA) is researching processes for making biofuel from forestry 'residue' such as woodchip and wood pulp, from Idaho, Washington, Montana and Oregon.[66]

Forest 'residue' could not supply sufficient biomass for scale production of jet fuel. Almuth Ernsting of Biofuelwatch researched use of wood in power stations throughout Europe, and discovered that 'deadwood, branches, leaves and twigs and even tree stumps are increasingly defined as "residues" even though they are essential for recycling nutrients and thus keeping soils fertile, for biodiversity and for carbon storage'. Demand for these 'residues' outpaces production, leading to increased use of logs and whole trees.[67] Scale production of cellulosic biofuel would raise the spectre of monoculture plantations. Moreover, it offers no solution to the food versus fuel issue. The amount of fertile land is finite, and biomass requires nutrients, whether it is edible to humans or not. Smolker explains that 'the distinction between food and non-food biomass is nonsensical, because of course underlying all plant biomass growth, is the soil, water and nutrients that are essential to plant growth, and are increasingly in short supply'.[68]

On 19 June 2012, one day before Rio+20, the UN Conference on Sustainable Development in Rio, an Azul Airlines Embraer jet flew over the city, using fuel made from Brazilian-grown sugarcane. Embraer issued a press release claiming 'another major step towards a sustainable air transportation industry'. Adalberto Febeliano of Azul Airlines trivialised the issue of growing a crop for industrial use on farmland, saying 'Brazil has abundant arable land, which allows for the growing of sugarcane in ways that do not displace other crops, such as food.'[69]

It is feasible that this edible crop will be incorporated into the jet fuel supply. Byogy, a San José-based biofuel producer, has formed a subsidiary to source large volumes of Brazilian sugarcane, and in a joint venture with Brazilian ethanol producer Itapecuru Bioenergia, aims to produce 19 million litres of jet fuel per year by mid-2014. Qatar Airways, which has already demonstrated its commitment to alternative fuels with its use of GTL, has invested in the programme.[70]

A few days after Azul's sugarcane flight, on 28 June 2012, corn-derived fuel supplied by Gevo was used in a Thunderbolt jet test flight.[71] Gevo's receipt of a US patent for fermentation technology for processing corn into fuel marks a step towards commercialisation.[72]

The first ever flight powered by 100 per cent biofuel used carinata, an edible crop similar to camelina and also known as Ethiopian mustard. With support from several Canadian government agencies, 40 farmers in Canada's mid-western prairies were contracted to grow carinata. In October 2012, the fuel was used for a Dassault Falcon corporate jet flight from Ottawa to Montreal and back.[73] The firm that contracted the carinata production for the test flight, Agrisoma Biosciences, shared its experience of growing the new crop in a regional agricultural magazine. It was grown alongside canola, an edible crop. Yields were higher than for canola, but carinata was not a miracle crop. Spraying was required to rid the crop of thistles and there was insect damage.[74]

Representing the interests of the world's airlines, IATA published a 'Fact sheet: alternative fuels', containing a list of 'Sustainable sources of biomass'. It is a wish list rather than a realistic assessment of the industry, stating that 'Biofuels should be made from a wide variety of sustainable, non-food biomass sources that include algae, camelina, halophytes, jatropha, switch grass and municipal waste'.[75] It states that algae 'Can produce up to 250 times more oil per unit area than soybeans', even though it has only supplied a minute proportion of fuel for a few test flights. Camelina, edible and highly nutritious, is referred to as an 'energy crop'. The document states that jatropha 'can be grown on degraded land and is resistant to drought'. Yet overwhelming evidence to the contrary was acknowledged in a report by the European Commission and representatives of the biofuel and aviation industries: 'It is yet unclear at which commercial conditions future large scale supply of e.g. jatropha oils can be realized from degraded land due to much lower yields than previously expected.'[76]

No flights have taken place using fuel made from switch grass, municipal waste or halophytes, plants that thrive in salt water. Mexican carrier Interjet planned a flight using salicornia, an oilseed halophyte. Between 2–3,000 kg of oil were anticipated from a 1 hectare plot. The actual yield was just 80 kg.[77] IATA's list omits three edible crops, sugarcane, corn and carinata, even though each has been used in test flights and steps have been taken towards commercialisation.

Together with more fuel-efficient aircraft, adoption of biofuels is a key strand of aviation's greenhouse gas emission reductions strategy. IATA and airlines frequently state that biofuels offer 80 per cent greenhouse gas reductions compared with conventional kerosene. FoE regards this figure as 'wildly optimistic and unscientific', maintaining that comprehensive life-cycle analyses 'consistently show that most of the currently used biofuels are worse for the climate than fossil fuels'.[78] For all the hype over biofuels, IATA expects the share of global jet fuel consumption to be modest for the foreseeable future, asserting that between 3 to 6 per cent is 'achievable by 2020'.[79] The drive to supply the world's fleet with biofuels fails to address dependence on fossil fuels, while threatening to compound climate change and convert large areas of land from feeding people to feeding planes.

3

Local environmental impacts

Localised Air Pollution

In addition to the long-term, global effects of greenhouse gas emissions, aircraft emit a cocktail of other pollutants which are damaging to respiratory health. Communities living near airports bear the brunt, suffering the highest concentrations. Debi Wagner documents 17 years of investigation of pollution from Sea-Tac Airport (Seattle-Tacoma) in her book *Over My Head*. Pollutants emitted by aircraft at take-off and landing include nitrogen and sulphur oxides, formaldehyde, benzene, unburned hydrocarbons, ozone, carbon monoxide and soot. Once pollutants are dispersed into the atmosphere, combining with pollution from road transport and other industries, it is difficult to ascertain the source of emissions, and the proportion for which aviation is responsible. Wagner explains that the aviation industry 'hides behind the ambiguity of emission identification'.[1]

Sea-Tac maintained that more pollution was emitted by road transport than planes. All airports can use this defensive argument, as a network of 'feeder roads' is essential for throughput of passengers and cargo. But analysis of FAA data showed high levels of toxic pollutants from planes, emitted within the few minutes of take-off. A DC-10 take-off taking two minutes emitted the same amount of nitrogen oxides as 21,530 cars. A Boeing 747 idling on an airport apron awaiting take-off for ten minutes emitted as much sulphur oxides as half a million cars.[2] Wagner found that the US regulatory framework to protect people from pollution emitted by road transport, and all other industries such as incinerators and refineries, did not apply to aviation, which she described as a 'giant, unregulated, unmonitored, exempt, dangerous polluter nobody understands'.[3]

The State Department of Public Health (SDPH) responded to pressure to survey health data for the areas around Sea-Tac. Between 1992 and 1995, cancer rates in communities living within 5 and 8 km of the airport were 10 per cent higher than the average for the state. The rate of glioblastoma, a type of brain tumour associated with exposure to hydrocarbons and formaldehyde, was particularly high among people living within 1.6 km of the airport, 75 per cent higher than the state average. Analysis of heath data for people living in the post code nearest to Boeing Field Airport, to the north of Sea-Tac, also showed high rates of ill health. The life expectancy of 70.4 years was nearly six years less than nearby Seattle. The asthma rate was 57 per cent higher, the cancer death rate 36 per cent higher and the rate of respiratory disease 26 per cent higher.[4]

A 2002 study found that aircraft emissions from Chicago O'Hare Airport were partly responsible for higher than average rates of cancer. There was evidence of cancer 'hot-spots', with rates up to 50 per cent higher than the overall local average, in communities living underneath flightpaths. Risk assessments for expansion of operations at two Californian airports, Oakland and Santa Monica, warned of increased cancer risk in neighbouring residential areas. The projected risk far exceeded the recognised significance threshold of 10 in one million, up to 22 in one million for people residing near one of Oakland's runways and as high as 26 in one million in the event of increased piston aircraft movements at Santa Monica.[5]

Benzene and toluene are carcinogenic, and an Australian study discovered that emissions from aircraft occur mainly as a result of incomplete fuel combustion during landing, so concentrations are higher over airport areas. There is no safe dose of benzyprene; it is so highly carcinogenic that it can cause tumours in laboratory animals exposed to doses as low as a few millionths of a gram. Benzyprene was detected in soil, vegetation, water and snow around airports. Aircraft using Sydney Airport were estimated to release up to 2 kg of benzyprene annually into surrounding communities.[6]

Wagner has uncovered strong evidence that localised pollutants from aircraft increase cancer in communities near airports. It is difficult to ascertain the exact causes for ill health; there are many pollutants, interacting with genetic factors, but this does not alter the certainty that there is a problem and action must be taken: 'One thing is for sure, statistics and evidence say there is a higher risk for people living near and working at an airport… People should be warned. They should be removed.'[7] Wagner's research raises concerns for airport communities worldwide.

Particulates, minute solid and liquid particles emitted by industrial processes and vehicles, lodge in the lungs causing respiratory and heart problems. Research by the Massachusetts Institute of Technology (MIT) attributed 2,000 premature deaths a year to aviation-related particulates emitted at take-off and landing. The MIT study also estimated that nitrogen and sulphur oxides from planes flying at cruise altitudes cause 8,000 premature deaths per year, far away from airports. Most of these pollutants are emitted over North America and Europe, but are carried eastwards over Asia by prevailing winds, where they combine with ammonia from farming to form particulates. Nearly half the deaths occur in India and China.[8]

Noise impacts on communities living under flightpaths are a focal point for campaigns against aviation expansion. John Stewart, leader of the campaign against expansion of Heathrow, redresses the neglect of noise as an important health issue in his book *Why Noise Matters*.[9] Noise is not just an annoyance. High levels and prolonged exposure cause demonstrable health problems, both psychological and physiological. In 2001, an estimated 30 million people worldwide were 'exposed to disturbing levels of aircraft noise'; the number will have grown significantly since then. Aircraft noise is particularly stress-inducing because it contains a high proportion of low-frequency noise, which destabilises the human body. Night flights cause the most stress because the noise continues as daytime noise has subsided, causing sleep disturbance.

A 2005 study of the effects of aircraft and road traffic noise on children's health in the United Kingdom, Spain and the Netherlands found impaired performance in reading comprehension and memory.[10] A Swiss study of 4.6 million people between 2000 and 2005 linked daytime aircraft noise levels of 60 decibels and above to an increase in coronary heart disease. Long-term exposure, for 15 years or more, was associated with a 50 per cent increase in the risk of a fatal heart attack.[11] A study of 4,681 people living near Heathrow, Berlin Tegel, Schiphol, Stockholm Arlanda, Milan Malpensa or Athens airports for at least five years, found that each 10 decibel increase in aircraft noise corresponded with a 14 per cent increase in the risk of hypertension, a rise in blood pressure which increases the risk of heart attacks, heart failure and strokes. In the noisiest houses the level of aircraft noise was 30 decibels higher than the quietest, making the risk of hypertension 40 per cent higher. The research also discovered that night-time aircraft noise causes a rise in blood pressure while people sleep, even if they do not wake up.[12]

New aircraft are quieter, but the flurry of publicity surrounding Boeing's 787, or 'Dreamliner', exaggerated the noise reduction. For example, a magazine advertisement claimed that Boeing was testing aerodynamic designs which would enable the 787 to 'fly 60% quieter than ever before'. The UK Advertising Standards Authority upheld a complaint that this statement was misleading, issuing an adjudication which stated that the noise reduction would be barely discernible for some people living within the noise footprint of the aircraft.[13]

When quieter planes are added to an airline's fleet, older, noisier aircraft often remain in service. So the overall effect is mitigation of the increase in aircraft noise, rather than a reduction. Frequently, old passenger aircraft are converted to freighters, increasing the noise burden on communities living in the shadow of cargo airports. Experiments with operational measures to reduce noise have focused on continuous descent. Another possibility is to land planes at a steeper angle to reduce the amount of low-level flying over residential areas. Stewart and his co-authors do not anticipate significant noise reduction from either of these techniques, and aviation growth offsets any gains: 'the projected growth in numbers is likely to nullify any advances in technology or operation procedures'.[14]

Sweet Poison

When temperatures dip below freezing, ice builds up on planes parked on the tarmac. Sometimes fringes of icicles can be seen dangling from the edges of a plane's wings and tailfin. Even the smallest particle of ice can alter the plane's aerodynamics and cause an accident. Before take-off, booms mounted on trucks spray planes with deicing fluid, made of ethylene or propylene-based glycols mixed with water. The most recent fatal accident attributed to inadequate deicing occurred at Tyumen Airport in Russia, on 2 April 2012. A passenger plane which had been parked in the snow crashed into a field shortly after take-off and caught fire. Thirty-three of the 43 people on board were killed.[15]

Glycols, recognisable by a distinctive sweet odour, are harmful to human and animal health if ingested, but the main problem arising from airport operations is the discharge of runoff into waterways. Natural bacteria break down glycols, but this process depletes oxygen levels in water. When deicing fluid is discharged into a body of water that is not large or fast-flowing enough to dilute glycols to a sufficiently low level, fish and other aquatic organisms choke to death. At its worst, glycol pollution creates 'dead zones' devoid of aquatic life.

Heathrow was fined $21,000 for exceeding the maximum

limits for discharging surface water runoff containing glycols into a nearby lake in April 2008. The airport exceeded its glycol discharge limits and hundreds of stickleback, perch and tench were killed. Thousands more fish were relocated to another lake nearby, and recreational facilities at the lake were closed for a week for a clean-up effort. An Environmental Agency spokesperson described the incident as having a 'devastating impact' on the lake's fish population.[16]

Deicing fluid management at US airports with freezing winter conditions is highly variable. Strict regulations for management and disposal of used glycol-based antifreeze products, categorised as hazardous waste, are not applied to airports. Some airports routinely discharge untreated deicing fluid; others have built complex systems to collect waste fluid and either treat it to remove glycols, which can be recycled, or break glycols down with bacteria and oxygenate the water before it is discharged into waterways. Deicing fluid is sprayed at high pressure in an unconfined, outdoor environment, so even the best treatment systems only capture a proportion of glycol runoff. In 2010, the Environmental Protection Agency (EPA) estimated that nearly 80 million litres per year of deicing fluid drained from airports into surface water.[17]

Portland Airport, in Oregon, spent $31 million on a system to collect glycol runoff in 2006, but the holding tank was not big enough. Discharge into the slow-flowing Columbia Slough damaged the habitat of juvenile coho and chinook salmon. Dozens of water quality violations resulted in a state fine of $82,500.[18] A new treatment plant, using bacteria to break down the 227,000 litres of glycol-based deicing fluid used per year, became operational in 2012.[19]

Buckeye Brook, a spawning ground for blueblack herring, runs through the Rhode Island city of Warwick. The river was known for its spectacular herring run each spring, before decades of overfishing, rubbish dumping and waste chemicals from a landfill site took their toll. By the 1970s, the herring run had diminished to a trickle. T. F. Green Airport joined the list of polluters with its discharge of deicing fluid. From the early 1990s to the mid-2000s, after ice storms, the sweet smell of glycols was noticeable to communities living downstream from the airport outfall. An orange coating on vegetation and rocks was identified as glycol-eating bacteria. The Buckeye Brook Coalition coordinated a clean-up campaign and 2011 saw the best herring run in the nine years since monitoring began. T.F. Green Airport had reduced the concentration of glycols in deicing fluid and used vacuum trucks. But there was still room for improvement as the trucks only captured an average of 35 per cent of glycol runoff.[20] In 2011, the airport committed to further reductions in glycol pollution, agreeing to build a $25 million collection system.[21]

Cincinnati/Northern Kentucky Airport discharges glycols onto Gunpowder Creek, and paid $125,000 in fines for permit violations between 1992 and 2001.[22] A $50 million treatment plant failed to stem the pollution. Glycol concentrations were so high that the creek stopped freezing over in winter.[23] Ongoing campaigning and packed-out public hearings resulted in a more stringent discharge permit and more pipes to collect from runway deicing pads. In 2005, for the first time in many years, the creek froze over in winter.[24] The airport also reduced glycol consumption by using a forced air stream to remove some of the ice from aircraft. The efficacy of the glycol-reduction measures was demonstrated when glycol use in winter 2008–09, nearly 2.5 million litres, was less than half the amount used in 2003–04.[25]

Not all airports have responded positively to pressure to reduce glycol runoff. Gerald R. Ford Airport in Michigan discharges unfiltered runoff into Trout Creek, which used to teem with fish but is now barren. William McCarrel, the sole resident on the airport stakeholders committee, observed that every winter, a month after the start of the deicing season, a film appeared on the creek, which would build up and form a 'gelatinous mass'. In 2011, the airport decided that a wastewater plant or deicing pad would be too expensive, and sought permission to build a pipeline to pump about 350,000 litres per year into Thornapple River.[26]

Anchorage, Alaska's main airport, discharges glycols into Cook Inlet, a geographically isolated habitat for a genetically distinct population of Beluga whales. Winter 2010–11 saw levels of biological oxygen demand (BOD) and chemical oxygen demand (COD), the measurements for glycol contamination levels, consistently between 15 and 40 times higher than EPA limits. This might have been partially attributable to late snowfall. Under normal weather conditions, snow absorbs glycol runoff, which is then released gradually, diluted with water, in the spring melt. Lack of snow meant excess glycol went straight from the airfield into the drains.[27]

A proven alternative to glycols already exists, but the low level of take-up is disappointing. Infrared deicing technology uses light waves to break down the crystal structure of snow and ice. There is no toxic waste stream, and greenhouse gas emissions are just one-tenth of the emissions from conventional deicing trucks, which burn fuel continuously as they sit on the tarmac. Infrared deicing is in use, and has proved reliable, but only at a small scale, alongside conventional deicing methods, at several airports including Oslo, Beijing, Rhinelander in Wisconsin, Dallas/Fort Worth, Newark and JFK.[28] Infrared deicing was effective throughout an ice storm at Newark in March 2007, when each Boeing 747 deiced using glycols required up to 19,000 litres of fluid.

An infrared deicing hangar at JFK handles between five and seven planes per hour, a small fraction of the airport's 1,200 daily aircraft movements.[29] JFK continues to discharge untreated water containing deicing chemicals into Jamaica Bay, the expanse of wetlands passengers see when flying into or out of the airport. Brad Sewell of the Natural Resources Defense Council (NRDC) described the bay as 'New York City's ecological crown jewel'. It is an oasis for migratory birds and teeming with marine life hosting 80 different fish species, porpoise and turtles.[30] In 2011, NRDC successfully sued the New York Department of Environmental Conservation to update guidelines on monitoring of toxins, enforcing frequent measuring and testing of chemical runoff from JFK, marking a major victory in the longstanding campaign to clean up Jamaica Bay.[31]

On Flood Plains

Airports built on flood plains in Asian regions with patterns of heavy, concentrated rainfall can exacerbate flooding. The airport's runways and apron replace porous ground with an impermeable concrete surface, blocking the natural absorption of water. Flood prevention measures, including boundary walls, containment lakes, culverts under runways and submersible pumps, protect the airport. But excess water which is channelled away from the airport site raises the water level in neighbouring communities.

Expansion of Chennai Airport, the biggest in southern India, has encroached on the Adyar River, which winds through the city into the Bay of Bengal. India was lashed with unusually heavy rains in autumn 2005, and in November, people living near the adjoining railway station held a demonstration against the discharge of rainwater from the airport into their community.[32] At the beginning of December Chennai's departure and arrival halls were inundated with water[33] and a section of the 20-year-old outer boundary wall collapsed.[34] A new wall to prevent water from flowing into airport grounds displaced excess water, and following heavy rains in November 2008, villages hemmed in between the airport and the river were flooded.[35]

Chennai Airport then began extension of its second runway into the path of the Adyar River, building a 200 m long bridge over it. The bridge is held aloft by 477 pillars and 2,440 prestressed concrete girders, making it strong enough to bear the weight of the Airbus A380. The bridge is 2 m above the 2005 flood level, and an airport official said that the 'entire structure is built with a flood-free mechanism' and would not interfere with the flow of the river. But the bridge was built on open land over which the Adyar River used to flow. The neighbouring communities of Pozhichallur, Pammal and Nandambakkam blamed the bridge over the runway when, following two days of heavy rain in November 2011, water was released from a reservoir upstream. The river swelled and 50 houses were flooded.[36]

Urbanisation on flood plains alongside Mumbai's arterial river, the Mithi, has made the city more flood prone. Mumbai Airport is one of the worst offenders. The first runway was built over the river, and extension of the second runway created a bend in it. The airport is thought to be partly responsible for the annual submergence of parts of the suburbs of Kurla and Kalina, under up to 2 m of water.[37] When Mumbai received over 94 cm of rainfall on 26 July 2005, the highest ever recorded for the city in a single day, the Mithi River burst its banks. The city suffered widespread flooding and more than 900 people lost their lives. Mumbai Airport was closed for two days, and reporter Nidhi Jamwal wrote that it 'resembled a swimming pool with the Mithi river flowing over the runway'.[38]

After the floods subsided, the state government embarked on a programme to reduce the risk of flooding from the Mithi River. This encompassed widening and deepening the riverbed, removing slums along the riverbank, reducing waste dumping, removing silt, expanding storm water drainage capacity and building more pumping stations. Jamwal criticised the scheme as 'only creating a façade of a flood-proof Mumbai'. Flood prevention was used as a pretext for forcible removal of slums, while the government remained 'tight-lipped on large encroachments such as Mumbai airport'.[39] By 2009, stretches of the Mithi River upstream and downstream from the airport had been widened to 100 m, but the airport section of the river, channelled beneath the runway, was still a narrow pinch point, just 27 m wide.[40] The airport took action to protect itself from flooding, raising the height of the main runway by 1 m in time for the start of the monsoon season in June 2011.[41] A year later, two streams had been desilted and two culverts blasted with dynamite through rock under the runway.[42]

Jamwal only learned of plans for a second Mumbai airport when she spotted a blue sign reading 'Site for international airport, Navi Mumbai' when travelling along a highway near the coast, where the Panvel creek flows into Mumbai's deep natural harbour. The 20 sq. km site is crossed by the Ulwe and Ghadi rivers, covered by pools of water and mudflats, with mangroves along the shoreline.[43] Journalist Kalpana Sharma warned that destruction of mangroves would make the area more susceptible to flooding. Mangroves are uniquely able to withstand coastal conditions, thriving in the combination of saline and fresh water. Acting as a buffer between land and sea, mangroves help stabilise water levels in a wide catchment area, absorbing rainfall and tidal surges, their interwoven roots preventing erosion.[44]

The Navi project threatens to disrupt drainage patterns over the entire region. Approval appears to be a foregone conclusion. Jamwal was one of just 30 attendees of a public hearing, boycotted by residents of the 18 villages standing to lose land to the development, some of whom waved black flags in protest. It was 'wrapped up in an hour'.[45] Coastal Regulation Zone notification, ensuring tight control over construction, was amended in order to allow conversion of mangrove forest to an airport.[46] Another regulatory hurdle was removed in 2012, when the Environment Ministry's Expert Appraisal Committee approved two roads leading to the site. Sections over mangroves are to be built on stilts.[47]

Bangkok's Suvarnabhumi Airport, built at sea level on a boggy site known as 'cobra swamp', opened in 2006, encircled by a flood wall 23.5 km long and 3.5 m high. Within two years the wall had subsided by 1 m and a programme to dredge 20 drainage canals, and build a new 10 km canal to channel water into the Gulf of Thailand, began.[48] In 2009 residents of single-storey dwellings in the neighbouring Lat Krabang district were knee-deep in water for a month. They blamed the airport for worsening flooding. Before it was built floodwaters had receded quickly into the swamp, which acted as a natural water retention area.[49] Suvarnabhumi was declared floodproof in 2010, upon completion of ponds big enough to hold up to 4.6 million cu. m of water, and two emergency pumps capable of draining 1 million cu. m of water per day.[50]

Suvarnabhumi's flood protection proved effective in October 2011 when, following months of heavy rain, Thailand's worst floods in half a century killed 562 people. But floodwaters breached the perimeter of Bangkok's second airport, Don Muang. The wheels of parked planes were submerged in water and the main road to the airport became a thoroughfare for motorboats. But the upper floor of the terminal provided a refuge for 350 people, who camped out amidst the check-in counters and baggage belts.[51] Don Muang Airport reopened in March 2012, after four months of pumping and draining.[52]

Fuel Leaks

Jet fuel pipelines are equipped with sophisticated systems to operate pumps and valves to prevent leaks, and shut down the flow automatically should a leak occur. When these systems fail, the smallest hole can result in spills of large volumes of fuel. Jet fuel is pumped under pressure and leaks can spread quickly, far from the airport site into rivers and sewer systems. When jet fuel permeates into groundwater it can spread slowly for many years, causing contamination far from the source of the leak.

In November 2006, 1.5 million litres of fuel leaked into storm water pipes from OR Tambo, on the eastern outskirts of Johannesburg. Contamination was detected 1.5 km away in protected wetlands, and autopsies on dead ducks which had ingested the fuel revealed that their insides had been eaten away. Local ecologists found that 4–5,000 cu. m of soil had been contaminated, and expected the effects to be evident for over ten years.[53]

At the beginning of 2012 communities living alongside Wilson Creek in Milwaukee complained of a smell of oil. The source of the leak was not discovered until late February. The decades-old pipeline supplying Mitchell Airport, owned by Shell, had a 2 mm hole, about the size of the tip of a pen. By the time the spill was contained, 34,000 litres of jet fuel had leaked into the sewer system and the Kinnickinnic River.[54] Another Shell pipeline, supplying Grantley Adams Airport in Barbados, leaked on several occasions between 1995 and 2003. Eighty hectares of farmland to the north of the airport were contaminated, ruining fertile black soil which had grown many kinds of vegetables.[55] By the time Shell agreed a compensation package, in 2010, about 25 of the farmers affected by the spill had abandoned their land.[56]

Jet fuel leaks can remain undetected for long periods. A leak was discovered in a pipeline running only 1 m deep under an environmentally sensitive marshland area near one of JFK's runways in autumn 2008. Six months later over 340,000 litres of fuel had been recovered and the full extent of the spill was still unknown.[57] In November 2007 a leak was discovered in the supply pipeline to aircraft stands at Heathrow's Terminal 1. A valve was losing about 7 litres per minute, but it was not known how long it had had been leaking. An investigation revealed that the leak detection system had had not been working for five months. Boreholes were sunk to extract the fuel, and by June 2010 nearly 140,000 litres had been recovered. The fuel remaining in the ground was still spreading, risking contamination of an aquifer feeding into four rivers used for drinking water.[58]

Pipelines spring leaks far away from airport boundaries. On 14 July 2007 a pipeline ruptured in a horse pasture near Huntsville, Texas. Jet fuel spilled from a 1.5 m split in the pipeline and over 1 million litres poured into Turkey Creek, spreading over 7 km downstream. Fish, wildlife and trees were killed at the spill site.[59] A jet fuel pipeline supplying Israel Defense Force (IDF) bases, running under the unique mountains, rivers and waterfalls of the Negev nature reserve, was struck by a tractor in June 2011.

Ironically, the accident took place when workers were testing the pipeline as part of rehabilitation work. It took emergency crews five hours to plug the leak, and by this time more than 1.5 million litres of jet fuel had spilled into the Nahal Zin stream. Nature and Parks Authority inspectors said the clean-up, involving transfer of contaminated soil to a treatment centre to extract the fuel, would be a 'Sisyphean' effort.[60]

Leaking underground tanks and pipelines are difficult to repair. In May 2010 King Shaka, the new airport in Durban, South Africa, with its 6 million litre fuel farm, was preparing for opening in the build-up to the football World Cup. [61] Seventeen serious leaks were discovered in pipelines and pumps underneath the 230,000 tonnes of asphalt laid down for runways and taxiways, and managers were concerned about the possibility of an explosion on airport grounds. More than 8,000 valves were found to be defective, and the repair operation required excavation of large sections of pipeline buried 7 m deep.[62]

Extracting fuel from soil and groundwater involves heavy-duty machinery, but is of limited effectiveness. By the time a leak was discovered at Wheeler Sack Army Airfield in Jefferson County, New York, in 2006, over 1.3 million litres of jet fuel had leaked from storage containers into the ground. Four years later, the federal government approved a $6.5 million clean-up contract. It was expected this would entail digging 240 wells, and that although the latest vacuum-enhanced skimming would recover about 90 per cent of the fuel, the remaining 10 per cent would remain in the ground.[63]

Jet fuel was discovered leaking from pipes under a loading facility at Kirtland Air Force Base in Albuquerque in 1999. The fuel system was built in the 1950s, and had probably been leaking for decades. By 2010, jet fuel was detected over 150 m underground, sitting on top of the groundwater, raising concerns that water from ten of Albuquerque's water wells could become unsafe to drink.[64] The full extent of the spill is still unknown, but in May 2012 the New Mexico Environment Department estimated that over 90 million litres had leaked. This is more than double the volume of the Exxon Valdez disaster in 1989 (in which an oil tanker collided with rocks off Prince William Sound, spilling crude oil which spread along more than 2,000 kilometres of Alaska's shoreline).[65]

Fires Far Away

Leaks in airport fuel supply bring the risk of fire, since when exposed to air, kerosene evaporates and forms clouds of highly flammable vapour. In August 2010, two men were convicted of plotting to blow up JFK's fuel farm and underground pipelines running under the Queens neighbourhood, aiming to kill thousands of people.[66] The prospect of terrorist attacks on vast quantities of highly flammable fuel, pumped along pipelines running under densely populated areas, sounds alarming, but the plot was unfeasible. Fuel can only ignite if it is exposed to air, and fuel farms are protected by airport security. Unauthorised use of the heavy machinery required for digging underground and puncturing thick steel pipelines would be highly conspicuous. Any irregularity in the flow, temperature or pressure of fuel supply to JFK would immediately be detected by the SCADA (Supervisory Control and Data Acquisition) satellite network, which monitors the pipelines supplying many of the world's airports.[67]

Fuel tank walls are strong, but not invulnerable. An air strike or a ground-to-air missile can cause a puncture. On 21 April 2010, the Lam Luk Ka oil depot in Bangkok was targeted during anti-government protests. A grenade fired from the motorway, just 200 m away, hit one of the depot's 19 tanks, T-401D, which supplies Suvarnabhumi Airport. The tank, holding 9 million litres of fuel at the time, was set alight and the fire took an hour to extinguish. The grenade made a 4 cm hole in the tank but did not ignite the main body of fuel as it did not penetrate the double-layered steel walls.[68]

The possibility of terrorists targeting airports' fuel supply is a concern, but the everyday reality is a litany of leaks and fires caused by equipment failure and human error. Overall, considering the global scale of operations, airport fuel supply is well managed with a good safety record, but, when accidents do happen, the effects on people and the environment are serious. I discovered a greater number of fatalities from fires far away from airport sites, at fuel depots where kerosene and other petroleum products are stored and distributed, and refineries where oil is processed to make jet fuel.

The Buncefield fuel depot, 30 km north of Heathrow airport, exploded on 11 December 2005, injuring 43 people and forcing 2,000 people to evacuate their homes. The explosion was audible from over 200 km away and the plumes were visible from space.[69] A fire raged for five days, the biggest in peacetime Europe.[70] At the time of the accident, Buncefield supplied about half the 21 million litres of fuel per day used by Heathrow, and was holding 35 million litres of fuel, mostly aviation fuel and petrol for vehicles.[71] The investigation concluded that the tanks caught fire after 250,000 litres of petrol had leaked from a tank and ignited.[72] A lengthy and complex corporate criminal trial concluded in June 2010. Five firms were found guilty of safety breaches. Hertfordshire Oil Storage Ltd, jointly owned by the oil conglomerates Total and Chevron, was singled out for failing to prevent the accident and limit the effects.[73] The safety of Total's UK aviation-related operations failed again on 30 June 2010, when a worker was killed in a fire at the firm's Lindsey Oil Refinery in Humberside. The fire ignited when crude oil was being processed into jet fuel.[74]

An explosion at a petrol and jet fuel depot in the city of Bayamon in Puerto Rico, on 23 October 2009, triggered a fire which spread to 21 of the 40 tanks on the site, and sent out 2.8 magnitude earthquake-type ground shocks which were felt in several neighbourhoods. Firefighters battled the blaze for two days, over 1,500 people were evacuated and thick smoke billowed over the area.[75] Graffiti reading 'Boom, fire, RIP, Gulf' in three locations in the vicinity raised suspicions that the fire was started intentionally. The investigation concluded that the cause of the explosion was a fuel leak, which occurred while one of the tanks was being filled, but the cause of the ignition remained unidentified.[76]

On 29 October 2009 a fire broke out at the Indian Oil Corporation fuel depot in Jaipur, northwest India, and raged for 12 days. Half a million people were evacuated, and plumes of smoke were visible 10 km away.[77] The depot had capacity for up to 35 million litres each of gasoline, diesel and kerosene. At the time of the blaze the depot held 24 million litres of diesel, 7 million litres of gasoline and 1 million litres of kerosene. Six of the eight people working at the plant were killed, 150 were injured and at least 80 were treated in hospital for burns.[78] It transpired that the fire began as workers were preparing to transfer kerosene and petrol though a pipeline. Provision of fire-fighting equipment was inadequate and a computerised system for sealing off storage tanks had been dysfunctional for months.[79]

A serious accident was narrowly averted at the AGE Refinery in San Antonio, Texas on 5 May 2010. A tanker truck exploded at a loading dock, injuring two workers. More than 100 firefighters worked for six hours to contain the fire and prevent it from igniting 12 nearby tanks of jet fuel. Fire chief Charles Hood said that, if the tanks had caught fire, the area 'could have seen a major explosion big enough to kill people a half-mile away'.[80]

Underground jet fuel pipelines are entangled with gas, petroleum, and water pipelines and run through populated areas. If pipelines are punctured by heavy machinery during construction and maintenance work there is the risk of explosion. In November 2004 a jet fuel pipeline supplying San José Airport, running under Walnut Creek in San Francisco, exploded during construction of a water supply pipeline. Five workers were killed and four suffered serious burns.[81] Workers had accidentally cut into the fuel pipeline, resulting in a huge explosion and a fireball several storeys high.[82]

Road tankers supplying fuel to airports are more vulnerable to spills and fires than pipelines, as traffic accidents frequently result in leakage of fuel and highly flammable vapour. Amounts of fuel carried in tankers are relatively small, thousands of litres as opposed to the millions in refineries and depots, but accidents can occur in populated areas. On 27 June 2010, a tanker carrying jet fuel to T. F. Green Airport in Rhode Island flipped over on its side in the town of Foxboro, just 35 m from people sleeping in their homes. All the fuel, over 45,000 litres, gushed out. Firefighters from 14 communities joined the airport hazmat team, covering the spill in foam to prevent it catching fire. It was fortunate that the tanker skidded onto grass. If it had crashed into hard pavement, it would have been likely to produce sparks, igniting the fuel into a dangerous fireball.[83]

The outcome of a collision between a jet fuel tanker and a bus on the outskirts of the city of Erode, in Tamil Nadu, India, in November 2011, was not so fortunate. Eight people, one of whom was a child aged just two and a half, lost their lives. The tanker caught fire immediately and six of the people died instantly, their bodies charred beyond recognition. The other two victims died in hospital.[84]

4

Threats to wildlife and farmland

The Winged Menace

Pilots often refer to birds as the 'winged menace' because 'bird strikes' are a risk to aviation safety. Collisions are inevitably fatal for birds, as they are sucked into, then minced up in, the plane's engines. In some instances they leave craters, or holes, in the nose or fuselage, or cracks in the windshield. Large birds like geese, herons and eagles, or dense flocks of smaller birds such as swallows or starlings, sometimes referred to as 'feathered bullets', can destroy a plane's engines. Occasionally large birds crash through the windshields of light aircraft, leaving pilots splattered with blood.

Complex programmes to keep birds away from the site are an essential component of airport operations. Grass alongside runways is treated with chemicals to kill insects, rodents and worms which provide food sources for birds. All over the airport site, plants that attract species that birds feed on are replaced. Loud, alarming noises are used to frighten birds away, including explosives, firearms, sirens and the distress calls of target species. Predatory hawks are trained to chase away flocks of smaller birds. But birds tend to adapt to attempts to frighten them away. When this happens, birds deemed to pose a risk are removed or killed, usually with poison, gas or bullets. Nests are destroyed, or eggs covered in vegetable oil to stop them hatching. In the United

States, USDA Wildlife Services, which conducts the majority of lethal bird control at airports, including military bases, killed 164,918 birds in 2007 and 136,890 in 2008.[1]

Bird strikes can appear dramatic. It is not unusual for a plane's engine to catch fire, forcing an emergency landing. But aircraft are designed to withstand the impact, and accidents causing fatalities or injuries are rare. The worst bird strike on record occurred when a plane struck a flock of starlings and crashed into Boston harbour in 1961, killing 62 passengers. On 15 January 2009 a dramatic bird strike in New York drew attention to the risk. A flock of Canada geese destroyed both engines of a US Airways Airbus A320 shortly after take-off from LaGuardia. The pilot, Captain Chesley Sullenberger, landed the plane safely in the Hudson River, averting a major accident which would probably have killed everyone onboard, and many people on the ground in this densely populated area.[2]

In the United States, public pressure and freedom of information requests forced the release of FAA bird strike data which revealed that, between 2000 and 2008, collisions with birds more than doubled at 13 major airports including Denver, Dallas/Fort Worth, Chicago O'Hare, Hobby in Houston and JFK. Over 112,000 incidents were reported in this period, resulting in five fatalities, 93 injuries and serious damage to 3,000 aircraft. Minor bird strikes were more frequent than the data suggested. The voluntary reporting system only recorded about 20 per cent of incidents, and 91 airports had failed to meet their obligations to conduct a formal bird strike risk assessment.[3] Richard Dolbeer, bird strike adviser to the FAA said, 'Birds and planes are fighting for airspace, and it's getting increasingly crowded.' He raised particular concerns over rising populations of large birds such as Canada geese, and an increase in bird strikes further away from airports.[4]

The Hudson River incident triggered intensification of efforts to keep birds away from airports. A programme to kill Canada geese living within 8 km of JFK and LaGuardia began in June 2009, and a year later the radius was extended to 11 km.[5] By July

2010 the Canada geese population near LaGuardia had been reduced by 80 per cent.[6] Visitors to Prospect Park in Brooklyn noticed that almost the entire population of 400 Canada geese had suddenly disappeared. They had been herded into a nearby building where they were gassed with carbon dioxide.[7] The culls failed to prevent an increase in the number of bird strikes at JFK, from 127 in 2005 to 257 in 2011. USDA has proposed extending the cull to other species: mute swans, double-crested cormorants, blackbirds, starlings, crows and rock pigeons.[8]

Oakland Airport sits adjacent to protected wetlands and one of its runways juts into Oyster Bay. On 23 December 2009, 2,000 cormorants, gulls and pelicans flocked around the end of the runway. Bangers and screamers, called 'pyrotechnics', failed to frighten the birds away, so dozens were shot. The shooters did not check that the birds were dead, and injured birds were found lying among the corpses on the shoreline. Wardens collected about 60 dead and injured birds.[9] Yet like many airports, Oakland's artwork plays on aviation's association with the grace of birds in flight, belying its hostility towards avian visitors. A glass mural, 50 m long and 3 m high, depicts a flock of imperial cranes from an ancient Chinese painting layered over a satellite image of the area.[10]

Philadelphia Airport is adorned with artworks suggesting an affinity with birdlife. A permanent sculpture, consisting of six groupings of 6,749 small pewter birds, suspended from cables which transform them into different shapes, supposedly represents the 'poetry of flight'.[11] Twee art installations in 2010 included birds made from origami and viewed through a telescope.[12] Outside the passenger terminal, 35 staff monitor birdlife on the airfield and freshwater tidal marsh surrounding it, removing nests and shooting problem birds.[13]

Tampa Airport in Florida hosts a permanent exhibition of life-size sculptures of 63 seabirds, made of bronze and other metal alloys. Pelicans with a 2 m wingspan are suspended over the escalators and roost in a mangrove tree in the ticketing area.[14]

Tampa's strategies in its battle against birdlife include keeping an owl near the runway to frighten smaller birds, and sending firecrackers into the air to disperse them. If these measures fail, airport employees have the right to fire live ammunition. They are protected from fines if they kill a rare bird like a bald eagle.[15]

A 2010 update on new methods to keep birds away from the world's airports listed imitation hawks and foxes, dead birds, radio-controlled model aircraft, gongs in Beijing, slingshots in Kenya and electrified mats to reduce the number of worms near runways in New Zealand.[16] A company based at Christchurch Airport developed a new type of grass treated with a fungus that makes birds sick, claiming it would deter them from returning to the area without causing harm.[17]

New radar technology could reduce bird culls, alerting air traffic control when high numbers of birds are in airport flight-paths. Yet take-up has been slow. The FAA approved use of avian radar at commercial airports, but only as an adjunct to established bird-control activities.[18] King Shaka was the first major commercial airport to trial a radar bird detection system. This helped to allay wildlife groups' concerns that the project could place a globally significant birdlife population in jeopardy. Every summer, the largest colony of barn swallows in the world, between 3 and 5 million birds, migrates from Europe to nest in the area under the approach flightpath.[19] When King Shaka became operational the bird radar unit was accompanied by traditional methods to frighten birds, namely lasers, pyrotechnics and four border collies trained to chase them away.[20]

Loss of Green Space

There is no ideal site for airport expansion. There are always negative impacts on people and the environment on and around the site. Expanding airports in the outskirts of cities gobble up green space. Manchester Airport in northern England is encroaching on a designated 'green belt' that was intended to prevent urban sprawl. The Stop Expansion at Manchester Airport campaign is resisting construction of a business park on an oasis of trees, meadows and ponds with rare newts.[21] Hamilton Airport, to the west of Toronto, is surrounded by prime farmland. A development for freight companies on 830 hectares was approved, even though the vacancy rate at established business parks in the area is as high as 85 per cent. Projected infrastructure costs of $353 million, including roads and a sewage pipeline would be a high level of expenditure for a development anticipated to generate $52 million annually in tax revenue by 2031. In October 2010, 50 activists planted garlic on the land to highlight the threat to local food production.[22]

Frankfurt quashed protest against expansion into forests to become the biggest airport in Germany. Opposition to a third runway, proposed in 1965, led to an eleven-year legal battle. When protesters who had camped out in a forest area threatened by the project were evicted in 1981, the level of violence between protesters and police was likened to civil war. Two weeks later, a protest drew 100,000 demonstrators. On opening the third runway in 1985 the regional government declared there would be no further expansion, only to recommend a fourth runway in 2001.[23] Of the land used for Frankfurt's fourth runway, 162 hectares was forest. When construction began in January 2009, protesters camped out in the trees for months in an attempt to prevent the development. [24] On 20 October 2012, the day before the opening of the new runway, 20,000 people gathered at the airport to voice their opposition. Ever since, protesters have gathered in the terminal on Mondays, staging lively demonstrations to highlight the impact of aviation expansion on neighbouring communities and the global environment.[25]

It is simpler to plan and construct a new airport on undeveloped land, called a 'greenfield airport', than to remove and reconfigure established urbanisation. Developers seek out sparsely populated sites that are easy to connect to urban centres with land transportation networks, reasonably flat, with a plentiful supply of fresh water yet not prone to flooding. These are also the best conditions for arable farming, so plans for greenfield airports often spark conflict over a threat to land used for food production. Once a site has been earmarked for a new airport, the pressure for the development to go ahead can be inexorable. Approval and construction can drag on for decades, resulting in protracted protests from communities left living in limbo. The good news is that opposition campaigns can be effective, leading to airport projects being abandoned, compromises reducing the number and length of runways, or the selection of an alternative site.

A new airport for Nantes in western France, on farmland to the north of the city, was first mooted more than 40 years ago, to serve as a hub for Concorde.[26] The airport was approved in February 2008, and in 2011, as preparations for construction began, opposition erupted into protests over the threat of loss of farmland, pollution and waste of public money. Smallholder families facing eviction have been supported by what Heathrow campaign veteran John Stewart described as a 'vibrant coalition of local residents, environmentalists, sympathetic politicians and direct action activists'. In July, 4,500 people gathered to form the outline of a plane and the message 'we will win'.[27] Six months later, thousands of protesters descended on Paris, on bicycles and tractors.

The campaign against the new airport escalated throughout 2012. Beginning on 10 April, six people held a hunger strike over a 28-day period. Michael Tarin, a farmer, endured without food for the entire time. The hunger strikers were supported by thousands of demonstrators who, complete with tractors, calves and sheep, repeatedly occupied Nantes city centre. On the site, protesters camped out in evacuated homes and built wooden cabins. By October, 150 activists had occupied the site. Police evacuated and destroyed the camp, inspiring activists from across Europe to flock to the site to help rebuild it. In December, there was a week of violent clashes when hundreds of police, firing teargas and rubber bullets, attempted another forcible eviction. There were injuries on both sides and the number of people occupying the site at any one time reached 500. Prime minister Jean-Marc Ayrault created a dialogue commission to determine the future of the project, but opponents demanded the withdrawal of police forces from the area as a prerequisite to their involvement.[28]

Campaign groups in the city of Pickering, to the west of Toronto, have endeavoured to prevent land acquisition for a new airport for 40 years. A 75 sq. km site, mostly prime farmland, was selected for a second international airport to serve the city in 1972. The federal government of Ontario expropriated the land and successive rounds of bulldozing and evictions met with spirited resistance. The Land Over Landings campaign formed a Land Trust, aiming to protect the land in perpetuity for farming.[29]

The initial site for a new airport for Dhaka, Bangladesh's capital, covered over 100 sq. km, predominantly wetlands, south of the city, in Munshiganj. The area is a valuable habitat for numerous rare bird species, and farmers cultivate rice, fish and oysters.[30] In December 2010, 30,000 protesters formed a human chain 8 km in length.[31] A few weeks later, a demonstration by about 20,000 villagers, mainly farmers, became violent. Fifty people were injured and a policeman was killed.[32] Assessment of three potential alternative sites, on the other side of the Padma River, began a month later.[33]

Construction of Narita, Tokyo's main airport, on farmland invoked the biggest protests in Japan's post-Second World War history, involving 1,500 farmers and residents. A series of violent clashes between police and protesters began with the commencement of site surveying in 1967. The airport opening, over a decade later on 20 May 1978, was delayed for two months, because protesters occupied and damaged the control tower. Protests resulted in ten deaths, three of whom were riot police officers.[34] The inauguration ceremony in 1972 required a heavy riot police presence. A steel tower was erected at the southern end of the Runway A to obstruct landings and takeoffs. It remained in place until it was removed in 1977, only to be replaced by a 'unity shed' built on its foundations, which prevented the installation of 900 m of approach lights at the end of the runway. Aircraft approaching from the south can only use 3,250 m of the 4 km runway, but relaxation of safety standards governing approach lights in 2011 raised the prospect that it might become fully operational.[35]

Narita's Runway B was short of its intended length by 320 m when it opened in 2002, because of resistance to land acquisition. This made it too small to accommodate the jumbo jets for which it was intended. Displaying a remarkable tenacity, two farms, which have used organic methods since the 1970s, remain to this day, just 400 m from the southern end of the runway, surrounded by walls and only accessible through a tunnel. Noise levels, from 90 planes a day flying as low as 40 m overhead, often exceed 100 decibels.[36] Runway B only became fully operational in 2009, when the transport ministry extended it in the opposite direction.[37]

The activism that impeded development of Narita, along with Japan's high population density, led to the construction of offshore airports, on land reclaimed from the sea. Yet Kobe, Centrair, Kitakyushu, Kansia and Haneda airports also met with community resistance, because of the damage inflicted on marine wildlife habitats and fishing grounds. Kansai, originally planned for 1 km offshore in Osaka Bay, was built 5 km farther out to sea, following protests from fishing cooperatives. The airport is built on 20 m of alluvial sand and silt instead of the solid seabed of the original location. Liquefaction destabilised the foundations, delaying opening until 1994. Ever since, Kansai has sunk a few centimetres every year.[38] Haneda Airport protrudes into Tokyo Bay, and the fourth runway was delayed by compensation talks with fishing cooperatives, who lost their fishing grounds to the land reclamation.[39] Residents of the coastal village of Henoko have protested over plans for a US airbase and military port since 1997. Land reclamation would remove a habitat for turtles, corals, sea grass and the one of the last remaining feeding grounds of the Okinawa dugong.[40] The United States offered a compromise in 2011, proposing to build the runway on stilts further offshore.[41]

On Indian Farmland

Greenfield airports form a central plank of aviation expansion in India. Two major greenfield airports, on the edges of the industrial cities of Hyderabad and Bangalore, are already operational. Farmland in several villages was acquired for Hyderabad Airport, which opened in March 2008.[42] Journalist R. Uma Maheshwari visited people who had been relocated to an airport 'colony' in 2010. She found that many were living in small rooms and 600 families were still fighting for compensation. Little of the employment which had been promised had materialised. A small number of people had low-paid casual jobs, as trolley boys and janitors. Outside the passenger terminal, among the colourful flower beds, she spotted a group of women in fluorescent jackets. They had become day labourers, tending flowers on the land they used to farm. The commute to and from work swallowed up a quarter of their meagre wages.[43]

Bangalore Airport opened three months after Hyderabad, in June 2008. Two thousand farmers from 13 villages in Devanahalli, a rural area north-east of the city, lost their land to the airport. Farmers with land ownership documents received compensation from the Karnataka State Government, but this was just one-twelfth of the market value of the land just one year after the airport opened. Those without the documents received no compensation, even if they had cultivated the land for decades.[44]

The Karnataka State Government's attempts at land acquisition for a greenfield airport on the outskirts of the city of Bellary, 250 km to the north of Bangalore, met with farmer protests throughout 2009. In February, police responded to a *rasta roko*, or roadblock, by firing rubber bullets at protesters.[45] A group of Bellary farmers marched all the way to the governor's office in

70

Bangalore in March, demanding that land acquisition proceedings be brought to a halt. They were joined by farmers who had lost their land to Bangalore Airport, persisting in their demands for a market rate for their land.[46] In early July an effigy of the *Government Gazette* announcing the project, which misleadingly categorised the land as barren even though it was irrigated by a canal and growing two crops per year, was burned in a mock funeral.[47] A few weeks later, farmers drew 18 bullock carts to Bellary, then untied the bullocks and drew the carts through the main streets of the city themselves to demonstrate outside the deputy commissioner's office.[48]

Protests continued into 2010. In March, 50 people attempting to make their voices heard during a ministerial visit were arrested.[49] Sustained resistance proved successful, achieving a victory against appropriation of agricultural land. Karnataka High Court allowed petitions from 70 farmers challenging land acquisition in 2012. Construction of Bellary Airport come to a halt and 100 landless agricultural labourers sought permission to recultivate parcels of land already in government possession.[50]

All over India there are tumultuous protests against land acquisition for greenfield airports. Rural communities' campaigns against displacement are pitched against a government policy drive. Civil aviation minister Praful Patel announced in 2010, 'If you have enough land, you can set up a greenfield airport. We will support the project.' He promised 'all possible' assistance.[51] Projects only go ahead after many stages of clearances by various regulatory bodies, but state governments have extensive powers to acquire farmland for airports and other industrial purposes such as mining, dams, power plants, factories, business parks and road networks. In many instances, inadequate compensation and rehabilitation programmes mean that farmers lose their livelihood as well as their land. Rural people's concerns over prospects for rebuilding their lives are justified. Rapid industrialisation has enriched a portion of India's population, but inequality has widened. About 230 million Indians, more than one-fifth of the population, suffer hunger and malnutrition.[52] Building on farmland adds to pressures on food supplies.

Ecological and political groups in Aranmula, a UNESCO-designated heritage village in rice paddy fields on the banks of the Pampa River in Kerala, have battled against a greenfield airport since 2003. The first plane, a two-seater microlight, landed on the 'slushy' runway, just a muddy clearing, in 2005. By 2010 the state government had given clearance for land acquisition for a full airport covering over 200 hectares.[53] Protests escalated, and activists obstructed construction, pelted stones at the developer's office, and broke through a police cordon protecting it.[54] N.K. Sukumaran Nair, general secretary of Pampa Parirakshana Samiti, an environmental group which has worked to protect the river for 20 years, said that wetlands were being converted illegally.[55] Regulatory obstacles are likely to be removed. A special meeting of the state cabinet was scheduled in May 2012, to discuss amending the Kerala Conservation of Paddy Land and Wetland Act in order to accelerate land clearance for the airport.[56]

Plans for a four-runway greenfield airport in Sriperumbudur, on the outskirts of Chennai, threaten to displace 37,000 people from 20 villages. The site contains 77 lakes, 120 ponds and 10,000 trees. Farmers cultivate rice paddies, mangos, jasmine trees and vegetables. On at least three occasions, villagers drove away officials sent to survey the land.[57] On 12 August 2010, 3,000 people from 26 villages demonstrated against the project. Police attacked them with a baton charge.[58] Communities' perseverance in blocking the new airport might be overwhelmed by the high level of backing from government. Sriperumbudur is a signature project in the Tamil Nadu Vision 2023: Strategic Plan for Infrastructure Development.[59] Furthermore, established physical infrastructure means that the site is hardwired for airport development. Inaugurating an aviation fuel pipeline supplying Chennai Airport, Patel said: 'This (pipeline) also passes through

Sriperumbudur where another airport is planned. Once it comes up, the pipeline will be extremely useful.'[60]

Land acquisition for a second airport to serve Goa, the tourist magnet on India's west coast, began in May 2010. The site, to the north of the city, covers 10 sq. km of fertile land on the Mopa plateau, where 15,000 people make a living from agriculture. If the project goes ahead, 4 million cashew trees will be felled, along with mango, jackfruit, betel nut and coconut trees. Residents of five villages formed the Mopa Airport-Affected Farmers' Committee to fight land acquisition. The group's secretary, Sandip Kambli, was adamant that what the group wanted was not money, but to retain their land and livelihood: 'We don't want any compensation for our land. Our land is a valuable treasure left behind for us by our forefathers and from time immemorial.'[61] In May 2011, officials sent to value and demarcate land were chased away.[62]

This determination not to part with land at any price is echoed in a farmer's response to plans for a greenfield airport in Kushinagar, Uttar Pradesh. Akhilesh Kumar said:

> This is our ancestors' land. The land is cultivable. We grow rice, wheat and other crops here. It is the only source of our income. How can we give this land away? We will get monetary compensation but what good is that? We can buy food with it for some time but what are our coming generations going to eat?[63]

The Buddha died in Kushinagar, making it a key destination in the Buddhist circuit of monuments and relics dotted over northern India and southern Nepal. The airport plan is linked to proposals for a grandiose tourism complex, centred on the world's tallest bronze statue, a 154 m high Buddha. This also threatens to encroach on farmland. A 1,262-day peaceful protest, involving 2,300 farmers, ended in August 2010 when the government announced that the tourism project would not proceed if they refused to give up their land.[64] In 2011, in the face of continued resistance, the project was scaled back.[65] But the airport found special favour with the state government. It was revived as a priority project in 2012 and the developer was offered 24 hectares of land as a sweetener, to build a hotel.[66] Concreting over agricultural land for an airport does not reflect the Buddhist teachings of interconnectedness and sanctity of all life. The most authentic pilgrimage to honour the life of the Buddha would be to retrace his steps literally, making the journey on foot.

India has one of the world's largest and comprehensive rail networks, yet the greenfield airport programme is for connectivity between smaller cities.[67] Capacity expansion for domestic flights constitutes an unnecessary and environmentally damaging duplication of rail services. India is already the world's fastest growing domestic aviation market. Between 2001 and 2011, the number of domestic passengers quadrupled from 13 million to 52 million, outpacing a tripling of international traffic growth to 38 million passengers.[68]

Communities are being uprooted for proposed greenfield airports which, like the Bellary project, might not go ahead. Sceptics within the industry are of the opinion that traffic projections for greenfield airports are unrealistic, pointing out that, of 115 airports run by the Airports Authority of India (AAI), 44 are not operational. The majority are closed because they are not economically viable.[69] Aviation industry consultancy Centre for Aviation (CAPA) notes the lack of an integrated national transport plan identifying the economic basis for new airports, and points out that many greenfield airport projects have 'overlapping or insufficient catchment areas'. CAPA also confirms suspicions that the true goal of some projects is land acquisition, rather than provision of air services:

> In certain cases, regional airports appear to be exercises in securing land for commercial activity, in others they are driven by political considerations ... all too frequently they seem to be floated without taking into account whether there is a market that can support viable air services.[70]

But the Indian government is pulling out all the stops to subsidise domestic aviation. In 2012, a government panel approved a proposal to allow airlines to import jet fuel directly, thus bypassing sales tax on fuel for domestic flights. This extraordinary legislative manoeuvre could save India's heavily indebted carriers $510 million per year, with commensurate loss of revenue to state governments.[71]

5

Green Garnish

Green Power

Flight remains fossil-fuel-dependent, but airports host some impressive solar, wind and geothermal installations which contribute to the energy supply for airport buildings. The most notable success is in solar energy, and airports boast some of the world's largest arrays. The photovoltaic solar panel display on the roof of Auckland Airport's arrivals area is the largest in New Zealand, measuring 300 sq. m.[1] Adelaide Airport has the second biggest grid-connected rooftop solar power system in southern Australia.[2] A solar system in a drainage area of the Virgin Islands's King Airport will be the biggest in the territory.[3] Passengers flying in or out of Düsseldorf have a view of 8,400 solar panels covering an area the size of six football pitches, one of the largest in Germany. A real-time display monitor in the departure hall shows how much energy has been generated.[4]

Solar installations need to be enormous to provide a signifi-cant proportion of airport buildings' energy requirements, even if they are basking in year-round sunshine. Dubai Airport hosts the biggest solar panel array of any airport in the Middle East, but this merely offsets the energy consumed by the lighting and plasma screen displays for an exhibition of historical photo-graphs.[5] In California, Long Beach Airport has six 3 m high steel poles outside the south baggage claim area, topped with photovoltaic arrays that shift and tilt to track the sun. These 'solar trees' generate less than 10 per cent of the airport's overall energy needs. Oakland Airport's solar power system generates about 5 per cent of the airport's power requirements.[6]

Two major solar farms at Denver Airport, soaking up sunshine over 300 days of the year, only supply 2.5 per cent of the airport's energy requirements.[7] A third installation, 19,000 panels, switched on in summer 2011, took the total to 6 per cent.[8] One of the solar arrays, measuring 3.6 hectares with 7,400 panels, provides almost 100 per cent of the energy requirements of the 10.3 million litre fuel farm.[9] Instead of replacing fossil fuel dependency, solar power has been harnessed to fill planes' fuel tanks with kerosene.

Solar installations are highly visible on airport sites, and the energy production, measured in kilowatt hours, is heavily promoted via websites, press releases and annual reports. In contrast, tanks containing millions of litres of jet fuel are out of sight and rarely merit so much as a mention. Each litre of kerosene type jet fuel provides 10.43 kilowatt hours of energy. I discovered the volume of jet fuel dispensed at three airports with solar power – Chattanooga, San Francisco and Schiphol. These airports' solar output barely registers in comparison with the energy content of the kerosene pumped into planes' fuel tanks.

Chattanooga, a small airport in Tennessee, has a 3,398 panel solar farm covering 1.8 hectares on the west side of the main runway. The solar farm is prominent on the home page of the airport's website, linking through to pages about how solar energy is generated and inviting people to book in for an educational tour. You can calculate the amount of energy generated over different time frames.[10] I used the website to calculate that, in the first half of 2012, the solar farm generated 758,667 kilowatt hours (kWh) of energy. Assuming a similar energy output for the remainder of the year, the solar farm generated 1,517,334 kWh of energy in 2012. This is equivalent to the energy provided by 145,411 litres of jet fuel. The amount of jet fuel dispensed to airlines, nearly 12.5 million litres in 2010, was buried in the website, in the masterplan.[11] Chattanooga Airport provided about 86 times more oil-derived energy to aircraft than it generated from its solar farm.

Chattanooga is only a minor airport. At San Francisco, the second busiest airport in California after Los Angeles, the disparity between the energy provided by solar panels and that supplied to aircraft is of a higher order of magnitude. There are 2,800 solar panels on the roof of Terminal 3, and a smaller installation on the engineering building. San Francisco Airport's 2011 sustainability report states that these solar facilities generated 747,000 kWh of energy in 2010.[12] This is equivalent to the energy provided by 71,586 litres of jet fuel. The report does not mention the volume of jet fuel the airport supplied to airlines. I discovered this figure, over 3.182 billion litres in 2011, in an announcement by Fitch, a credit rating agency.[13] The energy content of the kerosene San Francisco Airport dispensed to aircraft was 44,450 times greater than the energy generated by its solar facilities.

Schiphol Airport unveiled 9,500 sq. m of solar panels in July 2011. The array is expected to provide 440,000 kWh of energy per year, equivalent to the amount of electricity consumed by 120 households.[14] The airport dispenses approximately 4.38 billion litres of jet fuel per year,[15] providing 45.7 billion kWh of energy. If Schiphol were to produce the same amount of solar energy as it supplies to aircraft, in the form of kerosene, an installation 103,874 times the size the established array would be required. This would be an unfeasibly massive installation covering 987 sq. km of land – 4.5 times the area of the city of Amsterdam.

Airports are among the true pioneers in geothermal energy, drilling deep into the earth's crust to tap into heat from underground. As with solar power, this contributes to the energy supply for airport buildings. Orly, in the outskirts of Paris, was the first European airport to use geothermal energy, drilling 1.7 km below its site to access the 15,000 sq. km Le Dogger hot water reserve.[16] Schiphol, Oslo and Zurich airports are partly powered by geothermal energy. North American airports tapping into geothermal energy include Calgary, Denver, Nantucket in Massachusetts, Portland Jetport in Maine and Oakland in Michigan.[17]

Several airports, including Schiphol, Brisbane, Detroit Metropolitan, Bangalore and Hong Kong, have incorporated used cooking oil into the fuel mix for ground vehicles. This is preferable to using biofuels derived from food crops, but the volumes are insignificant compared with the throughput of aviation fuel. Hong Kong Airport collected about 3,000 litres of used cooking oil per month in 2009–10, for use in ground vehicles. The airport's annual report, entitled *Our Green Airport*, affords this more coverage than the new fuel farm, the largest of its kind with capacity for 388 million litres. Aviation fuel is pumped from offshore tankers under the ocean to the airport, through two 4.5 km pipelines.[18]

A growing number of airports appear to be at the vanguard of wind energy, with turbines on top of passenger terminals and other buildings. In fact, aviation is less incompatible with wind energy than solar and geothermal. Wind farms under flightpaths can be an obstruction to aircraft and there are concerns that turbines, even if situated at some distance, might interfere with radar equipment. Visually imposing wind turbines have been erected at many US airports including Minnesota, Detroit and Burlington in Vermont, but the height is limited by air space restrictions. Twenty wind turbines on Boston Logan's administration building, overlooking the harbour, supply 100,000 kilowatts of electricity per year. This is just 2 per cent of the building's energy consumption.[19]

East Midlands, the United Kingdom's biggest cargo airport, installed two 45 m high wind turbines, sufficient to provide 5 per cent of the airport's energy usage. Calculations by local campaigners showed that, once the flights to and from the airport are taken into account, the wind turbines reduced the airport's carbon dioxide emissions by just 0.05 per cent.[20] Within weeks of unveiling the turbines the airport objected to a farmer's proposal to install a smaller 30 m high turbine in a field nearby, stating that the spinning blades might cause 'radar clutter'.[21] Liverpool Airport, on England's north-west coast, also sports wind turbines while opposing similar installations under the flightpaths. There are two 15 m high turbines on the approach road, but the airport attempted to prevent the erection of a larger 76 m turbine 20 km inland, claiming it would create a blind spot on its radar.[22] Tensions between wind energy and aviation expansion are emerging throughout the United Kingdom, as half of the proposed wind farms in the country face opposition from airports.[23]

Greenwash

Boston Logan Airport, built largely on landfill in Boston Harbor, has grown to comprise over two-thirds of the land area of East Boston. The airport met with spirited resistance at many stages of expansion. In the 1960s encroachment over one of Boston's most popular beaches, Wood Island Park, was met with sit-ins and marches.[24] Neptune Road, a tree-lined street leading to the sea, was fenced in by the airport and planes came in to land over the residents' backyards. The campaign to save the residents from eviction was lost in 1973–74, but the last house was not demolished until 2009.[25]

One protest at Boston Logan, on 22 April 1970, was part of a groundswell of grassroots activism which proved to be pivotal in the evolution of the environment movement. A crowd of students assembled in the lobby, and at 6 pm they were joined by members of the Boston Area Ecology Coalition. They carried six black wooden coffins. A demonstrator lay in each coffin and others lay on the floor nearby, several of them wearing gauze facemasks. One of the coffins had the word 'biocide' and the names of several airlines written on it. This 'mock funeral', involving 100 people, was held as a protest against aviation expansion, deaths from air pollution and government funding for manufacture of supersonic aircraft. The police arrived just 15 minutes after the demonstration began, forcibly removing all the protesters from the building. Thirteen people were arrested on charges of disorderly conduct and trespassing.[26]

On the same day, about 10 per cent of the US population, about 20 million people, were involved in gatherings, teach-ins and practical environmental action across the country. This, the first Earth Day, pushed environmental issues up the agenda. By the end of the year, the EPA had been created, paving the way for landmark legislation: the Clean Water Act, Clean Air Act and Endangered Species Act.[27] Earth Day has been held on 22 April every year ever since, spreading worldwide to become an international campaign of environmental action and pledges.

Since the 1990s, citizens' voices on Earth Day have been drowned out by corporate greenwash. Environmentally damaging industries, such as oil, car manufacturing and agribusiness giants, have appropriated the occasion, turning it into an overblown celebration of superficial environmental improvements.[28] Association with a global movement also lends an air of legitimacy to corporate environmental awareness campaigns. Firms cast themselves as environmental experts and exhort people to make lifestyle changes. Earth Day information campaigns make no difference to firms' environmental performance, and shift the onus for saving the planet onto individual citizens.

In recent years, airport public relations departments throughout the United States have gone into overdrive on Earth Day, promoting initiatives which have zero impact on, and detract attention from, the core operation of servicing aircraft. Boston Logan Airport is an enthusiastic participant. On Earth Day 2007, a scheme to encourage passengers and taxis to drive to the airport in hybrid, alternative fuel vehicles was unveiled.[29] Earth Day 2009 saw a blitz of publicity about green initiatives including using recycled materials in asphalt and recycling aluminium, paper and plastic waste from passenger cabins. Children gave out postcards impregnated with wildflower seeds.[30] The airport launched an iPhone app to help passengers share taxi rides to and from the airport on Earth Day 2011. Employees and tenants participated in a hazardous waste collection, bringing in items such as paint, weed killer, batteries and computers for recycling or safe disposal.[31]

Denver plugged its solar energy, energy efficiency and recycling programmes, and distributed reusable shopping bags printed with a new sustainability logo and the slogan 'DIA: Sustainability with Altitude'.[32] An Earth Day Environmental Fair at Sea-Tac showcased energy and water conservation, waste reduction and wildlife management, and urged people to buy recycled products and take up composting, cycling and telecommuting.[33] San Diego lined up its fleet of electric vehicles outside the terminal, publicised its recycling and screened a film about a single person's impact on the earth's resources.[34] Philadelphia Airport presented awards to staff for volunteering, recycling and conservation activities.[35] Students planted rhododendrons and other decorative plants at the entrance to Yeager Airport in West Virginia.[36] Atlanta Airport promoted environmentally friendly cleaning products, energy efficiency in the home, and held a solar-powered bluegrass concert.[37]

Airports around the world celebrate Earth Day in a similar vein. Coimbatore, the second largest airport in Tamil Nadu, ditched plastic bags in favour of biodegradable ones.[38] Karachi Airport bussed in a group of children and kitted them out in Earth Day hats and T-shirts. They listened to a lecture about environmental awareness and global warming, then helped collect litter from around the airport site and plant trees.[39] Riga, Latvia's main airport, held a 'Greenhouse Effect' event in the terminal, with displays and discussions and works of art on the themes of climate change and sustainable development.[40]

Airlines' contributions to Earth Day 2012 were characterised by irrelevance to the environmental damage caused by flying. JetBlue and Virgin America planted trees. Southwest Airlines sponsored Earth Day Dallas and gave away 200 composting bins. Continental and United Airlines tackled one of the least resource-intensive aspects of their operations, the boarding passes, asking passengers to use mobile phones in lieu of the paper version. In return, the carrier made donations to Conservation International's Protect an Acre project. Alaska Airlines offered an incentive to fly, an Earth Day only 10 per cent discount, and donated air miles to the Nature Conservancy.[41] Delta Airlines cajoled passengers to 'go 'green' by making donations to forest conservation projects in Louisiana and Belize.[42]

Every March, airports around the world participate in Earth Hour, simultaneously turning off lights and electrical appliances for one hour, to symbolise a global call for action to combat climate change. In 2010, Abu Dhabi Airport turned off the lighting on the second runway. The reduction in carbon emissions will have been infinitesimal in comparison with the flights. Arrivals and departures scheduled for the appointed hour used the other runway.[43] In Singapore, Changi switched off decorative and non-critical operational lights, but the power supply to the plasma screens and public address system remained uninterrupted, in order to broadcast the airport's green message.[44] In 2012, the fifteen 30 m high multicoloured pylons illuminating the entrance to Los Angeles Airport were lit up in solid green for an hour, then switched off for Earth Hour.[45]

World Environment Day, a UN Environment Programme (UNEP) environmental awareness campaign held on 5 June, offers airports yet another opportunity to tout dubious green credentials and expertise. Auckland Airport claimed it would be 'leading by example' on World Environment Day on 5 June 2008, and proceeded to give tips to staff and travellers on 'how they can help save the planet'. Members of staff were bombarded with 24 email messages in 24 hours, promoting the airport's actions such as paper recycling and tips for greening the home and garden. Only one email was connected with flying, a plug for Air New Zealand's 'Eco Day'.[46] Kuala Lumpur Airport held environmental themed talks, exhibitions, performances and a treasure hunt, and urged passengers to purchase trees for planting in the 'Green Park' outside the terminal.[47]

By 2012, several Indian airports were scheduling activities for World Environment Day. A 'green brigade' drafted into Bangalore Airport encouraged passengers to take home a plant. Mumbai Airport hosted performances and distributed jasmine plants and baggage tags with a World Environment Day message. Hyderabad held competitions in writing environmental slogans and essays, and planted saplings outside the terminal. On land owned by Delhi Airport 150 trees were planted.[48] Mangalore Airport planted 100 different species of trees on its premises.[49] Beyond airport sites, trees under flightpaths must be removed, or kept below a certain height, to prevent obstruction to aircraft.

The Bihar state government used World Environment Day to promote its target to plant 2.4 million trees over the next five years. Simultaneously, the state moved a step closer to approving Patna Airport's plans to fell, or trim, 2,000 trees in the adjacent Sanjay Gandhi Zoological Park, a haven of biodiversity hosting 300 different species of trees. The trees, some exceeding 7.5 m in height, had been identified as impeding visibility for aircraft approaching the runway.[50]

Passenger Processing

Airports refer to their management of air passengers – funnelled through check-in, security, customs, baggage reclaim, waiting lounges, corridors and aerobridges – as 'passenger processing'. Contained within this system, the rest of the airport site is out of sight and out of bounds, and passengers' sensory experience is tightly controlled. The infrastructure supporting the flights is concealed, and typically the overriding impression is of being in a shopping mall. More terminals are being designed to route passengers through malls. Building its biggest walkthrough store at Sydney Airport, Naunce Group, one of the world's biggest airport retailers, explained that 'in an airport environment where passenger flows can be controlled, more and more walkthrough concepts are being introduced', and that sales are up to 20 per cent higher than in traditional stores.[51] The layout at Hyderabad Airport, filling up with outlets selling newspapers, books, watches, toys, sportswear, electronics, jewellery, games and confectionery, is designed to surround people so they bounce from store to store. This is described as the 'pinball effect'.[52]

Passenger terminals provide a captive audience for advertising. Frankfurt Airport is an example of how promotions cover ever more of the visible surface. A 127-page brochure sells advertising space on glass bridges, three-dimensional installations along the approach road, the welcome tower, flags at the terminal entrance, banners at gates and check-in, backlit displays covering entire corridors, columns extending up to the ceiling and onto the airfield inside 100 jet bridges. An 'ambient corridor' is bathed in colours of light associated with particular brands. Smaller spaces are up for sale, on flight information panels, seating areas, baggage pushcarts, passenger information monitors, car parking ticket dispensers and tickets. Movement catches the eye, so space is available on scrolling lightboxes, sliding doors, lifts, moving stairways and walkways. Static displays are being replaced with digital animated sequences. Advertising extends beyond passenger terminals, with 30 m high towers along the exit and approach roads and panels on the interior and exterior of buses.[53]

Dubai Airport proclaimed its promotion for Motorola mobile devices, launched in June 2012, as the world's longest indoor airport advertisement. The display, incorporating illuminated panels, was installed alongside the entire 223 m length of a moving walkway, which takes five minutes to transport passengers between the Terminal 1 check-in and duty free. Within three weeks, Motorola reported a 40 per cent upturn in sales in Terminal 1.[54] Denver signed an advertising deal for the largest digital signage display of any US airport in 2012, comprising 70 flat-screen televisions with 1.8 m screens, six overhead video walls, four high-definition video towers 8 m in height, and touch-screens sending hotel and other travel information to passengers' mobile devices.[55]

Digital technology brings new techniques to get our attention. The advertising industry is curious about passengers' reaction to digital messages in the bathroom mirrors at Chicago O'Hare. They are activated when someone walks in and looks into a mirror.[56] New innovations in digital billboards portend a convergence of advertising and surveillance technologies. Billboards can be fitted with software which ascertains viewers' age, gender, attention span and demographic profile, and targets advertising messages accordingly. Sony plans to test a prototype at JFK.[57]

The relentless commercialism of retail and advertising, dominated by international brands, is juxtaposed with artworks suggesting the very opposite, that the airport is public space celebrating the distinctiveness of the local area. A growing number of airports are adorned with whimsical representations of local culture, landscapes and wildlife. The Colorado landscape is a recurrent theme at Denver Airport, which claims to host 'one of the most extensive airport art programs in the world', with paintings, photographs, mosaics, statues, artefacts and sculptures. A fountain acts as an 'audible reference' to rivers and waterfalls.[58] The entrance to Houston Hobby is graced with a stainless steel sculpture of a bird's nest 9 m wide, supported by three pillars in the shape of tree trunks.[59] Schiphol has a gallery of Dutch masters' paintings.[60] The main concourse of Delhi's Terminal 3 has a row of giant copper hands jutting outwards in traditional 'mudras' dance gestures. Vancouver Airport is crammed with spectacular carvings and totem poles made by aboriginal people. McCarran in Las Vegas has large sculptures of a snake, a horny toad and other desert creatures.

From above, airports look much the same. Satellite images show a uniform picture of grey runways in a variety of alignments, grey aprons and access roads, and a monotony of grey rectangular buildings. But an airport's passenger terminal, its public face, is a different matter. Functional concrete boxes are giving way to iconic buildings evoking the unique characteristics of the destination. Denver's passenger terminal is topped with white fibreglass peaks resembling the views of snowcapped Rocky Mountains. Soekarno-Hatta Airport in Jakarta resembles a traditional Javanese *pendopo*-style pavilion built on columns. Fujairah Airport in the UAE has a traditional-looking Arabian-style façade with arched windows and marble flooring. The cast-iron entrances and exits of Cape Verde's Boa Vista Airport are modelled on a *kasbah*, or walled fortress. The roof of New Doha Airport's main passenger terminal is wave-shaped. Kruger Mpumalanga, in north-east South Africa, has a thatched roof, blending in with the distinctive savannah grasslands of the region with clusters of trees and shrubs.

Elaborate airport gardens are becoming obligatory, providing passengers with green oases. Changi is the most striking example. There is a five-storey 'green wall' of climbing plants and a waterfall at baggage reclaim, a fragrant garden, a cactus garden, a lagoon with water lilies and koi carp, a sunflower and lights garden, a fern garden, a rooftop garden, and the world's first airport butterfly garden. Dammam Airport in Saudi Arabia belies its desert location thanks to gardens supplied by its own plant nursery.[61] Two 'zen gardens' in Dubai's Terminal 3 host hundreds of plants, offering a peaceful respite for passengers. The creation of the gardens was far from tranquil. Seven 8.5 m tall monkey puzzle trees tower over the other plants. These trees, each weighing more than one tonne, were grown in Florida and flown to Dubai in a Boeing 747.[62]

More than 922,000 trees, plus shrubs, cacti and flowers and lush green lawns, were planted inside and outside Delhi's Terminal 3. Some of the most prominent plants were imported. Orchids were flown in from Thailand and palm trees were flown in from Mexico.[63] The gardens are a green garnish over 600,000 cu. m of concrete and 200,000 tonnes of reinforced steel, one of the biggest infrastructure projects in India.[64] An influx of construction equipment included floor-rolling machinery from Bahrain, eight vibratory soil compactors, ten electronic sensor pavers and 13 cranes from Germany, rolling machinery from Australia and roof sheeting machinery from Singapore.[65] At Chennai Airport's new terminal, elevated walkways transport passengers through 'vertical gardens', steel lattice structures more than 10 m high covered with plants.[66]

In addition to living plants, airports are beginning to transform dull corridors and waiting areas with sophisticated electronic simulations of nature. Schiphol has a 'park' area with images of real parks projected onto the walls, digital butterflies flitting around and sounds of birdsong, bicycle bells and children playing.[67] Two airbridges at Christchurch in New Zealand immerse arrivals passengers in a multi-sensory simulation of key tourist attractions, the West Coast forest and the beaches of Abel Tasman National Park. Floor-to-ceiling images are accompanied by sounds of birdsong, and smells of the natural environment are pumped in. On exiting the airbridges, passengers are channelled into customs, where the largest video wall in Australasia projects images of mountains, lakes and forests.[68] At Atlanta Airport, a similar art project, called Flight Paths, is scheduled for completion in January 2014. A 137 m underground corridor is being turned into a 'virtual forest' with a canopy of trees, simulated sunbeams, rainstorms, fireflies and birdsong.[69]

Shops, advertising, artworks, architectural flourishes and gardens give passengers plenty to look at, as airport security scrutinises them ever more closely. Security has intensified since the 9/11 terrorist attacks. Biometric systems identify people by physical traits such as iris, fingerprint and facial features. As the departing airport of both of the planes which hit the World Trade Center, Boston Logan has been at the forefront of this escalating security. It was the first airport to install whole-body imaging machines revealing detailed images of passengers' bodies under their clothing[70] and installed a 2,000 camera video surveillance system in 2010.[71]

Security is another airport function that is being more effectively concealed. In 2011, London Gatwick Airport claimed a world first when it deployed 'iris at a distance' technology. Automated gates scan passengers' irises on entering and leaving the departure lounge. In combination with facial recognition, the system tracks their movement through the airport.[72] New scanners can capture an iris image from people in motion, at a distance of over 3 m. They do not have to consciously look into the scanner.[73]

Acquris, a firm specialising in airport security, produces cameras for low-light conditions, covert cameras which can be embedded in everyday objects, and the world's smallest camera, the size of the head of a matchstick with the supporting electronics on a separate circuit board which can be located several metres away.[74] New laser-based molecular scanners, which analyse passengers' bodies, clothes and luggage, take invasion of privacy to a new level, revealing people's blood circulation, adrenaline levels and the contents of their intestines. Plans to introduce the scanners at airports throughout the United States have been justified on security grounds, to detect traces of explosives, other dangerous chemicals and drugs. Passengers will be oblivious, as the scanners can be fired from 50 m away.[75]

Perceptions matter. Airports manipulate passengers' impressions because it influences their behaviour. Making the airport environment more pleasant, hiding the infrastructure and technology supporting flight, and presenting a veneer of art, advertising and greenery, keeps the environmental damage it causes out of sight and out of mind. Exposing the supply chain of products, looking beyond labels and marketing campaigns, reveals the impacts from resource extraction, manufacturing and distribution. We need to apply this type of analysis and campaigning to buildings and transportation systems, the infrastructure that we experience from within. Understanding the reality of aviation infrastructure is a necessary step towards changing it, and making a transition to a more sustainable transportation system.

6

Air Cargo

Multimodal Cargo

The world's major freight gateways are 'multimodal', integrating air services with surface transport. Shanghai port, the largest in the world, is at the mouth of the Yangtze River, which carries 80 per cent of China's waterborne transport.[1] The Port of Hong Kong's drive-in multistorey logistics centre is 20 minutes from the airport.[2] A high-speed rail freight terminal is being constructed at Schiphol Airport.[3] Al Maktoum Airport is linked to Jebel Ali port, the world's largest human-made harbour, by a logistics corridor.[4] Memphis, combining airport, river port, road and rail, is 'quadramodal'.[5]

Standard-sized corrugated steel containers, introduced in the early 19th century, eased the transfer of goods between ships, trucks and trains. You can see stacks of these containers at ports, truck depots and rail terminals. The first time I saw a loaded container ship coming into a port I was astounded by its size, and that it could be piled so high with containers and not topple over. Container ship capacity is measured in 20 ft equivalent units (TEUs), referring to the standard length of these containers. Ever-larger vessels ply the oceans. In July 2005, Samsung completed construction of two 9,200 TEU ships, 337 m in length and 46 m wide, with capacity for 1.2 million televisions with 74 cm screens, or 50 million mobile phones.[6] In February 2009, the Samsung-built *MSC Daniela*, the first of new generation of mega vessels with a capacity of 14,000 TEUs, made its maiden voyage from

Asia to Europe.[7] By 2010, Maersk, the world's largest shipping firm, was placing orders for 18,000 TEU ships, necessitating a new generation of cranes to extend across 22 rows of containers.[8]

The Panama and Suez canals are being widened, and new trade routes are opening up alternative shipping routes between east and west. A deepwater port at Dawei, Burma, accessible by land via tunnel blasted through mountains on the border with Thailand, will enable ships to bypass the southwards loop around Singapore.[9] As Arctic ice melts, geopolitical tensions are heightening over control of the Northwest Passage, a sea route between the Atlantic and Pacific, which skirts around the thinning edges of the receding ice cap. In 2010, vessels began to transit the passage without the assistance of Russian nuclear icebreakers. A ship carrying 40,000 tonnes of iron ore from Norway to China travelled through in just eight days, and a icebreaking ore carrier completed a round trip from Norilsk in Siberia to Shanghai and back in 41 days. The usual route, via the Suez Canal, would have taken 84 days.[10]

Air cargo faces intense competition from ocean transport. Transportation by air offers shippers the advantages of unmatchable speed, reliability and security. But larger container ships have reduced the unit cost, and the fleet has quadrupled since 1990. Per unit weight, transporting cargo by air is about ten times more expensive than by container ship. Moreover, shippers have adopted supply chain visibility tools that used to be the preserve of the air express industry. Container ship tonnage grew an average 8.9 per cent per year between 1980 and 2011, outpacing air cargo growth.[11] As we have seen, carbon emissions from transporting goods by ship are a small fraction of emissions from air freight. Instead of increasing air cargo capacity, governments should facilitate this modal shift.

Air cargo volumes exceeded 93 million tonnes in 2011.[12] Only about 1 per cent of the weight of internationally traded goods is transported by air, but this small proportion accounts for about 40 per cent of the value. As air freight is more energy-intensive than surface transport, keeping the weight down is imperative. Goods are carried in pallets made of lightweight woods such as balsa covered in netting, or in unit load devices (ULDs) made of aluminium or lightweight plastic. Types of goods that are air freighted include consumer products, industrial equipment, small packages, documents and perishable food and flowers .[13] Air transport does not compete with maritime for intercontinental transport of bulk commodities: oil, coal, metal ore, aggregates and grains. In contrast, air is the preferred mode for gems and precious metals. Ninety-nine per cent of the estimated $200 million worth of diamonds that enter and leave Antwerp each day are transported via Brussels Airport.[14] A centre for processing and export of jewellery, precious metals and stones, Dazzle Park, is under construction in the high security zone adjacent to Karachi's Jinnah Airport.[15]

Consumer goods are air freighted to coordinate availability of new products with marketing campaigns. Fashion garments have been rushed to the stores since the early years of air freight. In 1935 clothing, together with perfume, was the main cargo carried by Air France.[16] In 2007, apparel, textiles and footwear accounted for 17 per cent of world air cargo.[17] Publication of the latest *Harry Potter* book in 2000 was a major operation for Memphis based FedEx and online retailer Amazon.com. A fleet of 100 planes and 9,000 trucks distributed 250,000 copies of the book, weighing 300 tonnes, across the United States in 24 hours.[18] Dozens of extra planes were chartered for the launch of Apple's iPhone 5 in September 2012.[19]

Planes also deliver goods that are vested with cultural value. As tourists fly around the world, freighters deliver some of the artworks and museum exhibits that attract them. In 2006, Etihad Crystal Cargo of Abu Dhabi flew 186 Picasso paintings from Paris to Abu Dhabi, and a 4 tonne statue of Buddha from Colombo to Beijing.[20] In 2007, an army of 2,000-year-old life-size terracotta warrior statues, 42 crates full, was flown from Shanghai to Ontario.[21] Luxembourg-based Cargolux reported flying 'enormous bronze sculptures' in 2008.[22] Freighters deliver heavyweight items for sporting events. As part of the city of Sochi's successful bid to host the 2014 Winter Olympics, Volga Dnepr flew a 63 tonne ice-skating rink to Guatemala.[23] Ten charter flights from Germany, London Stansted in England and Kuala Lumpur in Malaysia carried 32 Porsches, 13 racing cars, media equipment, car accessories and specialist fuel to the 2007 Formula One race in Bahrain.[24] FedEx carried 500 horses from Liege to the United States for the 2010 World Equestrian Games. Ten flights each moved between 40 and 60 horses, accompanied by their grooms.[25]

Animals have been air freighted since the early days of aviation. KLM carried a cow on a Fokker aircraft to London in 1920, and has specialised in live animals ever since.[26] By 2009, KLM was flying more than 6,000 horses per year, thousands of ornamental fish, 16,000 dogs and cats, rhinoceroses and other animals for zoos.[27] Moscow-based AirBridgeCargo specialises in carrying large numbers of livestock on 747 freighters, and in March 2012 it flew 175 Aberdeen Angus cows on its first cross-polar flight, from Chicago to Krasnoyarsk, making fuel savings from the more direct route.[28] Far lower volumes of fuel are used when animal breeders use air services to deliver small vials of semen and embryos.

A pet-only airline, Florida-based Pet Airways, launched in 2009. Five aircraft began flights between five major US cities, offering an average one-way fare of $250. Pets are carried in the main cabin, with in-flight attendants.[29] Airport staff deal with a menagerie of hapless creatures that are smuggled in, or discovered in abandoned luggage, attempting to return them to their natural habitat, or find a place in a zoo. If no home can be found, or if quarantine requirements are not met, they are destroyed. In 2001 440 squirrels arrived at Schiphol from Beijing, en route to a fur dealer in Greece, without the correct documentation. KLM staff duly followed procedures, putting the squirrels through a shredding machine.[30]

Flying Refrigerators

Perishable cargo, requiring temperature control, encompasses some types of chemicals, electronic, photographic and medical equipment and pharmaceuticals. But the bulk of the volume consists of fresh produce: fruit, vegetables, fish, meat and flowers. In 2010, perishables accounted for between 14 and 18 per cent of air cargo.[31] An unbroken 'chill-chain' of refrigeration is required to keep produce fresh. Airport cold storage facilities, called 'perishable centres', are comprised of zones maintained at a range of temperatures. Frankfurt Airport's 9,000 sq. m perishable centre has 18 different climate zones and handles 200,000 tonnes of fresh produce per year.[32]

Fresh produce is carried in insulated containers, or temperature-controlled planes, which are like giant flying refrigerators. By 2009, Cargolux had a fleet of 16 Boeing 747 freighters equipped with four temperature-controlled zones ranging between 4–29ºC. Each can carry 100 tonnes of flowers. At the carriers' Luxembourg Airport hub, low temperatures are maintained with a vacuum cooler and ten cooling cells, and produce is loaded onto cool trucks.[33]

Emirates SkyCargo's Boeing 747-400 freighters have air-conditioned zones, and at its Dubai Airport hub, the Cargo Mega Terminal and warehouses are temperature controlled. A refrigerated dolly on wheels carries perishable cargo between the terminal and aircraft. Insulated with aluminium and powered by a diesel engine, plus electrical back-up system, the 'cool dolly' keeps perishables at temperatures as low as -4ºC.[34] This is quite a feat of refrigeration. Dubai runways swelter in summer temperatures as high at 45°C. Ironically, the temperature control of the chill-chain makes it a contributor to climate chaos and the overall warming trend. Carbon emissions from the fossil fuel energy used for refrigeration add to the emissions from transportation. The poor bear the brunt of climatic instability while the wealthy enjoy an abundance of fresh produce regardless of the weather, or the seasons.

Dubai Flower Centre, at Dubai Airport, opened in 2007, covering 34,000 sq. m, with capacity for a throughput of 180,000 tonnes per year, and plans for additional 10,000 sq. m sections built in phases.[35] Dubai has yet to rival Schiphol Airport as a global hub for flowers. Sixty per cent of world trade in flowers passes through Schiphol. After landing, flowers are trucked to Aalsmeer flower auctions for viewing by buyers, then back to Schiphol for re-export all over the world. Hundreds of trucks travel back and forth every day.[36]

The Netherlands retains its position as the world's largest exporter of cut flowers, with Colombia in second place.[37] Kenya ranks as the third largest flower exporter.[38] Volumes multiplied from less than 11,000 tonnes in 1988 to almost 122,000 tonnes in 2011. About 65 per cent are sold at auction in the Netherlands.[39] Cargolux is one of the main airlines carrying Kenyan produce to the Netherlands. The carrier's vice president, Pierre Wesner, remarked on how fresh produce exports were unaffected by conflict over a rigged election in December 2007, which dragged on into 2008. He said, 'Most flights from African destinations, with the exception of Abidjan and South Africa, come back to Europe via Nairobi, where there is still plenty of flower and produce traffic to fill up with despite the recent political unrest.'[40]

Eldoret, on the fertile Rift Valley plateau, was seriously affected by the conflict. Yet in February 2008 Eldoret Airport was reported to be 'buzzing'. Fish, fruit and flowers, which 'could not even find their way to markets in the nearest towns', were easily airlifted to international markets.[41] Four months later a new 240 tonne cooler was installed at Eldoret Airport, complete with X-ray scanner and sniffer dogs. Exports included fish, flowers, mangoes, bananas and avocadoes.[42]

South-east along the Rift Valley, lying northwest of Nairobi, Lake Naivasha is Kenya's main flower production area. The lake is almost surrounded by flower farms, which have lowered the water level. Flowers are 90 per cent water, so the flower farms are exporting Kenya's scarce water supplies.[43] Kenya suffered severe drought in 2009. Food yields were down by a quarter and livestock died of dehydration. The number of hungry people was estimated to be between 3.8 million and 10 million. Yet exports of flowers to Europe continued, not missing a single delivery day.[44] Flower production around Lake Naivasha was scaled down, but water was still used to clear dust from the roads along which flowers were trucked to the airports.[45]

Nairobi Airport opened a new perishables centre in July 2010. Big enough to accommodate four simultaneous Boeing 747 freighter loads and with capacity for 250,000 tonnes a year, it is the largest in Africa.[46] By the end of the year total cargo was over 300,000 tonnes and Nairobi overtook OR Tambo as Africa's biggest cargo airport. Growth was attributed to perishable produce, which accounted for 85 per cent of exports.[47] Only small amounts of Kenya's flowers are exported to the United States, but the Kenya Flower Council has launched a promotion campaign, focusing on the large-headed roses.[48]

Houston Airport opened a perishables centre in 2009, aiming to establish the airport as a 'key link in the cold chain'.[49] The 18,000 sq. m building has seven airside doors and 18 truck doors.[50] In the first year of operation the facility received only charter flights and trucks. Blackberries, mangoes and other fruits trucked in from Mexico were flown to Europe and Asia. Exports included Californian produce and Texan beef. Throughput was 1,814 tonnes, a minimal volume for a perishables centre of its size. The new facility had failed to lure flower flights from Miami.[51]

Miami Airport is the main hub for perishable imports to the United States, receiving 54 per cent of fish imports, 71 per cent of fruit and vegetables, and 89 per cent of flowers. Most imports are from Central and South America. Colombia is the airport's main trading partner.[52] Greenhouses have proliferated on the fertile Bogotà plateau, Colombia's main flower-producing area.[53] In 2007, the aquifer supplying the flower-growing area was so depleted that water was imported from other regions.[54] Colombia supplies 80 per cent of US flower imports.[55] Only 9 per cent of Colombian flowers find their way to Europe.[56] This interconti-nental flow was boosted by a notable shipment in June 2010. A Cargolux Boeing 747 delivered 40,000 Colombian flowers for Princess Victoria of Sweden's wedding. Roses, lilies, hydrangeas and carnations were sourced from 24 flower farms.[57]

Agricultural exports are integral to the Indian government's aviation expansion drive. In 2009, India's civil aviation minister, Praful Patel, said, 'We need to take the airports to the remotest regions so that our farmers can look at exporting agricultural and farm-related products to the world. This time will come.'[58] The number of hungry people in India reached 220 million in 2009, nearly one in five of the population.[59] Yet subsidies were lavished on airport perishable centres for export of fresh produce. Cochin, the biggest airport in Kerala, opened a perish-able centre for fruit, vegetables and meat in February 2009, fully automated with X-ray and camera surveillance.[60] The Kerala government and APEDA (Agricultural and Processed Products Export Development Authority), a government agency, spent $102,000 on the 1,672 sq. m complex with three cold storage units, a freezer and a parking bay for cargo planes.[61] At the end of 2009, AAI, the Ministry of Agriculture and APEDA reviewed incentives to boost perishable exports. Government-run airport perishable facilities reduced the processing fee, offered a nominal licence fee for seven years, and waived royalty payments to AAI.[62]

APEDA has long supported exports of perishable foods from India's north-eastern states. It introduced subsidies for transport of perishable produce to export hubs by road, rail and air in 2006. The air freight subsidy amounted to 50 per cent of the cost of transport to Mumbai or Delhi, or 90 per cent of the cost of transport to Guwahati or Kolkata. The subsidy applied to bananas, guavas, lemons, oranges, pears, pineapples, plums, ginger, passion fruit, kiwi, apple, cut flowers and bamboo.[63] The air freight subsidy was still in place in 2009.[64]

Another Ethiopia

Ethiopia has been associated with hunger since the famine of 1984–85 claimed nearly 1 million lives.[65] Ever since, more than 5 million Ethiopians have been dependent on food aid.[66] The Ethiopian government cites drought in its repeated appeals for food aid. Rainfall is unreliable in parts of Ethiopia, but the country has a wealth of fertile land with nutrient-rich soil, a temperate climate and ample rainfall. Ever more of this fertile land is dedicated to export crops. The government has leased millions of hectares to foreign investors, a process that accelerated in 2008 when many Middle Eastern and Asian countries sought to stabilise their food supply in the face of rising food prices. By 2009, fence posts demarcated land all over the Rift Valley region. In the Gambella region, an Indian company, Karuturi, leased more than 300,000 hectares to grow rice, wheat and sugarcane, and flew in John Deere tractors from the United States.[67]

Writing for *Open Democracy*, René Lefort called Ethiopia 'the world champion of "land grabbing"'. It is projected that 70,000 sq. km, twice the size of Belgium, will be leased to investors, predominantly foreign, by 2015. The government hands over land and water resources regardless of the food security needs of its own people. Investors have described the land as 'green gold' and welcomed the leases as 'tantamount to ownership'. Researchers have refuted claims that the land is 'abandoned' or 'unutilised', uncovering brutal resettlement programmes.[68]

Ethiopia's oilseed belt stretches from Humera in the north of the country southwards through the Amhara region to the Rift Valley. In February 2009, after good rainfall in key growing areas, a bumper harvest of oilseeds, pulses and spices was expected, and the government announced an export target of 720,000 tonnes.[69] At the inauguration of Humera Airport, in July 2009, transport and communication minister Deriba Kuma said the facility would help fast delivery of maize, sesame and other oilseeds to international markets. The government paid the construction costs of $16.1 million. At 3 km in length, the runway can accommodate aircraft up to the size of the Antonov-124.[70]

Ethiopia's export horticulture sector has boomed in recent years. Flower exports increased from less than $10 million in 2004–05 to nearly $170 million in 2009–10.[71] Investors were given cheap leases on plots of land for as long as 21 years. Incentives included a five-year tax holiday, and the state-owned Development Bank of Ethiopia loaned up to 70 per cent of costs.[72] In August 2010 four major flower farms relocated from Kenya to Ethiopia, attracted by the loans, along with provision of roads and electricity. The Kenya Flower Council responded with a plea for tax holidays and other rebates to make their produce more competitive.[73] This exemplifies a key problem of globalisation. Governments compete to reduce business costs in order to attract investors, frequently granting additional incentives should firms threaten to relocate. The result is erosion of tax revenues, wages and working conditions, a process referred to as a 'race to the bottom'. When the Ethiopian government turned its attention to support for the nascent fruit and vegetable export industry, the incentives were as generous as for floriculture. Investors were offered a tax holiday of up to eight years and 100 per cent tax exemption on export of goods and import of equipment.[74]

Addis Ababa Airport, to the south-east of the city, is Ethiopia's export hub for flowers, fruit and vegetables. Satellite images show the airport on the southern edge of the city. The lush green area to the south is one of the main flower production areas. In March 2009, between 1,300 and 1,500 tonnes of flowers were being flown out of Addis Ababa Airport each week.[75] In October 2009 the Ethiopian government issued an emergency food aid appeal for $121 million to feed 6.2 million people, blaming a prolonged drought that had devastated crops and livestock.[76] The following month, government-owned Ethiopian Airlines' chief operating officer Tewolde Gebremariam, interviewed in *Aircargo News*, said, 'Filling the aircraft with perishables bound for Europe is never a problem.' He explained:

> This is all a bit surprising in the middle of a massive global downturn and in a country whose government appealed on 22nd October for food aid to feed six million of its people caught by drought in the horn of Africa. But as well as the Ethiopia that regularly seems to feature in humanitarian appeals, there is another one in the Ethiopian Highlands with adequate rains and a booming perishables export sector, sending flowers, fruit, vegetables, meat and spices by air to Europe and the Middle East.[77]

In August 2010 Ethiopia announced annual earnings of $216 million from floriculture and horticulture exports. This marked a $51 million increase over the preceding year, totalling 1.8 billion cut flowers and 66,000 tonnes of vegetables, fruit and herbs. Haileselassie Tekie, director of the state-owned Ethiopian Horticulture Development Agency (EHDA), attributed this growth to government support and the participation of investors.[78]

The export earnings did not find their way to Ethiopia's hungry people. In February 2011 Ethiopia appealed for $227 million to feed 2.8 million people for six months, citing poor rainfall in the Somali and Oromiya regions, exacerbated by insurgency in the Somali region.[79] The following month, an export promotion exhibition was held in Addis Ababa. The organisers, the Ethiopian Horticultural Producers and Exporters Association (EHPEA) expected Ethiopia's earnings from horticultural exports in 2011 would reach $190 million.[80] A March 2011 report by the EHPEA and the EHDA detailed the favourable climactic conditions for export crops in the Rift Valley, North Omo, Amhara and Tigray. High rainfall and supplementary water for irrigation supported tropical, sub-tropical and temperate crops including mangetout, sweet peas, melons, chillies, ginger, pomegranates, passion fruit and avocadoes. Export horticulture provided few opportunities for local suppliers: 'Virtually all production equipment and inputs are imported from Europe, Israel, India and China.'[81]

Ethiopia's hunger crisis worsened, and the government appealed for $398 million of food and non-food aid in July 2011, stating that 4.5 million people were 'on the critical condition before they reach brink of starvation'. In addition to the native population, thousands of refugees arrived from neighbouring Somalia, fleeing war and drought.[82] Growth of Ethiopian Airlines' perishable exports continued. In September 2011, the carrier attributed a 20 per cent rise in cargo for the fiscal year, to 160,000 tonnes, to 'a surge in horticulture and meat exports'.[83]

On 20 September 2012, Ethiopian Airlines greeted the arrival of its first Boeing 777 freighter at Addis Abba. With a payload of 105 tonnes, and on-board temperature control, it is a giant flying refrigerator. Anticipating the addition of another five Boeing 777s to Ethiopian's fleet, Kuma said the aircraft would be used for export of horticulture products.[84] Haileselassie Tekie, director general of EHDA, told the Ethiopia Investor website that the Boeing 777s 'will be fully engaged in the transportation of vegetables and fruits to the international market' and that 500 sq. km of land had been allocated for vegetables and fruits.[85]

Simultaneously, the Ethiopian government issued another food aid appeal, requesting either $194 million or 314 tonnes of food for the following four months. Agriculture minister Mitiku Kassa said that the number of food aid recipients was 3.2 million, and numbers were growing because of lack of rainfall in some areas of the country.[86]

On 13 March 2013, Ethiopian Airlines inaugurated a new cold store at Addis Ababa Airport. Measuring 3,700 sq. m, it is big enough to store produce from four cargo planes. Gebremariam said the facility would 'serve the growing exports of perishables in general and horticultural products in particular'.[87] Netherlands-based Celtic Cooling had announced that it was building the cold store the previous August. Normally, components of refrigeration equipment of this scale would be transported by ship in 40 containers, but, in order to speed up delivery to Ethiopian Airlines, the cold store was flown to Addis Ababa.[88] The cold store is only a stopgap. The Ethiopian government is subsidising construction of a new perishable centre at Addis Ababa Airport, aiming for it to be one of the biggest in the world, outsizing Schiphol and Dubai Flower Centre.[89]

7

Industrial Cargo

Airlinked Assembly Lines

A considerable proportion of commercial air freight, nearly one-third, consists of materials, components and equipment for manufacturing. The first-ever Boeing 747 freighter commercial flight, on 19 April 1972, from Frankfurt to New York, carried 25 computerised knitting machines, an entire production plant weighing 73 tonnes.[1] Analysts MergeGlobal, advisors to key aviation trade bodies IATA and TIACA (The International Air Cargo Association), estimated that in 2007 raw materials, components and unfinished goods constituted 12 per cent of the world's air freight. 'Capital equipment', machinery and tools used to manufacture and deliver goods, accounted for 19 per cent.[2] Manufacturing has been broken down into stages, and components are transported between specialised sites dispersed around the globe. Use of air freight, in preference to surface transport, has been galvanised by the adoption of 'just in time' production techniques, whereby components are delivered as needed in order to minimise inventory costs.

Air freight is used extensively in global supply chains for electronic products. Dell's use of air freight for manufacturing computers is regarded as a bellwether of the industry. In 2001 chips from Japan, keyboards from Mexico, monitors and cooling fans from Taiwan, soundcards from France and floppy drives from Malaysia were being flown in to the final assembly plant in Austin, Texas.[3] Clothing is also assembled from

103

components. 'Fast fashion', the rush to supply new garments based on designs from the latest fashion shows, stimulates air freight of items like buttons. Apparel industry adviser Mike Flanagan explained, 'It's often difficult to find local suppliers of every component where a garment is being made, so air freighting components is much more widespread than air freighting finished garments.'[4]

Vehicle components have been air freighted since the 1920s. In the 1920s and 1930s, 25 per cent of European air cargo was made up of spare parts for machinery and vehicles.[5] Between 1928 and 1932, Ford, the US car manufacturer, flew 6,500 tonnes of components between factories in Detroit, Chicago and Buffalo.[6] Peugeot established an assembly line for heavy mechanical equipment and upholstery in Kano, Nigeria in 1975. By 1988, 130,000 tonnes of components had been air freighted in from Lyons in France, speeding up manufacturing of 20,000 cars per year.[7]

South Africa hosts over 200 firms making components for Audi, Volkswagen, BMW, Mercedes, Fiat and other car manufacturers in Europe. Vehicle components are a mainstay of the country's air exports. Seat covers, dashboards, catalytic converters, tyres, exhaust pipes and other car components accounted for 40 per cent of Swiss WorldCargo's air freight exports from South Africa to Europe in 2005.[8] The carrier described South Africa as a 'components paradise', explaining that, along with the attraction of low labour costs, the manufacturing process for catalytic converters for export to Europe 'involves the use of materials that are forbidden by EU law. Importing finished products that contain these materials is, however, permitted'.[9] This is an example of how globalisation enables firms to locate operations in poorer countries with less stringent environmental, health and safety regulations.

Firms' costs are further reduced by government incentives such as tax breaks. An article by Lara Sorinski, 'Air cargo saves the bacon', explains how tax breaks can outweigh the expense of outsourcing manufacturing operations: 'The amount of money that can be saved by taking advantage of certain tax incentives can often times outweigh other costs associated with global supply chains, including transportation.'[10]

Aircraft manufacturing has its own airlinked assembly lines. Boeing undermined the green credentials of its 787, or 'Dreamliner' when it converted four 747s to carry components and tools between production sites.[11] The refitted 747s have a bulbous top to accommodate engines, sections of the wings, fuselage and landing gear, and other large, awkwardly shaped components, which are flown between supplier factories in Italy, Japan, Kansas and South Carolina, then to the final assembly plant in Washington.[12] Michael Boyd of the Boyd Group aviation consultancy said, 'All Boeing does is design it and glue it together.' He describes how Boeing's outsourcing of production reduces the firm's responsibility for workers' rights: 'If there is a downturn in orders, Boeing does not have to face the challenge of what to do with a permanent, unionized work force.'[13]

Five modified freighters carry Airbus components between factories. The freighters, similar to Boeing's with a bulbous top, are nicknamed 'Beluga' because of the resemblance to the eponymous whale. The tailcone is flown from Spain, the vertical stabiliser from Germany, and other sections of aircraft from various sites in Europe to final assembly lines in France, Germany and China.[14]

Aircraft manufacturing supply chains are extending to India. In 2009, Airbus opened a facility for manufacture of metallic parts in Belgaum, Karnataka.[15] A Boeing MRO (manufacture, repair and overhaul) unit at Nagpur, located at the geometric centre of India, will be used for repair and maintenance of Air India's aircraft, and manufacturing floor beams for the 787.[16]

The Cargo Giants

The biggest freighters are used to carry 'outsize cargo', large and irregularly shaped consignments which will not fit in the usual pallets. In place of the usual side door, the nose of the plane pivots upwards, enabling loading of items which can be as large as the length or breadth of the cargo hold. Cargolux has a fleet of 16 Boeing 747-400s, which, in 2007, delivered escalators for shopping malls, flight simulators, satellites, mill wheels, helicopters, trucks and a 52 tonne rotor shaft.[17] Cargolux was the launch customer for the Boeing's 747-8, an expanded model offering operators the options of either taking on 20 extra tonnes of cargo or carrying extra fuel to extend the range.[18]

Boeing's new freighter is outsized by the Antonov-124's maximum payload of 150 tonnes. Volga-Dnepr's fleet of ten An-124s has delivered an asphalt plant from the United States to Russia, a 43 tonne kiln tyre from Milan to Mumbai for a cement works and a 73 tonne production line for glasswork manufacturing from the Netherlands to Ulyanovsk in Russia.[19] Three Antonov-124 flights delivered a whole train from Germany to China. Each flight carried two carriages, along with ramps and guide rails to manoeuvre the carriages from the plane onto the tarmac at Guangzhou Baiyun Airport.[20] The heaviest single item carried in an Antonov-124 was a 135 tonne power plant generator, flown from Düsseldorf to Delhi.[21]

When infrastructure crumbles in the aftermath of hurricanes, earthquakes and floods, heavy-lift freighters are chartered to deliver food, vehicles, generators, water purification equipment, medicines and temporary shelters. Devastation wreaked by Hurricane Katrina on the coast of Louisiana in 2005 triggered an influx of air charters. Volga-Dnepr sent eight Antonov-124 flights for the British, Netherlands and Italian governments, carrying water pumps, water purification equipment, prefabricated houses, tents and blankets.[22] The relief effort following the January 2010 earthquake in Haiti saw Boeing 747 flights from the United States, United Kingdom, China, the UAE, Dubai and Israel.[23] The Japanese government sent the Antonov-225 and nine Antonov-124 flights, carrying earthmoving equipment and tents.[24]

After the 2011 earthquake and tsunami in Japan, which killed about 18,000 people, the first civil flight to land at Sendai was an Antonov-124, carrying a specialist medical van for diagnosing and treating ophthalmological diseases. The subsequent flight delivered personnel, equipment and satellite phones, along with a helicopter to deliver food, water and clothing.[25] Radiation leaked from the flooded Fukushima nuclear plant, and four Antonov-124 flights delivered truck-mounted pumps to pour water and concrete from above, to cool the reactors and contain the leak. A 95 tonne concrete pumper truck flown out from Atlanta was the airport's heaviest ever piece of freight.[26]

Within hours of serious oil spills, the cargo giants are chartered to support attempts to contain slicks, and clean-up operations if oil reaches landfall. The biggest oil spill in history occurred in 1991, during the first Gulf War, when Iraqi troops retreating from Kuwait opened valves on oil rigs and pipelines. Between 5 and 10 million barrels of oil flowed into the Persian Gulf towards the shores of Saudi Arabia. Saudi oil firm Aramco's emergency response involved 30 cargo planes from the United States and Europe, which, together with ships, delivered 80 km of booms to contain the oil spill, 35 vacuum tanker trucks and 57 skimmers.[27]

Pollution from the *Exxon Valdez* oil spill in 1989 necessitated the closure of fisheries, and the collapse in fish exports reduced exports from Anchorage, Alaska's main hub airport. But the formation of an 'Exxon Air Force' led to an overall 60 per cent increase in traffic for the fiscal year.[28] Heavyweight equipment was delivered in C-5 Galaxys, military aircraft normally used to carry armoured fighting vehicles and helicopters.[29]

Hurricane Katrina wreaked havoc on oil infrastructure in the Gulf of Mexico, leading to the biggest oil spill since *Exxon Valdez*. Over 24 million litres of oil leaked from offshore rigs and pipelines, and an unknown amount spilled from hundreds of submerged petrol stations.[30] Glasgow Prestwick Airport handled an 8 tonne anchor for an urgent repairs operation on an oil rig off the coast of New Orleans.[31] The Gulf of Mexico was hit by another serious oil pollution incident on 20 April 2010, when BP's *Deepwater Horizon* oil rig exploded. Eleven workers were killed and the emergency response failed to prevent the worst offshore oil spill in US history.[32] An Antonov-124 delivered seven skimmer boats from France, and eight Boeing 747 cargo charters from Singapore brought over 400 tonnes of rubber booms and other equipment.[33]

Attempts to contain the spill failed, and as oil flowed towards the shore, two C-130s, large turboprop military planes, flew nine flights a day from Stennis Airport in Bay St Louis, each carrying 19,000 litres of dispersal chemicals which were sprayed on the oil through large nozzles like a crop duster.[34] The flurry of flights was of limited effectiveness, and an oily sheen reached the Mississippi Delta by the end of April. By the end of May, 160 km of Louisiana coast were polluted with oil, and birds, turtles and dolphins were found dead along the shoreline.[35]

For the Oil Industry

Oil industry equipment, for exploration, extraction, production and maintenance, is a major air cargo sector. Helicopters provide direct and rapid contact with the most remote oil rigs. Emirates Airline, Etihad Airways, Alaska Airlines and BA are among the airlines carrying equipment in the hold of passenger flights. Long pipes, rigs, pumping units, oil well caps and other heavyweight items are carried in dedicated freighters.

The earliest instance I found of the use of aviation in oil and gas exploration was in November 1920, in Canada's Northwest Territories. Two F13 Junkers, the first all metal aircraft, delivered prospecting equipment to the Mackenzie River Delta, where Canada's largest river system empties into the Beaufort Sea, on the western edge of the Arctic Ocean, and where vast gas deposits had been discovered under the frozen ground.[36]

Now, areas of permafrost in the arctic regions are melting. Fossil fuel extraction in northern regions has had to adapt to this stark evidence of climate change. Winter roads, made from compacted snow and ice, are viable for shorter periods. An article by Graham Chandler in *Far North Oil and Gas* magazine, in 2006, notes the decrease in the winter work season, during which temperatures are sufficiently low to build and utilise ice roads, from 220 days to about 100 days in the space of 30 years. This has elicited an increase the use of air transport, including the world's biggest helicopter, the Mi-26, used in Siberian oilfields since the 1980s. Chandler describes how the size of the helicopter, when sitting on an airfield, is not evident 'until you start walking towards it and it doesn't seem to get any closer'. The Mi-26 can accommodate complete drilling rigs. The rotor head is about three storeys high, and the eight-blade rotor 32 m in diameter.[37] The hourly fuel burn is 3,000 litres.

Melting ice roads are noted again in a 2008 article about Canada's oil boom, quoting David Gillen, professor of transportation policy at the University of British Columbia:

> One of the things that we are finding is that the winter roads that use the frozen tundra and lakes are becoming less usable and for shorter periods of time because the changes in weather patterns that are going on... It's much more logical to move it by ship or barge along the Mackenzie River, or by air.[38]

Bordering Northwest Territories to the south, in the Alberta province, extraction of thick, tarry bitumen from the tar sands has turned a pristine wilderness into a toxic dump. Environmental Defence, a non-profit organisation, describes the environmental impact of the tar sands, the world's biggest energy and open cast mining project, as a 'giant slow motion oil spill'. Every litre of bitumen that is extracted produces a waste water stream of up to 2,500 litres, known as 'tailings', contained in artificial lakes which covered over 50 sq. km by 2008. Some of the biggest dams in the world surround the tailing lakes, but approximately 11 million litres of contaminated water per day have leaked into lakes and groundwater.[39] Tailing lakes are acutely toxic to birds. In April 2008, 1,606 ducks died after landing on a tailing lake operated by Syncrude, one of the largest tar sands producers.

Many birds were so heavily coated in oil and waste that they sank immediately.[40]

Exploitation of the tar sands has brought an influx of heavy-weight oil and gas equipment to Alberta's main airports, Calgary and Edmonton. In 2004, Edmonton Airport was receiving Antonov-124s carrying 'oil field supplies from locations as far away as Houston, Germany, China and Japan'.[41] By 2008, Antonov-124s were a weekly sight at Calgary Airport, delivering large items like compressors and vehicles for the tar sands.[42]

Russian Antonov-124 freighters have a well-established role in providing support for the oil business. Polet Air Cargo undertook a particularly challenging logistics operation in October 2003. A 44 tonne piece configuration of valves used to control flow of oil from a well, named a 'Christmas tree' after what it resembles when assembled, along with 80 tonnes of other equipment, was delivered to an oil rig in the Gulf of Mexico. The shipment was flown in an Antonov-124 from East Midlands Airport in England to Houston, trucked to Galveston, then shipped out to the rig 200 km offshore.[43]

Volga-Dnepr's fleet of ten Antonov-124s, provide 'oil & gas transportation for almost all major companies of the world'. The carrier's website lists BP, ExxonMobil, Chevron-Texaco, Calgary Overseas, Canadian Oxy Offshore International and Lukoil. In the space of 18 months, 120 flights transported nearly 10,000 tonnes of oil equipment to Colombia for BP.[44] By 2011, Volga-Dnepr had delivered a total of 130,000 tonnes of oil and gas equipment.[45]

I attempted to track the Antonov-225's movements for March 2012, and discovered a series of oil-related flights. Two winches weighing 125 tonnes were flown from Glasgow Prestwick to Washington for a Shell oil project in Alaska.[46] A few days later, the Antonov-225 touched down in Calgary to pick up oil and gas equipment for its first-ever flight to Africa, which delivered compression packages and other instruments to extinguish a gas flare to Port Harcourt, Nigeria.[47] At the end of the month the

Antonov-225 took off from Milan, destined for Wichita, Kansas carrying components for an oil refinery. Three stops were made en route to refill the 348,000 litre fuel tank.[48]

Oil industry equipment is a mainstay for all-cargo airline Cargolux. By 2007, the carrier had built up a fleet of 15 Boeing 747s, describing the planes as 'ideally suited for outsized cargo, such as pipelines or oil-drilling equipment, which does not fit through the side cargo door of older, converted B747 aircraft'.[49] Alex Pansin, regional director for the Middle East and Africa, told *Arabian Business* magazine, 'In Sharjah and Dubai we have seen pieces between 38 and 40 tonnes each that are moved through the nose of the plane .... We have been carrying for the oil industry things you cannot imagine, all of which requires a crane.'[50]

Cargolux's hub in the Caspian region, one of the world's main offshore oil and gas production areas, is Baku, the capital of Azerbaijan.[51] Situated on the western shore of the Caspian Sea, Baku is the starting point of the first oil pipeline from the Caspian to the Mediterranean. The 1,768 km pipeline extends westwards to Ceyhan in Turkey, with the capacity to pump 1 million barrels of oil per day. As the pipeline neared completion in 2004, oil equipment was the 'predominant cargo' on Cargolux's 25 weekly flights to Baku.[52] The route of the pipeline reveals the geopolitical imperative, securing an energy supply to Europe without interference from Russia. Instead of running directly through Armenia, which has close ties with Russia, the pipeline takes a sharp curve northwards through Tbilisi, the capital of west-friendly Georgia.[53]

Cargolux began a weekly service to Tbilisi in November 2008, stating that the destination 'fits well in Cargolux's global route network in support of the oil and gas industry'. A few weeks later the carrier marked its 10,000th landing at Baku Airport. Since Cargolux's first landing at Baku in 2001, the number of parking positions for Boeing 747s had grown from one to ten, and several daily flights delivered oil drilling equipment from Houston, Calgary, Aberdeen, Singapore and Dubai.[54]

Extreme Oil

Cargolux extended its route network to Atyrau, on the northern shore of the Caspian Sea, in 2007, carrying cargo predominantly for the energy sector.[55] Previously renowned for fisheries, Atyrau is Kazakhstan's oil capital. It is the centre for exploiting the Kashagan oil field, the biggest oil discovery in the past 30 years, pushing the frontier of offshore oil in an extreme environment. Drilling operations 80 km offshore are supported by an artificial archipelago of five islands, built from 7 million tonnes of rock.[56] The sea freezes over for five months of the year, temperatures veer between 40°C in summer and -40°C in winter, and rigs are buffeted by fluctuating sea levels, strong winds and storms. Oil, 4.5 km beneath the sea bed under layers of rock and salt, gushes out at high pressure and contains up to 20 per cent hydrogen sulphide, a lethal neurotoxin.

As Kashagan prepares to commence production there are concerns that, should a blowout occur, it could be more catastrophic than the one that occurred in the Gulf of Mexico. The northern waters of the landlocked Caspian Sea are shallow, and high concentrations of hydrogen sulphide would be acutely toxic to marine life, ruining the habitats of endangered species such as the Caspian seal and Caspian sturgeon. One of the biggest blow-outs in history occurred at the onshore Tengiz oilfield, which is part of the same geological formation as Kashagan. The flame column appeared on 24 June 1985, reached a height of more than 200 m and took 13 months to extinguish.[57]

The island of Sakhalin, in the Okhotsk Sea, off the east coast of Russia, seven times zones and a nine-hour flight east from Moscow, is the base for another extreme offshore oil and gas project. Covered in a sheet of ice up to 2 m thick for half the year, Sakhalin's drilling platforms have to withstand ice floes. By 2011, seven out of ten of the largest oil wells on the planet were in operation at Sakhalin, most notably the world's biggest and deepest 'extended reach oil well', which accesses offshore oil fields via drilling on land down into the ground, then horizontally beneath the sea floor.

Sakhalin Airport demonstrated its capacity to handle the Antonov-124 in January 2011, when the giant freighter delivered two compressors for a gas distribution station.[58] Another Antonov-124 flight, on 5 May, delivered two lifeboats from Poland, for ocean transport to the Molikpaq drilling platform.[59] The platform is 16 km north-east of Sakhalin island. A steel 'spacer', filled with 278,000 cu. m of sand, anchors it to the ocean floor.[60] Lifeboats on the Kolskaya oil rig, further offshore, proved futile. On 18 December 2011 the oil rig capsized in a storm 200 km offshore. The rig was being towed back to the island by an icebreaker and a tow boat after completing a drilling mission, but overturned in winds of 70 km per hour and waves 6 m high. Rescuers pulled 14 people alive from the water but all four lifeboats were found empty. Four days later cyclone conditions meant there was no hope of survivors and the search was called off. The death toll was 53, but only 17 bodies were recovered from the water.[61]

Papua New Guinea's $19 billion liquefied natural gas (LNG) project, PNG LNG, led by ExxonMobil, in the mountainous country's southern highlands, is a striking example of how onshore oil production is encroaching on increasingly inaccessible terrain. Construction of production and processing facilities, connected by 700 km of pipelines, began in 2009. Gas fields and pipeline routes are carved out of steep slopes, in close proximity to thatched-hut villages and small terraced farms. As PNG LNG strives to meet the 2014 target date for commencing production, there are ominous signs of a continuation of the 'resource curse' exemplified by Papua New Guinea's history of gold exports, a paradox of plenty where mineral wealth aggravates conflict and export earnings fail to reach the majority of the population and alleviate poverty. There have been violent disputes over loss of land and livelihoods and environmental damage. Stanley Mamu monitors PNG LNG, documenting his findings on the blog LNG Watch.[62]

Expansion of two high-altitude airstrips serving PNG LNG has met with unrest. The Tari airstrip is used to ferry supplies. Five hundred landowners staged a peaceful protest in October 2011, demanding recognition of their stake in the project, the release of agreed funding and closure of a new landing site where Hercules 100 turboprop aircraft had brought loud noise, dust and fumes.[63] In September 2011 landowners from five clans brought construction of a new airport, Komo, to a halt for a few days. They locked the gate to the access road, demanding outstanding business development grants and other agreements to ensure they would benefit from economic development.[64]

A 5.2 km by 1 km corridor of land, previously forested and cultivated with coffee and sweet potato, was cleared for the Komo airstrip.[65] It has been constructed specifically for PNG LNG, for delivery of heavy plant equipment far faster than would be possible along narrow, dilapidated roads. PNG LNG documentation is peppered with its safety mantra 'nobody gets hurt', but in November 2011 a contractor working at the Komo airfield died of injuries sustained when a trench collapsed.[66] Komo's 3.2 km runway, longer than Port Moresby, Papua's main airport, and comparable with major international airports, can accommodate Antonov-124s. To level the undulating ground 10 million cu. m of earth were used.[67] The schedule for construction of a gas conditioning plant and wellpads anticipated delivery of 5,000 tonnes of equipment to Komo, carried in 100 Antonov-124 flights from Port Moresby, over a four-month period.[68] A quarry above the villages of Tumbi and Tumbiago was excavated to supply aggregate for the airfield.

Early in the morning of 24 January 2012, mud and limestone slabs from an area immediately to the north-west of the quarry cascaded downwards, obliterating the two villages. The Red Cross estimated that 60 people were buried alive under the debris. Mamu found that the government's reaction to the landslide typified its failure to regulate resource extraction effectively. Authorities acted like business partners, supporting ExxonMobil and its contractors. Just two days after the landslide, Papua New Guinea's National Disaster Committee (NDC) published a hastily assembled report, identifying heavy rainfall as the cause. Yet there were no previous problems with geological instability. The area had been inhabited for 600 years, withstanding heavy rain and earthquakes.

Indications that operations at the quarry might have been a key, or contributory, factor in the landslide, one of the worst ever recorded in the country, were swept aside. Landowners thought that excavations could have loosened the ground, and that the blockage of two rivers could have resulted in a build-up of water pressure which would eventually have given way. In the months leading up to the disaster, PNG LNG's own environment and safety consultants had flagged up failing safety precautions and inadequate risk assessment at the quarry. Within a week of the landslide, Clough Curtain Joint Venture (CCJV), the firm that developed the quarry, was awarded a new contract for the project's upstream infrastructure.

Calls for an independent inquiry, backed by international landslide expert Professor Dave Petley and credible testimony from local people with intimate knowledge of the landscape, went unheeded. Several weeks later, humanitarian aid had not been released and 3,000 people were still living in temporary shelters. Resumption of PNG LNG took precedence over helping surviving victims, or respect for the dead. A section of the access road to the Komo airfield site was covered by landslide debris, but even though bodies lay unrecovered, bulldozers removed debris so that the road could be reopened. Landowners formed a blockade and delayed the reopening of the road for two weeks, but by the end of March 2012, bereaved relatives watched as heavy vehicles ran over the remains of the dead.[69]

A month after the landslide, in February 2012, there was another fatality at the Komo site. A worker was run over by a front-end loader, a construction vehicle used to pick up and dump materials.[70]

Remote Resource Extraction

Aviation has long played a pivotal role in mining minerals, metals and previous stones, facilitating extraction from remote regions inaccessible by land routes. Exploitation of rich gold deposits in the Bulolo Valley, near Papua New Guinea's northern coast, began in the 1930s, when the country was under Australian administration. Writing in *Flight International*, the world's oldest aviation magazine, in 1935, Lord Sempill, a British peer, bemoaned the inconvenience of using 'native carriers', indigenous people, to carry equipment to mines. Carrying heavy loads over heavily forested and mountainous terrain, and needing to stop for food, they 'could travel only about five miles a day'. Colonisers also had to contend with the 'danger of attacks by uncivilised natives who, not unnaturally, resented the coming of the white man'. So a fleet of 15 aircraft was dedicated to the mine. Between 1930 and 1942 the mine was supplied entirely by air. A specially adapted plane flew eight 1,000 tonne dredgers to the mine. They were dismantled for the flight, then reassembled.[71]

Gold mining activity in the Bulolo Valley has surged in recent years. Recommissioning of Bulolo Airport, in 2009, was part funded by Harmony Gold,[72] which has developed the Hidden Valley open pit gold mine in a joint venture with Newcrest Mining. Community relations have been far from harmonious. Hundreds of indigenous settlements living downstream, along the Watut River, have protested over water pollution killing fish and a build-up of toxic sediment destroying crops. Restricted access to the river reduced income from small-scale alluvial gold mining. Riots broke out in June 2011, after two years of raising grievances which went unaddressed. People from affected communities clashed with mining companies and police, smashing up a project vehicle.[73]

Mining in inhospitable Arctic regions has always relied on air services. In the 1930s, Alaska recorded the highest air freight of any US state, due to mining activity, in particular the gold rush.

Some mines were dependent on bush pilots to deliver supplies in small planes. The Brevier Glacier was used as an airstrip to supply the Big Foot gold mine, 2,000 m above sea level near Valdez.[74] Some mines are only accessible by land in winter, via ice roads. Material for construction of an entire town to support Diavik diamond mine, in Canada's Northwest Territories, was transported along an ice road, which is only open from February to early April. The remainder of the year, the airport's gravel runway sees regular Boeing 737 flights.[75]

Winter temperatures in Mirny, Siberia, plummet as low as -56°C. When excavations for a diamond mine began in 1958, jet engines were used to melt layers of permafrost 480 m deep. The mine grew to 525 m deep and 1.2 km wide, making Mirny the deepest open-pit diamond mine in the world. Rock hauling trucks 6 m high take two hours to make the round trip along the spiral road between the top of the hole and the basin. Satellite images of Mirny Airport show the enormous round hole at the end of the runway. Airspace above the mine is off limits to helicopters, as there have been instances of the powerful downward air flow sucking them into the hole.[76]

Vast mineral wealth lies beneath Afghanistan's deserts and rugged mountains, including gold, iron, copper, lithium, cobalt and precious stones. Much of this was discovered by the United States, since it led the invasion of the country in 2001. Surveying and prospecting progressed in the midst of the conflict, and US Geological Survey caravans were escorted by armoured vehicles. In 2010 the United States valued Afghanistan's deposits at $1 trillion,[77] and *Aircargo News* reported growing air cargo traffic into the country, driven by heavy lift freighters carrying equipment for Chinese investments.[78] China is extracting Afghanistan's minerals, and US forces are providing indirect support. Purchase of a $3 billion controlling stake in the Aynak copper field, one of the largest in the world, in mountains in the Logar Province to the south of Kabul, made China the country's largest foreign investor. The United States committed more than 2,000 troops and security for the projected routes for a road and railway to transport the copper to China.[79]

Aviation's role in the scramble for Africa's resources began in the early 20th century, with surveys to prepare for the establishment of colonies and trade routes. In the 1950s, colonial interests in many areas of the continent triggered a boom in air transportation of mining equipment.[80] Today, well-known international carriers play a role in supplying mining equipment to Africa. Emirates SkyCargo announced an agreement with Astral Aviation in 2006, providing 'significant reach within Africa, enabling the cargo division to transport odd-sized machinery and shipments, such as drilling and mining equipment, from Australia to Mwanza'. Mwanza Airport, on the southern shore of Lake Victoria, the biggest lake in Africa, is the hub for Astral's extensive inter-Africa route network.[81]

By 2011, Astral's fleet of small DC-9 freighters was distributing cargo for 20 international carriers flying into Kenya, its website listing Lufthansa, Singapore Airlines and Qatar Airways. Flights to Zambia and DR Congo were driven by intensified copper mining, and a third weekly flight to Mwanza was being considered, due to growing traffic of gold mining equipment.[82]

8

Arms, Aid and Accidents

Arms and Aid to Africa

In many African countries, extraction of oil, and minerals used in the electronic, automobile, aerospace and defence industries, is linked with conflict. Armed groups control mining of resources the export supply chain, which are sold in exchange for weapons. A 2009 report by Hugh Griffiths and Mark Bromley for Stockholm International Peace Research Institute (SIPRI), 'Air transport and destabilising commodity flows', analysed the role of aviation in resource-related conflict in several African countries, including oil in Sudan, diamonds in Sierra Leone and Liberia, gold in Angola and coltan in the Democratic Republic of Congo (DR Congo). Mining areas tend to be geographically isolated, and depend on aviation to export mined minerals to global markets. Incoming flights were laden with extractive equipment.

SIPRI's report revealed that many of the carriers involved in illicit resource extraction were directly connected with conflict, as they were also engaged in arms transfers. Analysis of reports by the United Nations and other agencies revealed that 186 air carriers and transport agents had been involved with transport of small arms and lights weapons to Africa over the previous decade. A number of African commercial carriers, with close ties to the armed forces of the country in which they were registered, had repeatedly transported arms for state institutions and militias, breaking UN arms embargoes. Several airlines, all registered in Sudan with satellite offices in the UAE and involved in oil extraction, violated the UN arms embargo on the Darfur region of Sudan, including Azza Air Transport, Badr Airlines, Trans-Attico, Juba Air Cargo, Ababeel Aviation and United Arabian Airlines. The most blatant violation of the embargo occurred on 31 July 2006. A Badr Airlines Ilyushin-76 was photographed delivering Toyota pickup trucks mounted with machine guns to El Fasher Airport in broad daylight.

Overseas carriers have also been involved in arms trafficking to Africa, including several Central and East European airlines, all closely associated with arms manufacturers and ministries of defence. Ukrainian Cargo Airways, owned by the Ukrainian Ministry of Defence, was involved in transportation of arms for more than ten years. Reports by Human Rights Watch, Amnesty International and the International Crisis Group implicated the carrier in shipments of small arms to Tanzania, Angola and DR Congo. A number of intercontinental commercial carriers were found to be involved in arms trafficking. These carriers were linked to organised crime, and avoided detection by dispersing different business functions around the world, taking advantage of lax regulation. Shell companies and offshore business registries kept ownership opaque and helped carriers evade detection. Typically, airlines were set up in the guise of a holding company in the Caribbean, North America or Western Europe, which provided 'a degree of anonymity regarding ownership and capital flows'.[1] Aircraft would be registered in African, Central Asian or Middle Eastern states with little oversight of civil aviation. Other commercial intercontinental carriers had shared personnel, aircraft or offices with airlines which were involved in supply of illicit arms.

SIPRI discovered that air transport of resources and illicit arms to kill and maim people was tightly intertwined with delivery of humanitarian aid. At least 90 per cent of air cargo companies identified in reports of arms trafficking to conflict zones in Africa had been contracted by UN agencies, the European Union, North Atlantic Treaty Organization (NATO) member states, defence contractors and NGOs to deliver cargo for humanitarian aid, peace support, stability operations and defence logistics. Some carriers were simultaneously facilitating conflict in, and providing relief for, the same zones.

Several of the Sudan-registered carriers that had violated the arms embargo on Darfur held contracts with UN agencies. Ababeel Aviation held contracts with UN agencies including the World Health Organization (WHO). Juba Air was contracted by the UN Children's Fund (UNICEF). Aerolift, an international specialist heavyweight and outsize cargo carrier, supplied assault rifles, hand grenades, mines, machine guns, surface to air missiles, rocket launchers, anti-aircraft guns and anti-tank guns to the al-Shabaab militia, which controls much of southern Somalia, in 2006. In spite of this record Dyncorp, a provider of aviation logistics and security services to the US government, contracted Aerolift to support peacekeeping and humanitarian operations in Africa in 2008 and 2009.[2]

Interception of an Ilyushin-76 suspected of arms running in January 2010 revealed multiple connecting flights spanning the globe. The beginning of the flight plan was traced from Baku. From here it flew to Al-Fujairah in the UAE, Bangkok, Pyongyang in North Korea where it picked up its cargo, then back to Bangkok where it was discovered that the consignment, claimed to be spare parts for the oil industry, consisted of more than 30 tonnes of explosives, grenades and surface to air missiles. Had the plane not been intercepted, it would have continued to Colombo, back to Al-Fujairah, then on to Kiev, Tehran and finally to Montenegro, a distance of 24,000 km.

Attempts to determine the ownership of the plane unveiled multiple layers of leasing by a 'tangled web of shell companies' in the UAE, Hong Kong and Spain. All these companies were 'suspiciously new and previously unknown', and denied knowledge of falsification of the shipment. Ownership of the plane was tracked to Kazakhstan, but the North Korean company that sourced the weapons could not be found.[3]

The supply of illicit weapons can is extremely complex and difficult to trace, but SIPRI identified air transport as a potential 'choke point'. Aircraft must be registered, so transport of arms via air is relatively easy to detect. Rigorous monitoring and regulation of carriers' involvement in arms trafficking could stem the flow. SIPRI recommended addition of 'ethical transportation' clauses to peace, humanitarian aid and defence contracts, forcing airlines to choose between transporting aid and transporting arms. Furthermore, a number of carriers involved in arms trafficking could be excluded from aid contracts on the basis of poor safety records, which have resulted in a ban from EU airspace.[4]

Africa's Abysmal Air Safety Record

Africa has an abysmal air safety record. An air accident rate of 7.41 accidents per million flights in 2010 marked an improvement on the 9.94 recorded in 2009, but was twelve times worse than the global average of 0.61. Air safety is compromised by poor airport infrastructure, inadequate regulatory oversight and lack of skilled personnel.[5] The 2011 global accident rate was the lowest in aviation history, 0.37 per million flights, but the rate for Africa was nearly ten times higher, at 3.27.[6] African carriers dominate the list of airlines banned from EU airspace because of safety concerns. At the end of 2011 the ban applied to all registered airlines from 13 African countries: Benin, DR Congo, Djibouti, Equatorial Guinea, Liberia, Mauritania, Mozambique, Republic of Congo, Sao Tome and Principe, Sierra Leone, Sudan, Swaziland, and Zambia. In addition, airlines and aircraft from Angola, Comoros, Gabon, Ghana and Madagascar were subject to restrictions.[7]

Elijah Chingosho, secretary general of the African Airlines Association (AFRAA), complained that some of the banned airlines, including two recent additions to the list, Air Madagascar and Mozambique's LAM, had better safety records than some

European carriers, most notably Air France, which, since 1990 had had three fatal accidents, with a death toll of 348. Chingosho also claimed that the ban was partially motivated by protectionism, serving the commercial interests of Air France in particular, as nine out of ten of its most profitable routes were to Africa.[8] IATA also argued that the EU ban is too sweeping, stating that the list includes airlines that are safe, the underlying issue being lack of confidence in these countries' regulatory authorities. Western governments should help resolve this by assisting with implementation of effective regulatory oversight and safety management systems, flight data analysis and training to reduce the incidence of aircraft sliding off runways.[9]

In Africa, as elsewhere, most air accidents occur at take-off and landing, and the high rate of runway excursions means that, in addition to the death toll of passengers and crew, wreckage frequently kills people on the ground. Another key factor in Africa's high air accident rate is the use of old, poorly maintained planes, in particular Russian Antonovs and Ilyushins.

Aerolift crashed two Russian-built freighters in the space of 17 days. On 20 February 2009 the carrier's Antonov-12 caught fire after refuelling at Luxor Airport in Egypt, killing all five crew. A source at Luxor Airport said that the plane had been diverted to the airport because of a fuel leak, but took off again even though the damage had not been repaired.[10] Then on 9 March an Aerolift Ilyushin-76 carrying tents and water purification equipment to Somalia crashed into Lake Victoria following take off from Entebbe, Uganda, killing all eleven people on board. The US military flew in sonar scanning equipment which located the wrecked plane underwater in the lake, buried 10 m deep in silt with the tail fin sticking out.[11]

Between 2001 and July 2011 there were 19 fatal Ilyushin-76 crashes, with a total of 410 people killed.[12] The plane is banned from EU airspace, with exemptions for military operations and some humanitarian shipments. Writing in *International Freighting Weekly*, Alex Lennane explained why the plane is popular with cargo carriers, quoting Justin Bowman of Air Charter Service: 'The IL-76 is a very useful aircraft .... You can get very high, wide pieces into remote air strips, war zones and areas of political tension.' Comments from carriers showed that the ban is not strictly enforced. Bowman explained that it is possible to get exemptions in some countries: 'France is fantastic. If there is outsize cargo in the UK, you truck it to France and fly from there.' A comment by Volker Dunkake of Lufthansa Cargo Charter showed awareness that some shipments were not for humanitarian purposes: 'We do hear people claim the flights are for relief cargo, when we know they are not, because we saw the request.'[13]

Between 2005 and 2008 there was litany of accidents taking off from and headed for Khartoum, Sudan's main airport. All but one involved Ilyushin-76 and Antonov planes. On 3 February 2005 an Ilyushin-76 carrying aid from Sharjah developed problems with the fuel system and an attempted emergency landing failed. All seven crew died when the plane crashed in the desert and broke into pieces.[14] An Antonov-24 crashed on take-off from Khartoum on 2 June 2005, when one of the engines caught fire, killing one crew member and six passengers.[15] On 8 November 2007 a Juba Air Antonov-12 crash landed and caught fire when an engine failed shortly after take-off. The crew escaped unharmed but two airport guards were killed. The airline claimed that an eagle had been sucked into one of the plane's engines.[16] An Airbus A310 burst into flames on landing at Khartoum in stormy weather on 10 June 2008, killing about 120 people.[17] There was another accident involving a Juba Air Antonov-12 on 27 June. The plane, travelling from Khartoum to Juba, crashed at Malakal on the banks of the River Nile, killing seven of the eight people on board Three days later, on 30 June, an Ababeel Aviation Ilyushin-76 took off from Khartoum and exploded into a fireball, killing all four Russian crew.[18]

Antonov aircraft account for three of the seven fatal air crashes which have occurred in the Republic of Congo. On 5 September

2005 an Antonov-26 crashed in Brazzaville, the capital city, killing all of the plane's 13 occupants.[19] On 26 August 2009 an Antonov-12 cargo plane bound for Brazzaville, carrying food, a minibus and three cars, crash landed 11 km short of the runway in a cemetery, killing all six on board.[20] The next fatal accident, on 21 March 2011, was another Antonov-12, which burst into flames when it crashed into a residential area of Pointe-Noire. About 20 buildings including a school were destroyed. Reports of fatalities varied between 16 and 19, and there was uncertainty over whether some of the victims had been killed on the ground or had been stowaways.[21] On 30 November 2012 an Ilyushin-76 overshot a runway at Brazzaville. The plane destroyed a group of houses, crashed into a ravine and caught fire. All six people on board, and 25 on the ground, were killed.[22]

Crashes and Conflict in DR Congo

DR Congo has an appalling air safety record, with a series of fatal accidents at the capital Kinshasa's two airports, N'Dolo and Ndjili. Again, Antonovs and Ilyushin-76s feature heavily. The country's worst air disaster was on 8 January 1996, when an Antonov-32 cargo plane crashed into a crowded market after take-off from N'Dolo. Five of the six crew survived, but at least 300 people on the ground were killed and 253 were seriously injured.[23] Five months later, on 6 June 1996, an Ilyushin-76 crashed on take off from Ndjili, killing all ten crew and passengers.[24] On 8 May 2003 the rear door of an Ilyushin-76 opened after take-off from Kinshasa, killing seven people who were sucked out of the plane.[25] Another market, in the river port town of Boende, was hit on 29 November 2003 when an Antonov-26 bound for Kinshasa aborted take-off and overran the runway, killing 20 on board and 13 people on the ground.[26]

There were six fatal plane crashes in DR Congo in 2007. The accident with the most fatalities was on 4 October. At least 25 people were killed when an Antonov-26 cargo plane clipped treetops after take off from Ndjili, and crashed into a busy market in the shanty town of Kingasani.[27] There was another serious accident at Ndjili on 4 April 2011. A passenger jet made an unsuccessful attempt to land in heavy rain, and the plane broke in two and burst into flames. Only one of the 33 occupants survived. The plane was operating for the UN mission in the country.[28]

DR Congo is renowned for its mineral deposits including gold, coltan, tungsten, manganese and tin. Some of the country's most perilous airstrips, in densely forested, mountainous terrain and frequent cloudy, stormy weather, serve mines. Bukavu Airport, perched 1,720 m above sea level, is surrounded by even higher mountains. On 3 August 2006 all 17 people on board an Antonov-28 carrying mining products from Lugushwa were killed when the plane crashed into a mountain on approach to Bukavu in heavy cloud.[29] The flight was operated by Tracep, a DR Congo airline banned from EU airspace in 2006. Another Tracep plane, a LET-410, crashed on 21 October 2010, when the engines failed on the climb out, killing both crew.[30] There was another fatal Tracep Antonov-28 accident on 30 January 2012. The plane took off from Bukavu but crashed in a forest en route to Namoya, a gold mining area. Three crew were killed and two survived.[31] Two weeks later, on 12 February, a Gulfstream corporate jet overshot Bukavu's runway on landing. It slid down an embankment and split in two, killing three of the people on board and two farmers.[32]

Two humanitarian aid flights have crashed into the mountains surrounding Bukavu. An aid flight from Kinshasa crashed into the steep ridge of Mount Kahuzi on 1 September 2008, as it approached the airstrip in severe weather. All the plane's occupants died, two crew and 15 passengers.[33] Both crew of a LET-410, returning from delivering seeds for the World Food Programme, were killed when the plane crashed into a hill just outside Bukavu on 14 February 2011, minutes before it was due to land.[34]

The Kilambo airstrip in Walikale is the main transit point for cassiterite ore, which yields tin, from the Bisie mine. A number of accidents occurred when the airstrip was still in use as a road. A plane attempted an emergency landing on 9 November 2006, but the airstrip had been reopened for road traffic and it collided with vehicles, killing one of the occupants, then crashed into houses. On 15 February 2007 a small Cessna plane carrying food made three unsuccessful attempts to land in poor weather. A month later the rescue mission had still not found the wreckage.[35] Three months, later, on 17 May 2007, a cargo plane used to transport minerals caught fire three minutes after take-off and all three people on board were killed.[36] A 2008 report on artisanal mining in the area stated that on a typical day six planes flew four rotations, each carrying around 2 tonnes of cassiterite to Goma, the main export hub for DR Congo's minerals, and the wreckage of a plane could still be found next to the airstrip.[37]

Mount Nyiragongo, with an altitude of over 3,500 m, towers over the city of Goma. It is one of the most active and dangerous volcanoes in Africa, spewing very liquid lava that can flow at speeds of 60 km per hour. A major eruption in January 2002 resulted in a lava flow of nearly 10 km, in a stream almost 1 km wide. A third of the city was destroyed and 147 people were killed. Lava covered the northern third of Goma Airport's runway, where it cooled and solidified into igneous rock.

The Aviation Safety Network (ASN) database lists five accidents on the shortened runway. On 27 May 2003 an Antonov-12 overran the runway in strong winds, coming to a halt in a pile of lava. There was another Antonov-12 accident on 7 September 2007. The plane, carrying palm oil and other cargo, crashed into the petrified lava, killing all five crew.[38] On 15 April 2008 a passenger plane failed to take off in wet conditions, and skidded into residences just 100 m from the end of the runway. Three of the 94 people on board were killed, and there were 37 ground casualties.[39] Another passenger flight overran the runway in wet conditions on 19 November 2009. The plane collided with a pile of lava, injuring 20 passengers.[40] Eight years after the volcanic eruption, in January 2010, an operation to remove 135,000 cu. m of petrified lava from Goma's runway began.

Formally, civil war in DR Congo ended in 2003, but conflict continues, and airstrips serving mines are focal points. Walikale is in the mineral-rich east of the country, and armed groups control mining with extortion and violence. The imposition of a ban on mining in Walikale in 2007 proved futile, as ore was sent by road out of the area, then flown to Goma for export.[41] The national army, FARDC, was unable to provide security because some officers were colluding with militia groups. In 2009 both state and non-state armed groups were found to be confiscating minerals from miners, and demanding illegitimate fees. The United Nations discovered evidence that FARDC had requisitioned an aircraft which flew military goods to Walikale, then returned to Goma with cassiterite.[42]

DR Congo's president, Joseph Kabila, banned mining in Walikale and the North and South Kivu provinces, but the attempted intervention was ineffective. On 28 December 2008, 308 kg of cassiterite were seized at Bukavu Airport. A week later, police intercepted an attempt by traders, working with army elements, to ship 70 kg of cassiterite on a plane to Bukavu.[43] Army and rebel groups battled for control of the Kilambo airstrip when rebel groups attacked and looted 15 villages between 30 July and 2 August 2010. Two soldiers were killed, two pilots from a plane that had landed on the airstrip were kidnapped, and four aid workers were stranded near the runway, hiding from gunfire for over four hours.[44]

Because of its position on the border with Rwanda, Goma Airport was an entry point for arms during the 1994 conflict between the Tutsi and Hutu ethnic groups. Over a period of just 100 days 800,000 people were killed, mainly Tutsi civilians. Arms shipments from many countries landed at Goma, in violation of the UN arms embargo, and were transported across the border. There were reports of at least five air shipments of artillery, machine guns, assault rifles and ammunition from France, two planes each loaded with about 40 tonnes of arms from the Seychelles, a plane carrying 39 tonnes of arms from Spain via Malta, and a plane from Libya carrying surplus government stocks.[45]

From Reconnaissance to Rendition

Aviation's role in conflict dates back to hot air balloons. Stationary balloons, anchored with ropes, enabled observation and communication behind enemy lines during the French revolution in 1789.[46] When Paris was under siege in the 1870–71 Franco-Prussian war, balloons carrying pigeons were released to deliver mail, the only way the city could maintain contact with the outside world.[47] Dirigibles, powered and steered balloons, were of strategic importance in the First World War. The Allies deployed dirigibles to protect convoys at sea, and in the course of 284 missions, German dirigibles dropped over 480,000 kg of bombs on England, France and Belgium.[48] In the early years of the 20th century, some the earliest aeroplane models were used by the United States, United Kingdom, France, Germany, Austria, Hungary and Russia for observation and reconnaissance.[49] These countries became protagonists in the First World War, when the production of aircraft increased by a factor of 100. Bombers had a payload of up to 1 tonne. After the war the planes were used for civilian cargo.[50] During the Second World War millions of tonnes of troops, arms, supplies and fuel were flown by both sides.[51]

Commercial carriers have carved out a growing role in delivering military cargo to Iraq and Afghanistan. In a 2006 article entitled 'Cargo's hot market' Robert W Moorman writes:

> There's usually nothing worse for trade than armed conflict, but the fact is the ongoing strife in the Middle East are feeding large volumes of air cargo business. Carriers, forwarders and related businesses benefit by shipping materials to the region to support the conflicts or reconstruction efforts or the oil business infrastructure.[52]

Between January 2006 and mid-August 2007 contracts valued at $3.6 billion were awarded to carriers to support US forces in Iraq and Afghanistan. *Air Cargo World* reported that 'Pentagon-related air freight industry expenses have been soaring – and so has military-related revenue at the carriers and forwarders moving that freight.' Oregon-based Evergreen International Airlines topped the list of commercial carriers holding US defence contracts, with 738 contracts.[53] Evergreen's website proclaimed that the firm had 'provided support in every war, in continuous support for the US military since 1975'.[54] In the last quarter of 2007, US defence contracts to commercial carriers spiralled upwards. The total for 2006–07 was $5.6 billion. FedEx overtook Evergreen as the top beneficiary, awarded contracts to the value of $1.3 billion.[55]

Charleston Airforce Base, adjoining the civilian Charleston Airport in South Carolina, was flying out about 360 mine-resistant ambush-protected (MRAP) vehicles per month in March 2008.[56] Communities near the base had become accustomed to US Air Force C-5 and C-17 cargo planes flying overhead. But the fleet was ageing and overstretched, and contracts were awarded to Russian carriers, whose Antonov 124s, with twice the capacity of the C-17, can carry four of the 30 tonne vehicles, as opposed to two. A $300 million six-month contract to transport MRAPs was awarded to Volga-Dnepr and a smaller contract to Polet.

Relations between the United States and Russia, the two main cold war adversaries, remained strained, so the dependence of strategically important operations on Russian carriers was a cause of concern at the highest level of the US military. Air Force secretary Michael Wynne asked the House of Representatives Armed Services Committee, 'Did [we] truly envision that we would fly war supplies with Russian-made airplanes?'[57] Camille Allaz, a leading air freight historian, wrote that the market for the plane was 'kick-started by the first Gulf War in 1990–91'.[58] An Antonov-124 was used for a particularly sensitive operation in April 2001. After colliding with a Chinese fighter jet over the South China Sea, a US EP-3 spy plane made an emergency landing on the island of Hainan. It remained stranded until, following lengthy negotiations, China agreed that the plane could be disassembled and returned to the United States. Polet was awarded the contract and delivered the plane to Dobbins Air Base in Atlanta.[59]

Commercial carriers combine government military contracts with civilian cargo and humanitarian aid. Evergreen supported the relief effort to help victims of the tsunami in the Indian Ocean on 26 December 2004, sending water purification and mobile kitchen equipment to Sri Lanka.[60] Polet sent food and water from Japan and Europe.[61] The website of Australian carrier Heavy-Lift Cargo Airlines listed notable shipments including racing cars, up to 24 racehorses at a time, art works belonging to HM the Queen, Sir Richard Branson's hot air balloon, munitions, rockets, police riot control vehicles and UN Class 1.1 explosives.[62]

In the aftermath of the 9/11 terrorist attacks, US President George W. Bush launched the 'war on terror' against Al-Qaeda and any regime, organisation or individual deemed to support it. The CIA's programme of extraordinary rendition flights expanded dramatically. People suspected of involvement with Al-Qaeda, many of whom were innocent, were flown to many countries, including Syria, Egypt, Jordan, Morocco and Uzbekistan, for interrogation in clandestine prisons, where it was known that they would be tortured.

In his book *Ghost Plane*, Stephen Grey tracked rendition flights up until 2006, painstakingly piecing together flight logs and interviewing Central Intelligence Agency (CIA) pilots, chiefs and operatives, and prisoners. In the absence of official figures, Grey estimated the total number of extraordinary renditions at several hundred. In contrast with prisoners sent to the official prison in Guantanamo Bay, Cuba by the US Army, tied up with ropes in the noise and cold of the hold, CIA prisoners were often transported in luxury Boeing 737 and Gulfstream private jets. Hooded, and with their legs in shackles, they were unable to avail themselves of chilled champagne and in-flight films. A front company, Aero Contractors chartered flights from private companies. The CIA's use of civilian business jets meant that rendition flights were able to hide in plain sight, dropping in at civilian airports for servicing, including Washington Dulles, Frankfurt, Cairo, Stockholm Bromma and Glasgow Prestwick.[63]

Grey records three instances of Glasgow Prestwick providing refuelling services for planes used for rendition flights returning to Washington after transferring prisoners. A CIA pilot described the airport as a popular destination for refuelling stops, saying: 'It's an "ask no questions" type of place and you don't need to give them any advance warning you're coming.'[64] I looked at the airport's website, which did not mention the role in the logistics for torture, but two clicks away from the home page, announced the airport's capability to handle eight tonnes of Class 1.1 explosives, the 'highest capacity throughout the UK outside military airfields'.[65]

Grey's observation that one Gulfstream jet, used by the Boston Red Sox with the baseball team's logo on the tail, was simultaneously in regular use for rendition flights was confirmed in 2011. Invoices, receipts and correspondence revealed in a fees dispute in a New York court confirmed that, in between flying the Red Sox around, the jet, owned by businessman Philip Morse, had been made available to the US government at $4,900 per hour. One invoice for $301,113 tallied with an eight-day series of rendition flights through Alaska, Japan, Thailand, Afghanistan and Sri Lanka. The disclosed documents included crews' expenses claims for wine and biscuits.[66]

During his first presidential campaign, in 2008, Barack Obama wrote of 'ending the practices of shipping away prisoners in the dead of night to be tortured in far-off countries'. Since he took office, government facilities, including Guantanamo, have been maintained, and the United States still renders terrorist suspects to their countries of origin. Human rights campaigners have dismissed these countries' assurances not to mistreat prisoners as worthless.[67]

9

Concrete and Overcapacity

Stimulus and Subsidies

Launched in the wake of the global economic crisis, Barack Obama's 2009 stimulus programme was a bold attempt to create jobs by rebuilding the US infrastructure. Funding went towards home insulation, rebuilding roads and bridges, renewable energy, high-speed rail and rural broadband services. But the main effect of one element of the stimulus programme, a $1.1 billion package for airport upgrade, repair and expansion, was massive expenditure on concrete. Over two-thirds of the stimulus money for airports, $679 million, was spent on runways and taxiways. The biggest grant, $18 million, went to Washington Spokane, to renovate the runway and apron. Memphis received nearly $18 million for a new taxiway and improvements to the terminal, runway and perimeter fencing. Projects costing $15 million were approved at Los Angeles, Washington-Dulles, Baltimore-Washington and Kahului in Hawaii.[1]

A sizeable proportion of stimulus funds, $100 million, benefited a minute number of people, as it was allocated to airports serving remote communities, recreational flyers and corporate jets. Three airports in Alaska, Akiachak, Fort Yukon and Ouzinkie, an island with a population of 165, each received $15 million. Purdue University Airport in Indianapolis, mostly used by students, administrators and a basketball team, received

$1.45 million to raise its fence and build a barrier to prevent animals burrowing underneath. Williamson-Sodus Airport, near Lake Ontario in New York, mainly used by 200 private members, received $555,000 stimulus funds to resurface its runway.[2]

Use of stimulus finds to support underused minor airports was heavily criticised. John Murtha Airport, only two hours' drive from Pittsburgh, handling just three flights per day, sometimes with passenger numbers outnumbered by security staff, received $800,000 to repave its alternate runway. This stimulus boost topped up $200 million of federal funds over the previous decade.[3] Greenbrier Valley Airport in West Virginia, serving a premium resort where the cheapest hotel room was $500 per night, received $2 million in stimulus funds to refurbish the terminal. The airport was handling an average of two commercial flights per day, each carrying between three and nine passengers.[4]

Stimulus funding for airports was in addition to regular federal Airport Improvement Program (AIP) grants, or airport construction grants. The AIP is a tremendous boon to the concrete and asphalt industries; more than half of the budget is allocated for construction and rehabilitation of runways, taxiways and aprons.[5] AIP is funded through excise taxes levied on users of the national airspace system, including a Passenger Facility Charge (PFC) – an addition to the ticket price, air cargo waybills and fuel taxes. The AIP budget remained unchanged since before the economic downturn through to 2012, at $3.5 billion per year. In 2012 there was a small reduction in AIP funding, to $3.35 billion, through to 2015.[6]

Since the economic downturn, a federal subsidy paid to airlines to serve remote rural communities, the Essential Air Service (EAS), has increased. EAS was created in 1978, to ease an adjustment to deregulation which had enabled airlines to drop unprofitable routes. It was envisaged that the subsidy would be phased out within ten years. More than 30 years later, the EAS is still in place, serving about 140 locations. The scheme cost $50 million in 2001, then in the aftermath of 9/11 terrorist attacks airlines withdrew services from small unsubsidised routes, and the budget spiralled upwards, reaching $136 million in 2009.[7]

The EAS has always been contentious. There is a case for the support granted to airports in genuinely remote communities, in particular Hawaiian islands and Alaskan destinations where roads are impassable in winter. But the EAS has supported several airports which are only a short distance by road from another airport. Opposition to the EAS intensified as the budget continued to rise, reaching $200 million in 2010. Some of the routes handled less than ten passengers a day, carried in tiny nine-seat aircraft. The level of subsidy per passenger ranged between as little as $6 to over $1,000 in some instances. The service between the city of Ely in the Nevada desert and Las Vegas was being maintained with a subsidy of $3,000 per passenger.

Eligibility for EAS was supposedly restricted to airports more than 113 km driving distance from a hub airport, but there were anomalies. Muskegon Airport in Michigan received the subsidy, even though it is only 64 km from Grand Rapids Airport, served by six airlines. Lancaster Airport in Pennsylvania fell within the upper limit, as it is 109 km by road to Philadelphia Airport. Yet the airport received EAS subsidy for flights to Baltimore Washington, the only commercial flight to serve the airport in a decade. This service was used by only 30 passengers per day.[8] In 2012, eligibility for EAS was restricted to flights averaging fewer than ten passengers, an upper limit of $1,000 per ticket imposed and new communities were blocked from receiving the subsidy. Yet the budget for the EAS was increased, to $214 million.[9]

Private jets, the preserve of the wealthiest, became a symbol of widening inequality and corporate excess in November 2008, when chief executives of the 'big three' US car manufacturers, Ford, Chrysler and General Motors, flew to Washington in corporate jets to appear before Congress to plead for a $24.9 billion bailout package.[10] There was further controversy when analysis of FAA flight records between 2007 and 2010, by the *Wall Street Journal*, indicated that executives' personal use of corporate jets far exceeded the level disclosed to shareholders, and was for leisure as well as business. The research revealed that 'dozens of jets operated by publicly traded corporations made 30% or more of their trips to or from resort destinations, sometimes more than 50%'.[11]

Tax breaks supported a quick turnaround to recovery in the US private jet market. John Rosanvallon, chair of the General Aviation Manufacturers Association, said:

> Flying hours are steadily on the rise, and there are two critical U.S. tax provisions in place that will help our industry recover. One is the extension of a 50 percent bonus depreciation allowance through 2011; the other allows companies to deduct the full cost of new planes from revenues.[12]

Obama made repeated calls to end the depreciation tax break for corporate jet owners. He mentioned the issue six times in a news conference in June 2011, and said this would bring $3 billion into the Treasury over a decade. But Obama's own administration had introduced the tax break. It was part of the 2009 stimulus package, and aimed to encourage purchase of private aircraft.[13]

An Airport to Nowhere

Vast amounts of concrete, and public money, were poured into Northwest Florida Beaches Airport, the first major new airport in the United States since Denver opened in 1995. The airport site is situated 15 km inland from the famous white-sand beaches, amidst dense pine forests and marshes. Journalist Hal Herring described the area as the 'last undeveloped expanse of Florida'. The wetlands are among the most biologically diverse habitats in the United States, a haven for black bears, red-cockaded wood-peckers and the endangered gopher tortoise. Rivers, creeks and springs, among the cleanest in the country, are vital for inshore fisheries, and flow into West Bay.[14] Construction of the airport began in 2008. Concrete was produced on site, at a rate sufficient to fill a mixing truck every two and a half minutes.[15] By May

2009, 2 km of slow-moving streams had been paved over. The porous wetlands were not strong enough to support conventional building foundations, so earth was excavated and filled in with reinforced concrete supported by steel poles.[16]

The airport was built in spite of six lawsuits from environmental groups and a non-binding referendum in which 56 per cent of citizens rejected the project. The wording of the question posed by the referendum outraged opponents, as it stated there would be no cost to taxpayers.[17] Voters were misled. Construction cost about $318 million, from federal, state and local government sources in equal amounts. Linda Young, director of the Clean Water Network of Florida (CWN), a coalition of 155 groups committed to safeguarding water resources, said that 'decision-makers have been hoodwinked into spending vast sums of public money on an environmentally destructive fiasco'.[18] Melanie Shepherdson of NRDC slammed the FAA's approval of the airport as illegal: 'The law is clear: The agency has to pick the alternative that is least damaging to the environment. And it failed to do that.'[19]

The airport authority attempted to assuage concerns over building on fragile wetlands by committing to storm and wastewater treatment systems exceeding the requirements of Florida law.[20] These standards were flouted during construction. CWN reported that even light rainfall resulted in uncontrolled mudflows. Water from above the airport site, previously absorbed by sponge like wetlands and forest then released slowly into West Bay, rushed over the impermeable concrete of the airport site: 'The torrents of mud from the site have clouded previously pristine waters flowing downstream from the airport site and accumulating in marshes, creeks, streams, fish beds and the estuary, causing a steady decline in habitat and water quality.'[21] In May 2009, the state of Florida imposed $393,849 in fines for 72 water quality violations and filling in a small area of wetland without a permit.[22]

Northwest Florida Beaches Airport replaced the old Panama

City Airport, just 13 km away on the coast. The choice of the airport location, enveloped by pine forests and far from population centres, appears illogical, but the rationale for the project is that it will facilitate development on the land surrounding it. Shepherdson explained that 'the airport to nowhere' will spur industrial parks, resort hotels, shopping malls and condominiums.[23] The airport is the lynchpin of the West Sector Bay Plan for commercial and residential development, described by Herring as 'the largest land-planning effort ever undertaken in Florida'. Randy Curtis, executive director of the Panama City–Bay County Airport Authority, said, 'The relocation of the airport is going to be the trigger to remake the entire Bay County area.'

The site for the airport was donated by St Joe, one of the largest private landowners in Florida. St Joe owns almost 290 sq. km surrounding the new airport, and stands to profit from development of beachfront residences and office, industrial, retail and hotel development around the airport. All these ventures will be more lucrative than timber. St Joe's 2009 *Annual Report* stated, 'We anticipate that the airport will provide a catalyst for value creation in the property we own surrounding the airport, as well as our other properties throughout Northwest Florida.'[24] Approval of the airport was aided by St Joe's considerable political influence, evident from donations to more than 100 state candidates between 1997 and 2002, at the maximum legal amount.

Some environmental groups were placated by St Joe's promise to set aside 162 sq. km of woodlands and shoreline as a preservation area, to remain undeveloped in perpetuity. Almost half of this area is merely the legally required mitigation for loss of wetlands habitat to the airport. St Joe failed to respond to repeated requests to formalise the preservation area by putting it in writing, and there was no recourse to federal law, as protection of geographically isolated wetlands had been removed in 2001. Herring pointed out that protection of a specific area of wetlands, in isolation from the wider ecosystem, is unworkable. The entire watershed depends upon the flow of water, now blocked by the concrete slab of the airport and access roads.[25] Young likened the preservation plan to saying 'we're going to preserve your arms and legs forever, but we're going to cut out your heart and liver'.[26]

Northwest Florida Beaches Airport opened in 2010. Passengers are greeted with a veneer of native flora and foliage. Goldenrods, purple muhly grass and yellow and pink Indian blanket flowers adorn the entrances to the airport and terminal, and the walkway between them.[27] Adjacent to the airport, a 28,000 hectare business park was built on newly deforested land. The first tenant, defence contractor ITT Corporation, was confirmed in September 2011, supported by a package of state and local incentives, including property tax abatement.[28] There had been further incidences of stormwater runoff damage to surrounding wetlands, and in September 2010 the Department of Environmental Protection ordered the Airport Authority to plant 600 trees, to replace 86 that had been felled.[29] Problems with stormwater runoff polluting creeks with dirt and sediment continued into 2012. The airport sought yet more government funds, $1.25 million, from the FAA or State Department of Transportation, to collect the excess water and use it to irrigate the plants around the airport entrance.[30]

The OMP Boondoggle

Overhaul and expansion of Chicago O'Hare Airport has been even more expensive than building Northwest Florida Beaches Airport on a greenfield site. The O'Hare Modernization Program (OMP) is one of the largest construction projects in the United States. Excavating the site in order to lay new concrete, extending some of the existing runways and moving operational buildings access roads and utilities, while the airport is still operational, is a complex and expensive exercise.

Unveiled in 2001 by Richard Daley, mayor of Chicago from 1989 to 2011, the OMP has expanded the airport footprint over the neighbouring communities of Bensenville and Elk Grove.

John Geils, president of Bensenville from 1985 to 2009, and Craig Johnson, mayor of Elk Grove, founded the non-profit Aviation Integrity Project (AIP) to investigate O'Hare expansion, and in 2004 it published a damning report by J. Terrence Brunner, who had served as executive director of the Better Government Association for 30 years. Brunner analysed 67,000 pages of documents that Mayor Daley had attempted to conceal from the citizens upon whom the project impacts, and attempted to uncover who had paid for the project. Daley's argument against disclosure was rejected by the Illinois Supreme Court, and the documents revealed an astonishing lack of public process. The extent of the plan far exceeded the 'modernization' which had been announced, entailing reconfiguration of seven intersecting runways to a new layout with six parallel east to west runways and two diagonal runways, and a 20-year timescale. Projected costs, $15–20 billion, were far higher than the $6.6 billion figure that has been disclosed.

Brunner found that O'Hare was rife with the corruption for which Chicago is notorious, citing many examples of cronyism, rigged hiring practices and political patronage. Contracts were frequently awarded without a bidding process to 'favored insiders' and at inflated prices. In return, contractors would 'shower contributions' on federal legislators and state officials' campaign funds. Some contracts were awarded to Mayor Daley's closest friends and family. Daley 'personally placed' two friends into the W.H. Smith newspaper concession, making them 'instant millionaires'. One of Mayor Daley's brothers received over $500,000 for insuring O'Hare contractors, and another brother received $2 million as a consultant to the O'Hare bond business.[31]

There have been more revelations of corruption at O'Hare in recent years. In 2009 Christopher Kelly, a roofing contractor, pleaded guilty to fraudulently obtaining $8.5 million in inflated contracts for projects at O'Hare.[32] In 2010 one of the owners of Azteca, a company contracted to supply concrete pipes, pleaded guilty to fraudulently receiving $9.6 million for two O'Hare projects. The contract was set aside for a minority-owned business, but another firm provided the services and paid a percentage to Azteca.[33]

The OMP is financed by a passenger facility charge added to the ticket price; United Airlines and American Airlines, for whom O'Hare is an important hub; federal funds; and O'Hare bonds issued by the City of Chicago, set against future revenues, which depend on increasing airport traffic. A downgraded bond rating brings the risk of rising interest rates sending OMP costs upwards. Since the beginning of the project, the Chicago Department of Aviation has repeated that the project will not require local or state taxpayer dollars. This ignores federal funds and the sheer expense. For example, in 2009 United Airlines was paid $163 million to relocate its cargo facility away from a new runway.[34]

Geils warned that most of the financial burden of 'the OMP boondoggle', a term for a project that is a waste of time and money, would fall on taxpayers.[35] He was right. As citizens adjusted to austerity budgets, federal funding began to flow in for more concrete at O'Hare. $5.5 million in stimulus funds was granted to replace concrete pavement on a runway, plus another $6.7 million to widen and relocate a taxiway.[36] In April 2010 an additional $410 million in federal funds raised federal support for the OMP to $747 million, the largest ever federal investment in an airport reconstruction project.[37]

Later that month, to mark Earth Day, O'Hare replanted five fully grown trees near the airport welcome sign. The press release addressed citizens as if they were still in primary education and needed to be educated about trees' basic biological functions. It explained that the trees would 'provide shade to reduce the ambient temperature in and around the airport, absorb storm water to reduce run-off and soil erosion, help remove pollutants from the air and provide oxygen while absorbing carbon dioxide'.

The Earth Day event formed part of O'Hare's 'months long effort to transplant more than 75 full-grown trees rescued from land immediately southwest of the airport'. The trees had been 'rescued' from the airport's own expansion, dug up from the village of Bensenville.[38] Bulldozing of 500 homes and businesses was still underway three months later, when Chicago blogger Robert Powers visited and observed the devastation: 'An entire neighborhood had been fenced off and was prepped for systematic destruction. Trees are down, fences are ripped out and piled in the street, grass has been stripped away.'[39]

O'Hare overcame its final land acquisition barrier in January 2011, when it gained possession of Bensenville's 170-year-old St Johanne's cemetery, the final resting place of 1,600 people, many of whom were veterans of the Civil War. More costs were added to the project; the City of Chicago paid $630,000 in compensation and the painstaking process of exhuming and relocating the bodies began.[40] Simultaneously, United Airlines and American Airlines began litigation to halt further expansion of O'Hare, on the grounds that the extra capacity would be unnecessary and expensive, and two major credit rating agencies, Fitch and Moody's, downgraded O'Hare bonds, predicting that the airport's debt would almost double to $11.4 billion by 2015.[41]

Continuation of the OMP was assured by the infusion of even more federal funds. The airlines' financial commitment to the project was reduced, and in March 2011 allocation of federal funds escalated to $1 billion, plus the last-minute injection of a further $155 million. The next phase of the OMP, the southern runway on land acquired in Bensenville, extends the footprint of the airport for future realisation of the full plan.[42] Brunner had raised the issue of the OMP swallowing a large portion of FAA discretionary grants shared among airports nationwide, estimating an allocation of $815 million.[43] In October 2011, the Chicago Department of Aviation acknowledged receipt of nearly $1 billion in discretionary grants.[44]

Overcapacity in Illinois

Capacity increase at O'Hare has already proved to be unnecessary. A new runway and a runway extension opened on completion of Phase 1 of the OMP in 2008,[45] but between 2006 and 2011 O'Hare's passenger numbers plummeted from 77 million to 66.6 million.[46] Yet plans for a third airport for the city of Chicago moved forward. The 97 sq. km site, consisting of farms and wetlands in Peotone, in the southern suburbs, had been selected in 1990. Residents have been in a state of limbo for over 20 years, as the State of Illinois and FAA vacillate over final approval for the new airport. By 2010, towns, villages and citizens' groups, supported by Shut This Airport Nightmare Down (STAND), had passed more than 30 resolutions and referenda against the airport, but the state of Illinois began a programme of eminent domain (compulsory purchase) on parcels of land.[47] In 2011, in spite of a multi-billion-dollar deficit, Illinois Governor Pat Quinn confirmed plans to borrow $110 million to purchase 1,000 hectares of farmland for the airport. George Ochsenfeld, president of STAND, said:

> This is wrong time, the wrong place to even think about project
> .... Right now, the state of Illinois is slashing funding for mentally
> disabled people and other vulnerable people and they want to spend
> $100 million to build an unneeded airport.[48]

Critics of the Peotone project pointed out that an established Illinois airport, also built on farmland, stands almost empty. MidAmerica, its passenger terminal covered with a striking white metal and glass atrium, adjoins Scott Air Force Base in St Clair County. The FAA contributed $220 million towards construction, and St Clair County $70 million. After the airport opened in 1998 there were no scheduled flights for two and a half years. Then four airlines in succession received financial assistance to serve the airport but withdrew after a short period, and the airport lost its single remaining passenger service in January 2009.[49] In eleven years of operations, from the airport opening until 2009, St Clair County covered operating losses ranging between $2–5 million per year.[50] Passenger flights did not resume until a twice-weekly flight to Orlando began in November 2012. In the interim MidAmerica's operating loss escalated, reaching $11.93 million in 2010 and $8.4 million in 2011.[51]

The FAA bears some responsibility for the MidAmerica Airport fiasco. The agency approved and provided funding for MidAmerica as a relief airport for Lambert Airport, 60 km away in the northwest suburbs of St Louis, just over the border in Missouri. But Lambert proceeded with expansion, and the FAA, bowing to political pressures, approved it and stated that a second airport was not viable.[52]

Two thousand homes, six churches and four schools were subject to eminent domain for Lambert's expansion. J. Desy Schoenewies, a lifelong resident of Carrollton, one of the neighbourhoods affected, was involved with residents' resistance to the loss of green space, parks and their homes: 'For almost 5 years, every house in our subdivision was tied with yellow ribbons to show solidarity against the large airport.' The encroachment of demolition and concrete was unstoppable, and she watched the wrecking crew demolish her old house on 24 October 2006. Within a year, all but 56 of the 2,000 houses acquired by the airport had been demolished.[53] The third runway cost $1.1 billion, but airport traffic declined by two-thirds between 2001 and 2010 and it was barely used. Excess capacity made Lambert an ideal setting for the George Clooney film *Up in the Air*.[54]

MidAmerica's attempts at developing cargo business pumped millions of dollars of public money into facilities that were barely used. A $7 million warehouse, largely financed by the FAA, was completed in 2005, but handled no international flights until June 2007, when seven DC-10 flights delivered Monsanto seed corn from Chile, destined for farms around the US Midwest.[55] St Clair County then spent $3.3 million on refrigeration equipment for the warehouse, and weekly flights of flowers from Ecuador and Colombia began in October 2008.[56] Within two years the flower flights ceased, and St Clair County spent another $3.5 million removing the refrigeration equipment and converting the warehouse for Boeing to make components for military aircraft. The State of Illinois gave Boeing $2.3 million towards the costs of setting up manufacturing.[57]

MidAmerica then pinned its future on becoming a hub for trade with China. The FAA paid $2.5 million to double the size of the cargo ramp to accommodate four Boeing 747 freighters. Airport director Tim Cantwell envisaged importing electronic and auto parts and exporting perishable produce, in particular berries and beef from the US Midwest.[58] St Clair County invested $2.2 million in another refrigerated warehouse, measuring 3,344 sq. m, but it is unlikely to create significant economic benefits for neighbouring communities. The warehouse is expected to create just 10–15 full-time jobs and 80 seasonal positions, and opportunities for farmers in the region to export produce are limited. The prime purpose of the airport warehouse is to act as distribution point for fresh produce from all over the United States and as far afield as Mexico and South America. In July 2012, as the warehouse prepared to commence operations, the tenant, North Bay Produce, anticipated arrival of blueberries from Michigan by truck and Mexican fruit by air, and boasted the region's first cold treatment for blueberries, to prevent the spread of Mediterranean and South American fruit flies.[59] The refrigerated warehouse welcomed its first shipment in November 2012. A Boeing 767 delivered $500,000 worth of berries from Argentina, for storage in the refrigerated warehouse before being flown to China.[60]

Lambert Airport's plans to utilise its little-used runway, for cargo flights, to become a hub for trade with China, hinge on authorisation of requests for up to $480 million in incentives, with exemptions from corporate, income and financial institution taxes and tax credits for developers to build warehouses.[61] Greg Lindsay, co-author (with John Kasarda) of *Aerotropolis: The way we'll live next*, expressed scepticism regarding the scheme's viability. He said there was plenty of cargo capacity in the middle of the United States, and the initiative might not outlast the tax incentives: 'the history of airlines and subsidies indicates that they can leave the moment the subsidies run out'.[62] Schoenewies drew parallels with stores full of Chinese goods, in particular Walmart, moving from neighbourhood to neighbourhood chasing incentives: 'Perhaps the irony here resides in the cheap Chinese goods we're looking to have land in St. Louis are the very goods that fill these roving big box stores.' She envisaged that, 'instead of vacant houses, the land of Carrollton may soon be filled with brand-new vacant warehouses sitting next to a vacant runway.'[63]

Airport capacity expansion in the United States is incompatible with a transition to more equitable use of aviation. Americans already fly more than the global average. Airbus's 2011 statistics showed that per capita, American citizens took two flights per year. Picking out a few examples, two flights a year is twice as high as Italy and Belgium's one flight per capita, 20 times higher than citizens of Equatorial Guinea at 0.1 flight per capita and 200 times higher than Lesotho at just 0.1. A considerable proportion of US passenger flights are short-haul, and surface transport is a feasible substitute. In 2012, 642.2 million domestic passengers, flying between destinations within the United States, accounted for 78 per cent of the 815.3 million total reported by the Department of Transportation.[64]

A high proportion of US air cargo is domestic, flying goods around within the country's borders. In 2011 domestic air cargo, at 17.2 million tonnes, accounted for 65 per cent of the total for North America.[65] The North American region covers Canada as well as the United States, but transborder traffic between the two countries is negligible, and the US accounts for 95.9 per cent of total cargo.[66] Domestic cargo traffic does not bring the much-vaunted economic benefits of air freight. It does not boost exports or enable other countries sell goods to wealthy US customers. The bulk of the volume could be transferred to road and rail networks. As with air passengers, US usage of air cargo is higher than the global average. In 2011, US air cargo accounted for 24.2 per cent of the world total of 202.4 billion revenue tonne kilometres (RTK).[67]

10

Counting the Costs

The Taxpayers' Burden

Aviation is heavily subsidised, placing a heavy burden on taxpayers, and reducing the costs for the frequent flyers who are the main beneficiaries. Governments provide a high level of financial support for airport construction, aircraft manufacture and sales. Airport operations, ancillary services, duty-free shops and aviation fuel are lavished with tax reductions and exemptions. This reduces funding for public services including health, education and environmental protection. Overall, aviation subsidies are regressive, transferring public funds to the wealthy, who fly more.

The majority of the costs of airport construction, upgrade and expansion is paid for by taxpayers or government financial institutions. This is also the case for the requisite 'network infrastructure' of roads, power, telecommunications, water supply and effluent treatment. Private investment in airports, in particular from airlines and construction firms, has grown, but by 2011 only 2 per cent of the world's commercial airports were owned or operated by the private sector. About 20 countries had leased or sold airports, including Australia, Canada, China, Germany, Japan, Malaysia, New Zealand, South Africa, Switzerland and the United Kingdom. Major US airports are operated by local or regional government in partnership with private interests. In Latin America, concessions bring private investment in airports while governments maintain control. There is little privatisation activity in Africa or the Middle East.[1] Building and operation of some of India's new airports is under a PPP (public–private partnership) model, but the 2011–12 budget allocated $2 billion for airport infrastructure development.[2]

Taxpayers prop up the Boeing and Airbus duopoly over aircraft research, development and manufacturing. Boeing is subsidised by the US government while Airbus is subsidised by Germany, France, Spain and the United Kingdom. The two firms have been embroiled in disputes over the value and legality of these subsidies since the late 1980s. Bilateral talks broke down in 2005 as Airbus applied for funding for development of its mid-sized A350, which is intended to compete with Boeing's 787.[3] Ever since, the two firms have submitted appeals and counter-appeals to the World Trade Organization (WTO). In 2009 Boeing claimed that Airbus had received a total of $205 billion. Airbus claimed that Boeing had received $305 billion.[4] Both sides claimed victory when the WTO issued a 598-page report in March 2012, upholding a ruling that Boeing had received illegal government loans. Boeing supported its interpretation of the ruling as a victory with claims that the European Union had failed to comply with WTO findings against Airbus the previous year, and that European government subsidies to Airbus were higher at $18 billion. It threatened to hit the European Union with sanctions worth $7–10 billion.[5]

Sales of Boeing and Airbus aircraft have received government support since the 1980s, in the form of export credit, which guarantees the financing of aircraft sold to foreign airlines. Ultimately, taxpayers underwrite the sales, and are liable should the foreign customer default. Airbus's exports are supported by the export credit agencies of the EU member states France, Germany, the United Kingdom and Spain. In 2008 alone this amounted to between $11 and $12 billion.[6] The US Ex-Im Bank's support for Boeing has led to the institution's reputation as 'Boeing's Bank'. Timothy P. Carney, columnist at the *Washington Examiner* and a long-term critic, described the US Ex-Im Bank as a 'poster boy for corporate welfare', transferring funds from US taxpayers to corporations via foreign buyers, with the vast majority of loans and guarantees going to 'a handful of large corporations'. Of $63.5 billion of Ex-Im Bank loans and guarantees between 1998 and 2005, $33 billion, 52 per cent, went to Boeing.[7] Since then, the amount and proportion of Ex-Im Bank's loans to Boeing has increased. In the financial years 2007 and 2008 combined, 65 per cent of loans, almost $10 billion, went toward the purchase of Boeing aircraft.[8]

Both Boeing and Airbus have increased aircraft deliveries since the global financial crisis. Recent growth in the global fleet is largely attributable to a rise in export credit to the two firms. Export credit for 2009 was estimated at $21 billion, almost double 2008 levels, and Airbus and Boeing delivered a record 979 aircraft. Export credit backed 34 per cent of Airbus's deliveries and 26 per cent of Boeing's.[9] Ninety per cent of the US Ex-Im Bank's 2009 loan guarantees, a total of $8.4 billion, were to Boeing, including $2 billion for Air India to buy 68 planes.[10] Polis Polycarpou, vice-president of aviation at DVB Bank, which specialises in transport finance, was crystal clear about the importance of this government support for aircraft manufacturing, saying, 'The export credit agencies saved the industry.' Without export credit, hundreds of orders would probably have been cancelled.[11] He was of the opinion that export credit accounted for 33 per cent of the total aircraft market in 2010, reducing slightly in 2011 to 30 per cent.[12] By the end of the year, the combined total of Airbus and Boeing deliveries exceeded 1,000 for the first time.[13]

Duty-free sales provide revenue for airports, and the tax exemption reduces revenue to national exchequers and gives an unfair advantage over other retailers. Prices in duty-free stores are generally lower than in regular stores, providing another perk for air passengers. The main product categories are alcoholic drinks, tobacco, fragrances and cosmetics, luxury clothing and electronic goods. International brands dominate, leaving few opportunities for local suppliers. Between 2001 and 2010, global airport duty-free sales grew 162 per cent, from $8.9 billion to $23.3 billion, nearly four times the passenger growth rate over this period.[14] Growth of duty free in the past decade has been concurrent with intensified security since 9/11, and makes a mockery of it. Outbound passengers go through the charade of having hand luggage checked for small sharp items like tweezers and nail files; airside, they can buy alcoholic beverages in large glass bottles that could be used to inflict serious injury.

Dubai Duty Free shopping space measures 18,000 sq. m across three terminals. When the new airport concourse is complete this will grow by another 8,000 sq. m.[15] In 2011 alone, Dubai Duty Free sales grew by 17.7 per cent, to $1.46 billion, from a total of 22.4 million sales transactions.[16] Even this growth rate was insufficient for Dubai to hold onto its position as the world's biggest duty-free operation. By the end of 2011, Dubai Duty Free was overtaken by Incheon, which reported sales of $1.53 billion.[17]

Since standard airport retail formats began to appear in India, in 2006, the country has reported the world's highest duty-free growth rate. Sales reached $215 million by 2011, with wines and spirits the biggest product category, accounting for 63 per cent of sales, equivalent to 489,000 9-litre cases of liquor. Sales at Delhi Duty Free, India's biggest duty-free shop, quadrupled over this period, to $72.7 million.[18] Interviewed in the *Moodie Report*, a travel retail magazine, CEO Steve O'Connor described two logistics options for delivery of products. Both of these bypassed domestic supply routes. Most alcoholic beverages arrived via Mumbai by sea, and the time between ordering and delivery could be as long as two months. A warehouse close to the airport offered a faster option, and several duty-free suppliers, including confectionery manufacturers, had begun flying in products direct to Delhi.[19]

In summer 2011, as Heathrow continued to lobby for approval for a third runway, arguing that capacity expansion would revitalise the UK economy, the airport ran an advertising campaign which explicitly poached business from London's West End shopping destinations. Outdoor sites, taxis and underground stations were emblazoned with multilingual displays flaunting the savings tourists could make by shopping at the airport, using the tag line 'See it in London, Buy it at Heathrow'.[20] At the end of the year, the airport stated that its gross retail income rise of 10.7 per cent, to $688 million, was 'led by duty free sales'.[21]

In a 2003 report, *The Hidden Cost of Flying,* Brendon Sewill estimated the annual value of tax breaks to aviation in the United Kingdom. Air passenger duty, introduced in 1993, brought in $1.48 billion, but this was heavily outweighed by the value of tax breaks, estimated at $16.6 billion. Airport duty-free sales cost the exchequer $658 million. Exemption from VAT (value added tax), applied to all goods and services except those deemed essential, saved the aviation industry $6.58 billion. Sewill outlined the extent of the VAT exemption, encompassing goods and services related to aircraft, airport operations and ancillaries:

> There is no VAT on any aspect of air travel, not on airline tickets, nor on purchase of aircraft, nor on their servicing, nor on their fuel, nor on air traffic control, nor on baggage handling, nor on aircraft meals. Everything to do with air travel, after passport control, is zero rated.

The biggest subsidy was tax exemption on aviation fuel. This drained $9.3 billion from the treasury. Sewill compared the price of tax-free aviation fuel with petrol for cars, which is subject to duty. For each litre of fuel, the price paid by motorists was more than quadruple the amount paid by airlines.[22]

The United Kingdom is among the majority of countries that do not levy taxes on domestic flights. Tax exemption on fuel for international flights is almost universal, and critical to the economic viability of aviation. Even with this subsidy, airlines' fuel bills constitute, on average, more than 30 per cent of operational costs.[23] Debate on the issue of fuel taxes is clouded by misinterpretation of the relevant provisions of the Chicago Convention, which serves as the international regulatory framework governing aviation. Contrary to common perception, the Chicago Convention does not prohibit tax levies on fuel for international flights. It merely precludes taxation of fuel already on board arriving aircraft. The prohibition does not apply to the far larger volumes of fuel dispensed at airports for outbound flights. The European Federation for Transport and Environment explains that governments introduced tax exemptions on fuel for international flights of their own volition, beyond their obligations as signatories to the Chicago Convention:

> The Chicago Convention ... prohibits the taxing on arrival of fuel already on board an aircraft. This prohibition, taken to avoid the dangers of double taxation, was widely extended by Governments in subsequent years to a general tax exemption for fuel on international flights. The prohibition was further enshrined in a very large number of bilateral aviation agreements.[24]

Flag Carrier Bailouts

Flag carriers, airlines designated by governments and recognisable by the display of the country's flag on the aircraft tail, enjoyed a heyday after the end of the Second World War. Governments established national airlines as strategic assets and to demonstrate presence on the global stage. Many governments maintain full ownership, or hold a majority share, in a flag carrier, but over the years preferential treatment, in the form of subsidies, partial or total monopoly on international routes, and landing slots at key airports has been reduced. Flag carriers became less dominant and the market opened up for new entrants. Then in 2009, as the economic downturn began, airline liberalisation was thrown into reverse. Governments in all the world's regions intervened with financial support packages to prop up ailing flag carriers, even as they imposed austerity programmes which had devastating effects on vulnerable citizens.

Four European governments bailed out flag carriers as debt crisis loomed. Malev, Hungary's national airline, received an emergency cash injection of $26 million to help pay for aircraft leases. Slovenia's Adria Airways received support from various government agencies, including $2.8 million from a state-owned restructuring company. The Latvian government increased airBaltic's share capital in 2009, but the airline's turnaround to profit was short-lived and in 2010 it slumped back into the red. In September 2011, Prime Minister Valdis Dombrovskis announced plans to increase airBaltic's share capital again, by between $97–136 million.[25] State-owned Croatia Airlines was given $136 million in 2012.[26]

Air Canada was propped up with $300 million in government loans in 2009. Half this sum came from Export Development Canada (EDC). In order to support the airline, EDC's remit, to support exporters and investors in expanding their international business was reconfigured to include domestic business.[27] Argentina renationalised its flag carrier, Aerolineas, and during 2011 the airline received $757 million in funds from the treasury, equivalent to $2 million per day. The funds went towards new aircraft and staff, but the number of passengers for the year decreased by nearly 7 per cent.[28]

The commercial success of Emirates, Etihad Airways and Qatar Airways is not representative of the Gulf region as a whole. Three Gulf national carriers received substantial financial support in 2010. Oman Air's authorised capital was increased from $780 million to $1.3 billion, Kuwait Airways received a capital injection of $128 million, and Bahrain's state carrier, Gulf Air, received a capital injection of just over $1 billion.[29] When Gulf Air hit financial trouble again, in 2012, the country's ruler, King Hamad bin Isa al Khalifa, issued a decree allocating $490.9 million to support the airline.[30]

As the financial woes of a cluster of Asian national carriers became evident at the beginning of 2010, CAPA declared the 'Year of the Asian Airline Bailout'. Japan Airlines, China Eastern Airlines, Air India, Garuda Indonesia, Thai Airways and Malaysia Airlines were set to receive a total of over $10 billion in restructuring programmes in the first three months of the year.

Within days of CAPA's report, Japan Airlines was rescued from bankruptcy with $6.6 billion. In August, the Thai government approved $467 million for Thai Airways.[31]

Bailouts to Asian flag carriers continued into 2012. The Sri Lankan government gave SriLankan Airlines a $100 million interest-free loan when it reported a record operational loss of more than $143 million.[32] Pakistan International Airlines has haemorrhaged millions of dollars per year since 2008. By June 2012, the carrier's net debts had spiralled to $1.3 billion.[33] In August, Prime Minister Raja Pervez agreed a raft of support measures. He approved a request for $4.5 million in assistance for lease of new aircraft, directed the Ministry of Finance to reschedule $1.55 billion in loans owed to banks, and assured the airline's management that he would support conversion of government loans of $84.5 million into equity.[34]

In March 2012 Air India, which had already received state support adding up to more than $640 million since 2009, received a $1.1 billion equity infusion, to cover gaping debts to jet fuel suppliers, airports for parking and landing charges, and staff who threatened strike action over salary arrears.[35] This injection of funding was nearly double the amount spent by federal government on new hospitals in three years. Prakash Gupta, head of Healis, a Mumbai based non-profit health research and advocacy organisation, was critical of the bailout, saying, 'Spending on health care is much more important than propping up an airline.'[36] A month later, Air India's outstanding loans and dues stood at over $1.3 trillion, and the government approved a debt restructuring programme for injecting $5.9 billion by 2020.[37]

The Namibian population suffer high rates of chronic malnutrition, yet the government has provided sustained financial support for Air Namibia. A $10 million bailout in 2009 brought total state support for the carrier, since 2000, to $246 million. Yet another Air Namibia 'turnaround strategy' was agreed in July 2011, at a cost of $222 million over the following three years.[38] Mauritania is unable to feed its own people. Yet the government established a new carrier in April 2011, with an initial fleet of three Boeing 737s, expecting fish exports to Europe to be an important part of operations.[39]

South African Airways (SAA) has been a recipient of serial bailouts. The airline was granted over $190 million for recapitalisation in 2006–07 and $235 million in 2007–08 for restructuring. This was followed by cash injection of more than $230 million in 2009, to support its 'turnaround strategy'.[40] SAA turned a profit in 2009–10 and 2010–11, but continued to receive substantial state support for expansion of its fleet and expansion of its route network. Following a $164 million preferential loan and a cash guarantee of $202 million in 2011, SAA requested a guarantee of between $500 million and $755 million. The Democratic Alliance, the opposition to the ruling Africa National Congress, pointed out that this would bring total public funds, providing a financial lifeline to the state-owned enterprise since 2007, to $1.46 billion, stating, 'We cannot continue using public money on SAA when so many of our people are without clean drinking water, basic sanitation and housing'.[41] In October 2012, in spite of widespread and vocal opposition, the treasury agreed a $597 million guarantee for SAA for two years, for operational costs and to purchase 20 aircraft.[42]

The United States does not have a flag carrier, but, over the past decade many of the country's major airlines, including US Airways, United Airlines and Delta Airlines, have filed for bankruptcy protection. This brought considerable tax benefits and forced creditors to agree restructuring programmes. Moreover, bankruptcy protection served as a trump card in labour negotiations, enabling airlines to void contracts and reduce staffing levels, wages and benefits. Following in the footsteps of its rivals, American Airlines filed for bankruptcy protection in November 2011, hoping to gain approval for a restructuring plan which would save billions of dollars and eliminate 13,000 jobs.[43] But bankruptcy proceedings could backfire on American Airlines. Unions outmanoeuvred management by negotiating a new labour agreement with US Airways, with no layoffs and higher pay, forming the basis for a buy-out. Steven Pearlstein of the *Washington Post* described the unions' actions as 'deliciously ironic', and marking an important challenge to airlines' use of bankruptcy as a corporate strategy:

> For years now, Corporate America has viewed the bankruptcy court as a blunt instrument by which failed executives and directors can shift the burden of their mistakes onto shareholders, employees and suppliers .... Now the unions at American airlines have taken another step in curbing this flagrant corporate abuse and restoring the rule of law.[44]

Economic Doubts

The aviation industry often insists that job creation, business growth, tourism and trade can only be achieved if a new airport, or a new runway, is built. But examination of the economic case for aviation expansion raises many doubts. HACAN (Heathrow Association for the Control of Aircraft Noise) commissioned Delft, an independent research organisation, to examine the economic case for the expansion of Heathrow to maintain the airport's global hub status. The ensuing report picked apart the methodology used to justify expansion, finding that suppressed business demand was overestimated and the economic impact per passenger overstated. Government estimates failed to factor in tax breaks or the likelihood that, if expansion does not take place, people will spend their money on something else.[45] Delft's analysis of the economic case for a greenfield airport in Nantes, the site of protests involving thousands of people, found that the costs exceeded the benefits. Passenger growth and economic growth projections were over-optimistic. Travel time savings were overvalued. All the cost projection scenarios were based on the assumption that the costs of aviation will continue to decrease.[46]

Analysis of aviation expansion in the United Kingdom, by Sally Cairns and Carey Newson, cast doubts on the argument that economic growth is highly dependent on aviation expansion.

Inward investment was not as fixated on accessibility as claimed. Availability of air services was just one of a range of factors influencing location decisions, including land price, labour costs, market size and political stability. Aviation's benefits in supporting business development were overstated. Government forecasts assumed that business travel would grow faster than leisure travel, when in fact the opposite trend was well established. By 2004, UK residents' international holiday flights outnumbered their international business flights by a factor of five. Comparisons with other European countries added weight to evidence that the relationship between transport provision and economic well-being is not straightforward. The United Kingdom had twice as many flights as France, but the same GDP.[47]

International tourism is highly dependent on aviation, and growth of this sector is held up as one of the key economic benefits of investment in aviation. But tourists' expenditure does not necessarily benefit businesses in host destinations. A 2008 report by the New Economics Foundation and World Development Movement discovered that a high proportion of income from tourism in developing countries 'leaks' from the region to foreign-owned airlines, hotels and tour operators, and in payments for imported supplies including food, drink and construction equipment. Kenyan people received little of the income from an all-inclusive safari trip. A UK-based tour operator and airline took a 60 per cent share of tourists' expenditure, the Kenyan hotel chain and safari company received 31 per cent, the Kenyan government 9 per cent. The local Masai community received nothing. European multinational firms operated 90 per cent of tourism services in the Maya Riviera region on Mexico's Caribbean coast, monopolising provision of hotels, shops, restaurants and bars. An estimated 92 per cent of the income generated by the European companies went to Europe.[48]

Aviation-driven tourism drains income from wealthy countries when citizens' expenditure on foreign trips outweighs that of incoming visitors. British air passengers spend more abroad than foreign visitors spend in the United Kingdom. Sewill's analysis of data revealed that, in 2005, UK residents' leisure flights abroad outnumbered overseas visitors' leisure flights to the United Kingdom by 41.5 million. This led to a 'tourism deficit' of over $19 billion.[49]

If a country's air freight imports are higher in value than its exports, it runs up an 'air freight deficit'. The United Kingdom ran up a considerable air freight deficit in 2007. The value of air-freighted exports was $50.8 billion, while the value of imports was nearly $83 billion.[50] Import–export imbalances in the volume, and value, of air cargo, are a global issue. Passengers tend to book return flights, but cargo is one-way only. A 2008 report by Seabury, advisers to the aviation and maritime industries, stated that for every 3–5 kg air freighted from China to Europe and the United States, just 1 kg was flown in the returning direction. Seabury anticipated that global trade lane imbalances, the 'result of underlying imbalances of consumption and production', would widen in most cases.[51]

Invariably, aviation expansion is announced with the promise that a large number of jobs will be created. Sewill's research in the United Kingdom exposed this as a 'cruel hoax'. Between 1998 and 2004, passengers passing through UK airports increased by 30 per cent, but employment at airports rose by just 3 per cent. Airport expansion plans routinely exaggerated prospects for job creation. Manchester Airport claimed that a second runway would lead to 50,000 new jobs at the airport. Subsequently this figure was revised to 18,000, but the media continued to quote the higher figure, as did the airport chief executive after planning permission was granted. The new runway opened in 2001. Five years later, the number of jobs at Manchester Airport was only 4,000 higher than a decade previously.

Low-cost airlines minimise staffing levels. Airport automation, from internet ticket purchasing to check-in and baggage handling, replaces human beings altogether. At Heathrow's Terminal 5, nine out of ten passengers need not contact staff until they arrive at the boarding gates. There are few local employment opportunities in associated industries such as fuel production and aircraft manufacture. A key argument for expansion is that enhanced accessibility results in businesses locating in the airport catchment area. But accessibility is a two-way street: airport expansion can support an outflow of investment and jobs.[52]

Jobs for Robots

Statistics from ACI, the airports' own international trade organisation, show that globally, employment on airport sites does not keep pace with capital expenditure on buildings, machinery and other airport assets. The *ACI Airport Economics Survey 2006* reported growth in capital expenditure from $36 billion to $38 billion, but the global total of people employed on airport sites had remained static since 2004, at 4.5 million. Both these trends, of escalating capital expenditure and stagnating employment levels, were well established. The report states:

> Over the past decade, ACI has found that employment at airports does not vary greatly from year to year. While there is a component of the workforce which increases or decreases with passenger and freight numbers, the physical plant of the airport tends to need a fairly stable number of employees to keep the expensive fixed assets functioning.[53]

ACI reported a decline in the number of people employed at the world's airports in both 2007 and 2008. 2007 was proclaimed as a 'banner year for international traffic', and capital investment reached a record $40.1 billion. But ACI's description of employment at the world's airports as 'stable', at 4.3 million, glossed over a reduction of 200,000 jobs from 2006 to 2007.[54] In its report for 2008, ACI stated that 3,975,000 people were employed at the world's airports.[55] This marked a further reduction, of 325,000.

Aviation is capital intensive, not labour intensive. Images in the aviation trade press are almost devoid of people, showcasing the latest heavy and high-tech equipment. Overhead shots show runways and grey rectangular buildings extending to a vanishing point on the horizon. Airport construction jobs, operating bull-dozers, dump trucks, diggers, soil compactors and concrete mixers and other heavy machinery, only last until the building programme is completed. Once they become operational, airports are a showcase for the latest in automation, systematically eliminating jobs.

Self-service check-in kiosks are standard at modern terminals, and new technology is beginning to automate other jobs which involve staff interaction with passengers. Schiphol was the first airport to install automated bag drop-off, installing 18 units by February 2012, followed by Paris-Orly and Bologna in Italy. Geneva Airport has introduced online self-service for reporting missing luggage.[56]

Luton, to the north of London, was the first airport to install 'virtual assistants', holographic video projections with the appearance and recorded voices of real people. 'Holly and Graham' began telling passengers how to prepare before entering the central search area in January 2011. Within a few months, similar virtual assistants, programmed to give messages in several languages, appeared elsewhere in the United Kingdom at Cardiff, Birmingham and Edinburgh, and at Boston Logan, Washington Dulles, Frankfurt and Dubai. The holograms have many functions: reminding passengers to have boarding cards ready for inspection, explaining restrictions on carrying liquids in hand luggage and giving directions for catching connecting flights. They also provide instructions should anyone find themselves perplexed by the touch screen check-in kiosks.[57]

Trained border officials are being replaced by unstaffed immi-gration booths. By 2012, electronic gates equipped with facial recognition and a biometric passport scanner were operational, or being tested, at airports all over the world, including the United States, the United Kingdom, Taipei, Songshan and Kaohsiung in Taiwan, Incheon, Soekarno-Hatta, Moscow, Sydney, Kigali, Schiphol and Narita.

Manchester was one of the first airports to trial facial recognition technology. A series of glitches has compromised efficiency and security. In 2009 a high rate of false alarms led to the build-up of long queues, so the machines were recalibrated from requiring an 80 per cent likeness to passport photographs, to just 30 per cent. Rob Jenkins, a leading facial recognition expert, said that at this setting, the machines would be unable to distinguish between people of markedly different appearance, such as Osama Bin Laden and actor Winona Ryder, or former UK Prime Minister Gordon Brown and actor Mel Gibson.[58] An inspection by the UK Border Agency in 2010 found that the gates in Terminal 1 had broken down five times in one week, on one occasion trapping a passenger.[59] A whistleblower reported that the system was unable to read Dutch or Lithuanian passports, failed to identify a woman banned from entering the country, and let a man through the gate even though he was carrying his sister's passport.[60]

If new automated systems for 'ground handling' of passengers' luggage and cargo are widely adopted, progressively fewer human hands will be involved. Schiphol Airport installed a baggage robot in 2011. Thirty-six cranes handle baggage along the 21 km conveyor belt transporting bags through the airport. Six robots at the end of the conveyor belt automatically load bags into containers.[61]

Machines to load cargo onto planes are in development. In 2010, the USAF Research Laboratory offered contracts to build a cargo 'robo-pallet', a mechanised platform with inbuilt navigation to load cargo onto planes autonomously. The USAF envisages that the 'robo-pallet', initially deployed in war zones, could have 'direct application' to civilian cargo handling.[62] Contracts were awarded for development of two automated pallet-loading systems, called 'roboloader' and 'i-pBot'. Both feature wireless networks to coordinate movement and stacking of pallets.[63]

Driverless 'robot pods' transport passengers and their luggage between the parking lot and Terminal 5 at Heathrow. Twenty-two pods run along tracks nearly 4 km in length. Each pod can accommodate four passengers and their luggage, and carry about 800 passengers per day.[64] Stockholm Arlanda, Venice, Schiphol and several US airports have expressed an interest in the system.[65]

A South Korean military airport has unleashed robotic scarecrows on its avian visitors. The 'Airport Birdstrike Prevention System' consists of four semi-autonomous robots, controlled from a base in the airport by a single person. The robots emit the sound of screaming hawks and dying birds at up to 100 decibels, fire lasers and collect information on bird concentrations and movements. The Korea Atomic Energy Research Institute (KAERI) hopes it will be adopted by civilian airports worldwide.[66]

Elaborate vending machines are replacing retail workers. Dallas/Fort Worth has a giant vending machine called Shop 24, selling sweets, snacks, milk, diapers and children's games 24 hours per day, 365 days per year. It looks like a small convenience store, and in place of a door there is a dispenser with a robotic arm.[67] An advertisement in the trade magazine *Asia Pacific Airports* for the 'Shopping Wall', a fully automated vending machine already introduced at Frankfurt and Schiphol, proclaimed that there are 'no staff costs'. Books, electronic goods, souvenirs, sunglasses, perfumes and watches are displayed in a glass case, and purchased using an LCD monitor and touch screen.[68]

Destinations in Their Own Right

Passenger terminals are filled with ever more shops, catering outlets and leisure facilities. As John Kasarda, the leading advocate of aviation-driven economic development, says, airports are becoming 'shopping, trading, business meeting and leisure destinations in their own right'.[69] Heathrow, Incheon and Dubai vie for status as the world's largest airport retail operation. Dubai topped the list for the first time in 2008, reporting sales of $1.1 billion.[70] Heathrow reclaimed the top spot in 2011, when sales reached $1.7 billion.[71] Changi boasts 230 shops, 110 food and beverage outlets plus cinemas, a sauna and a swimming pool.[72]

McCarran, the main airport serving Las Vegas, the gambling capital of the United States, has 1,500 slot machines, mainly used by passengers waiting for outbound flights.[73] Passengers can tie the knot in wedding chapels at Stockholm Arlanda and Schiphol. Incheon has a casino, two cinemas, an ice rink, medical centre, dry cleaning and a spa.[74] Spas offering massages, facials and other treatments are common at major airports, and at Minneapolis pets can be pampered too. The pet boarding service provides grooming and an exercise pool.[75]

Urban development clusters around airports, and passengers can avail themselves of accommodation, entertainment and yet more shopping in close proximity to terminals. Hong Kong Airport Regal Hotel has 1,171 guest rooms and 30 function rooms. The Sofitel Lux Le Grand hotel at Heathrow is the United Kingdom's third-largest conference venue, with 45 meeting rooms and a convention centre accommodating 1,700. Dallas/ Fort Worth's Grand Hyatt Hotel has 20 conference suites, 45 meeting rooms and more than 3,000 sq. m of function space.[76] The SkyPlaza complex, adjacent to Hong Kong Airport, contains a 3D IMAX cinema and the AsiaWorld Expo venue with capacity for 13,500 people.[77] Athens's biggest exhibition venue, the 50.000 sq. m Metropolitan Expo Centre, is located to the north of the airport.[78] Passengers exiting Christchurch Airport's international arrivals terminal find a trail of blue footprints painted on the ground. These mark the route to the International Antarctic Centre, a five-minute walk.[79]

All of these facilities, from the shops to the exhibition centres, are examples of airport assets that generate 'non-aeronautical revenue'. The facilities are airside, landside and on land owned by the airport, and are operated either directly by the airport or through concessions and leases. Airports use non-aeronautical revenue to cross-subsidise charges to airlines, or 'airport user charges'. This encompasses use of runways for landing and take-off, navigation, landing gates, passenger check-in, security, and handling of baggage and cargo. Yet, between 1978 and

2008, airport user charges accounted for just 4 per cent of airline operating costs.[80] Airport user charges are distinct from, and a mere fraction of, airlines' fuel bills, which account for upwards of 30 per cent of operational costs.[81]

Worldwide, non-aeronautical revenue is an important factor in airports' financial viability. The main income categories are retail, hotels, food and beverages, car parking, car rental, property and advertising. In 1990 about 30 per cent of global airport revenues came from non-aeronautical sources. By the mid-2000s this had reached nearly 50 per cent at major airports.[82] Non-aeronautical revenue also funds airport upgrade and expansion. Kasarda explains that 'non-aeronautical revenues have become critical to airports meeting their facility modernisation and aeronautical infrastructure expansion needs'.[83]

Atlanta, the world's busiest airport, raised 60 per cent of its revenue from non-aviation activities in 2009. This enabled the airport to charge airlines some of the lowest landing fees in North America. Atlanta's $376 landing fee for a Boeing 767 contrasted with $6,000, 16 times as much, at Toronto Pearson.[84] Every day 250,000 passengers passed through Atlanta's terminals, spending money in more than 200 retail, food and beverage and service outlets. Seventy new concessions, including branded stores, spas and a nail salon, were due to open by the end of the year.[85] By 2011 the proportion of Atlanta's revenue coming from non-aviation activities had increased to 63 per cent, and the landing fee for a Boeing 767 had reduced further, to just $301.[86] Expansion continued into 2012, as Atlanta prepared for opening of its new terminal. In May 2012 it awarded concession contracts for 24 retail units, including two large duty-free stores and 126 food and beverage units. The airport expected the rent to contribute an additional $23 million per year in revenue.[87]

Atlanta Airport pocketed more $95.7 million from car parking in 2010. Dallas/Fort Worth made more than $97 million.[88] Denver Airport earned more than $123 million from 40,000 spaces.[89] Airport car parking is a grudge purchase, and fees are highest when there is a high level of car dependency and poor public transport provision. Melbourne Airport was criticised over its car parking charges when it predicted that its 23,000 spaces would make a profit of over $131 million in the 2013 financial year – twice the amount from retail, a full 20 per cent of its income and a profit of 93 cents per dollar spent on parking facilities. The sole public transport option taking passengers all the way to the terminal, instead of dropping them off several hundred metres away, is the SkyBus.[90] Australia's other main airports – Sydney, Brisbane, Perth and Adelaide – generated a similar level of income from car parking in the 2011–12 financial year, making a 70 per cent profit. The chair of the Australian Competition and Consumer Commission, Rod Sims, pointed out that the commission had no power to regulate airport car parking charges or restrict earnings of 'monopoly profits'.[91]

Research conducted in 2012 by the *Independent* newspaper revealed that many UK airports, including Heathrow, Manchester, Liverpool, Birmingham, Edinburgh and Glasgow, charge more for 24 hours of car parking than for parking a six-seater light aircraft for the same period. Heathrow's Terminal 5 car park was the most expensive. The 24-hour fee of $81 was more than an off-peak flight to Aberdeen.[92]

Airports' position on major road networks means that landside facilities are ideally placed to draw on the local population from a considerable catchment area. Hong Kong Airport's SkyPlaza complex, with 37,000 sq. m of retail space, is aimed at neighbouring communities as well as travellers.[93] Changi is a 'choice shopping destination, not just for travellers, but also for local residents'. Footfall in public areas rose in 2009–10, after the introduction of new retail brands and promotion of the airport as a weekend destination for families, with activities like children's rides, car boot sales and a Segway circuit.[94] Hyderabad Airport aims to become 'a leisure destination for Hyderabad residents', and has a gaming area, hospital, business school, multiplex cinema and go-karting track. A 12 km flyover connecting the airport with downtown reduced the journey time from two hours to 40 minutes.[95]

Centrair, built on an artificial island 35 km from the city of Nagoya, tapped into the local market as soon as it commenced operations, hosting the 2005 World Expo with pavilions from many countries. In addition to air passengers, the event attracted 10 million local visitors. Subsequently passenger numbers and freight volumes flagged, but non-aeronautical revenue was boosted by retail and catering, a traditional Japanese bathhouse, beer garden, wedding chapel and weekly entertainment events such as concerts and film previews. In 2008 local sightseers spent an average of $15 per visit.[96]

When Incheon Airport opened in 2001, Gimpo was designated as Seoul's secondary airport, handling only domestic flights. At a stroke Gimpo lost the 70 per cent of revenue that had come from international flights, but the airport turned its excess capacity to its economic advantage, developing facilities to draw on the local market as well as visitors. Motorways and subways make the airport easily accessible for the entire Seoul metropolitan area. Seung-Sang Cho, project coordinator with Gimpo's operator, Korea Airports Corporation, said, 'We aim to create an airport city that will provide a place of rest and relaxation for local residents.' The terminal was remodelled into a discount supermarket and spinal care clinic. A car park and fields were repurposed for phased development of shops, hotels, movie theatres, exhibition halls, golf courses, a sauna, a nine-screen cinema, a convention centre, a wedding hall and a cancer clinic.[97]

Airports' evolution into a dual role, as commercial centres as well as transportation hubs, brings the very opposite of the stimulation of the local economy that aviation expansion promises. Instead of a flow of visitors boosting trade in neighbouring communities, the airport establishes itself as a competing urban centre. As airports, with their tenants and concessionaires, become destinations in their own right, they capture a growing proportion of income from the aviation-induced flow of people and goods, leaving less to filter into surrounding communities. Airports that develop land in order to that target their own catchment area as part of the customer base are economic parasites, extracting the everyday expenditure of local residents who are not taking flights, in order to cross-subsidise operation and expansion.

11

Real Estate and Revenue Streams

On Airport Land

Since the first airstrips in the 1900s, airports have been built on the periphery of, and to serve, established urban centres. But the 1990s marked a shift towards urban development on land surrounding airports, and new greenfield airports with substantial land banks to accommodate the full spectrum of urban functions. The airport forms the central core of this new urban form. Retail, leisure and cultural complexes, manufacturing, warehousing and office space, cluster around the airport and radiate outwards. Multi-lane highways and rail networks extend the airport's catchment area across the conurbation. John Kasarda is the leading exponent of this airport-centric development, and coined the term 'aerotropolis', meaning airport city, to describe it.[1]

The key to a full-blown aerotropolis is the airport's ownership of a large area of land beyond its boundary. The airport controls development on its land, to ensure that it increases the throughput of passengers and cargo and generates non-aeronautical revenue. Kasarda identifies the land-owning aerotropolis as a global phenomenon, stating that 'airports from Amsterdam to Zurich and from Beijing to Seoul have embraced the Airport City model to develop their terminal and landside areas as a pivotal means to financing airport operations'.[2]

Amsterdam's Schiphol was one of the first airports to become an aerotropolis, developing into an urban centre in its own right. A real estate division was established in the mid-1990s to oversee development of retail, hotels, entertainment venues, offices and logistics parks.[3] The airport's property portfolio has grown steadily ever since. For example, in 2010 Schiphol added 11,200 sq. m of space to an office building, established a land-operating company for development of logistics and business parks on 350 hectares south-west of the airport, and began to build a detention centre and court for the Dutch Military Police.[4] By 2011, more than 500 companies were located on Schiphol Airport land.[5] Business parks offer maximum floor space for storage and for trucks to manoeuvre. Over the course of 10–15 years a 20,000 sq. m building generates 10 per cent of its value in cash flow.[6]

Munich Airport was another early aerotropolis. The green-field airport, 38 km north-east of the city, opened in 1992, then expanded into its 16 sq. km site. By 2006 Munich Airport had grown into a rival city centre, with 215 retail outlets, post office, dry cleaners, hairdresser, shoe repairs, swimming pool, internet café, spa, microbrewery, beer garden, hospital and a multidenominational chapel. There is a venue for concerts and events including a Christmas market and ice-rink. The 'fly-meet-fly' Municon facilities, with 28 conference rooms and accommodating 554 guests, are promoted as an alternative to travelling to Munich city centre.[7]

Germany's other main airports have also expanded onto surrounding land. Frankfurt Airport's 22 sq. km of land was described by the Global Airport Cities website as 'the scene of one of the most ambitious airport real estate projects in Europe'.[8] The airport states that its 110 hectare Mönchhof site, alongside the new fourth runway, is 'the largest contiguous block of commercially zoned land now being developed in the Rhine-Main region'. By 2011 about half the space was occupied, predominantly by logistics and express delivery businesses.[9] Düsseldorf Airport purchased 23 hectares of vacant land in 2003, covering it with a business park with office blocks, showrooms, hotels and conference facilities, yet leaving ample green space and trees, all a five-minute walk from the terminal which has 110 landside shops, restaurants and bars.[10] The new airport for Germany's capital, Berlin Brandenburg, has 16 hectares in front of the terminal revenue for shops, restaurants, conference halls, hotels and offices, and 109 hectares of land set aside for the biggest business park in the city.[11]

Kasarda highlights Incheon, with 61 sq. km of land, as 'perhaps the most ambitious effort to develop an airport city and Aerotropolis'. The central core, Air City, is crammed with office complexes, hotels, shopping malls, convention centres and exhibition space, a water park and 'fashion island' with shows and stores. The surrounding Airport Support Community contains logistics industries, housing for airport area employees and their families, a manufacturing zone and more office complexes, shopping malls, convention centres, exhibition space and hotels.[12] In 2012, Incheon Airport reported that 65 per cent of its revenue came from non-aviation activities. Within a few years, Maglev (magnetic levitation) trains will connect clusters of hotels, shopping malls, business premises, an entertainment resort and a watersports centre.[13]

Airports Company South Africa's (ACSA) property portfolio encompasses land surrounding OR Tambo, Cape Town, King Shaka, six domestic airports plus the site of the old Durban airport which was decommissioned when King Shaka became operational. OR Tambo, the busiest passenger airport in Africa, is ACSA's flagship airport. Development of retail, hotels, offices, conference centres, museums and an industrial zone around OR Tambo captures visitors, and their expenditure, rather than channelling them into the surrounding region. ACSA's property brochure explains that the 'need to travel away from the airport for business purposes is minimised'.[14]

Every aerotropolis project claims to act as an 'economic engine' for its host region, galvanising tourism and trade. But the primary objective of the aerotropolis is to stimulate its own growth, through the symbiotic relationship between growth in air traffic and development on airport land. Passengers and cargo are funnelled through airport assets, thus maximising airport growth and revenue. The aerotropolis does not so much create wealth as concentrate it on its own property. Every aerotropolis claims that non-aeronautical revenues from land ownership make it self-sustaining, reducing or removing any dependency on government funding. But non-aeronautical revenue is only possible by virtue of governments allocating land to the airport, precluding income generation for any beneficiary other than the airport and its tenants.

The rise of the aerotropolis also erodes one of the most important benefits that can be gained from travel, the enhanced understanding of other cultures. Within the aerotropolis, passengers are separate from the wider community. They are well catered for and entertained, but their experiences are filtered by the airport's decisions over which facilities are hosted on its land.

Shops and Solar Panels

Shops, hotels and other facilities on land outside the airport fence are even better placed to capture trade from the host region than their counterparts within the airport complex. Two of Canada's main airports, Vancouver and Edmonton, own prime parcels of real estate. Vancouver Airport Authority's Russ Baker Way property is one of few remaining undeveloped sites suitable for commercial properties in the Metro Vancouver area. Development of retail, dining and an entertainment centre is under way. Edmonton Airport is developing retail, entertainment, hotel and office space on the one-third of its site that is not required for airside expansion. The land is well positioned to capture trade, on the interchange between two major highways, one of which is the CANAMEX Corridor linking Canada with the United States and Mexico.[15]

Several Australian airports support their operations and expansion by leasing land for retail centres targeting the local population. Canberra Airport's property portfolio includes the Majura Park retail complex, occupied by factory outlets, an aquatic centre, gym and a petrol station. Catering outlets include a McDonald's fast-food restaurant, the second in Australia to be delivered to the site in prefabricated modules, with all internal fittings already in place.[16] A factory outlet centre was one of the first developments on Brisbane Airport's 27 sq. km site.[17] The first tenant on Darwin Airport's 60 hectare precinct, a ten-minute drive for 80 per cent of the city's population, was a household goods and DIY store.[18] Adelaide Airport's land hosts the Harbour Town retail centre and an IKEA store.[19] A 22 hectare site owned by Avalon Airport is being developed into 'destination shopping'. Big box stores under consideration for tenancy include Costco, Woolworths hardware and IKEA.[20]

IKEA is a store for residents furnishing their homes. Goods such as sofas, beds, shelving and bathroom suites are the very opposite of the compact, lightweight products that can be accommodated in air passengers' baggage allowance. Yet airports, situated at key junctions on major road networks, provide ideal locations for the store. IKEA is the anchor tenant at the Cascade Station development along the main road to the Portland Airport, Oregon, which is part of the airport's property portfolio.[21] Key tenants at Athens Airport's retail park, the first phase of commercial development on 17.5 sq. km of land, include a 25,000 sq. m IKEA.[22]

Athens is one of a number of airports that have instigated solar energy projects to generate both energy and non-aeronautical revenue. When the airport opened a solar park alongside the runway, in 2011, it was the biggest airport solar installation in the world, covering 16 hectares. It is sufficient to supply 9 per cent of the airport's electricity usage.[23] The solar facility is expected to boost Athens Airport's non-aeronautical revenues.[24] In March 2012 the managing director of Cochin Airport, V. J. Kurien, said,

'Renewable energy is definitely one area we will be exploring for diversifying our revenue streams.'[25] Within three months, the airport began installation of a pilot solar power system on the rooftop of the terminal and feasibility studies for higher capacity systems on other rooftops and in the car park area.[26] Indianapolis Airport has approved a land lease agreement for the largest solar farm of any US airport. A total of 52,400 panels covering 30 hectares, highly visible at the airport entrance, will be sufficient to power up to 17,050 homes. Revenue from solar energy, estimated at $315,000 annually over 15 years, will lower costs for airlines and support airport operations and growth.[27]

Solar panels will enhance these airports' green image, but the main impact will be an increase in the amount of fossil fuel burned by airlines. The income generated from solar power will be used to cross-subsidise airport user fees charged to airlines and for airport upgrade and expansion. Lower fees attract more flights, increasing carbon emissions. A larger airport can handle more flights, increasing carbon emissions.

Cashing in on Green Space

Airports can generate revenue from land that is not built on, and remains as green space. Denver's main airport and the nearby Front Range Airport grow wheat on vacant land.[28] Houston Airport System, which encompasses Bush, Ellington and Hobby airports, began replacing wild grass with a type of Bermuda grass used for livestock feed in 2006, aiming to create one of the largest hay-baling operations in south-east Texas.[29] By 2008 the roads to Houston Airport were lined with hay bales, selling at $20 per bale. Once hay is harvested from the entire 809 hectare project area, annual revenue could reach $4 million.[30] A 2012 presentation about US airport income generation, by an FAA representative, stated that the biggest blueberry farm in the state of Georgia was on airport property, but did not specify which airport.[31] Victoria Airport, on the southern tip of Vancouver

Island, has grazing land with a herd of black and white dairy cattle, but land currently leased for growing corn and hay is to be turned into an industrial park.[32]

Non-food crops provide another income stream. Alabama's Huntsville Airport was built on a cotton plantation, and a cotton crop covering more than 1,200 hectares is among the top revenue earners, bringing in $500,000 per year. In Florida, Jacksonville Aviation Authority receives $300,000 per year from wood and straw harvested from 500 hectares of timberland at four airports.[33] Eldoret Airport, in the south-west of Kenya close to the border with Uganda, began planting 240 hectares of eucalyptus trees on its 1,200 hectares of land in 2007, planning to sell them to power firms for use as electricity pylons. The trees can grow to maturity within eight years. Eldoret had failed to fund its operations for ten years and anticipated that the income from the trees would be sufficient to run the airport for six years without state funding.[34] Kilimanjaro Airport began planting jatropha, a biofuel crop used for jet fuel, on half of its 110 sq. km estate in 2006, expecting that that this would be a 'good income generator'.[35]

Airports in the United States own 3,306 sq. km of grasslands, an area larger that the state of Rhode Island. A study supported by USDA has identified this grassland as offering unrealised potential for alternative energy production, predominantly solar and biofuels, providing a new source of airport revenue. Use of land for biofuel reduces biodiversity, but the report notes that airports 'offer one of the few land uses where reductions in wildlife abundance and habitat quality are necessary'. Certain biofuel crops, including strains of grasses, repel species that attract birds, so large-scale planting would reduce the risk of collisions with aircraft.[36]

Kuala Lumpur, Malaysia's main airport, on the southern edge of the city, opened in 1998, bestowed with 100 sq. km of land. A major tourist attraction, the Sepang Formula One racing track, was already operational, but the remainder of the land was agricultural.[37] At the airport, arrivals passengers are greeted with the sight of an arboretum densely planted with rainforest plants, complete with a waterfall. Outside the terminal, half a million trees, incorporating 400 indigenous species, were transplanted from the rainforest to form the 'Green Park'. It is a showcase for botanical biodiversity with an 'educational research area based on the varieties of plants available'. Visitors can 'experience Malaysia's rainforest first hand' and take part in environmental events.[38] An elevated 'jungle boardwalk' through the rainforest plants enhances the impression of being in a natural environment.[39] Kuala Lumpur has adopted the slogan 'the airport in the forest, the forest in the airport'. The architect, Kisho Kurokawa, claimed to have designed the world's first green airport, with the Malaysian rainforest forming 'an integral part of the airport's very structure', demonstrating a 'symbiotic relationship between nature and architecture'.[40] In reality, as with all airport greenery, it is merely decorative, irrelevant to the core operation of servicing flights.

The planting also disguises the airport's economic relationship with nature. Aerial photographs reveal that Kuala Lumpur is not an 'airport in the forest' at all. Aside from two small patches of transplanted forest on either side of the airport entrance, the airport is surrounded by grids of identical vivid green rectangles, extending outwards to the west. This is palm plantation, large tracts of which are owned by the airport. Each rectangular plot is demarcated by access roads, and if you zoom in closer you can see the trees densely planted in rows.

Kuala Lumpur Airport lectured people about rainforests and biodiversity as it reaped revenue from a monoculture plantation, producing palm oil to be sold on global markets. In 2008 Malaysia Airports made over $19.4 million from 79 sq. km of palm and coconut plantations around Kuala Lumpur, Subang and Kota Bharu airports. The vast majority of this sum was from 70 sq. km of palm around Kuala Lumpur. Other key sources of non-aeronautical revenue included $17.8 million from the Pan Pacific Hotel, $22.5 million from the Sepang Formula 1 circuit and $88 million from retail and food and beverage outlets.[41] Income from all these assets was not sufficient to balance the books. In November 2008 Kuala Lumpur Airport faced criticism over an annual government handout of $286 million to prop up its operations.[42]

Satellite photographs of the palm plantation around Kuala Lumpur Airport show angular greyish brown areas, where trees have been cleared for expansion of the airport and its non-aeronautical assets. Malaysia Airports's *2010 Annual Report* states that over 1,700 hectares of palm plantation had been cleared for construction of a new low-cost terminal and associated commercial development. Land that is built on generates higher returns, but palm remains a significant source of revenue. Replanting of palm plantations was identified as a key strand of Malaysia Airports's economic programme for the following 25 years. The *Annual Report* also expressed regret that part of the forest around the terminal entrance had been replaced with palm, reducing the airport's contribution to biodiversity. The forested area had provided a habitat for owls, bats and other wildlife, compromising the bird strike prevention programme.[43]

In 2011 the development area of Kuala Lumpur Airport's land bank was enlarged, and earthworks were in progress in preparation for construction of business premises, a factory outlet centre, a boutique hotel, a theme park, agro-tourism and golf courses.[44] Golf courses could help Kuala Lumpur Airport with its bird strike management. Swaths of manicured short grass are uniquely compatible with airport operations as they are unattractive to birds. Some of the world's most famous golf courses are on airport land. For example, Nine Eagles at Hong Kong Airport has the country's first island green and night lighting, Melbourne Airport Golf Club is known for its water features, and the Shenzhen Huangtian course, in southern China, overlooks the sea.[45]

Site Struggles

Kasarda notes that aerotropolises are 'emerging most vividly around Asia's newer international gateway airports', notably

Incheon, Hong Kong, Kuala Lumpur and India's main airports. He attributes the scale and rapid construction of these aerotropolises to 'powerful government bodies that simultaneously control the development process of the airport and its environs with relatively few social or environmental constraints'.[46] But some of these developments entail significant loss of wildlife habitats, farmland and wholesale displacement of communities.

Kuala Lumpur Airport is a convenient starting point for tours of the rainforest villages of Orang Asli, descendants of the earliest inhabitants of Peninsular Malaysia. Visitors learn about myths and legends, watch performances of traditional songs and dances, and observe crafts including weaving palm leaves into roofs for thatched huts. Few settlements remain because, throughout Malaysia, the majority of indigenous peoples' ancestral land has been seized for palm and rubber plantations and urban development. Members of the Orang Asli Temuan tribe were forcibly evicted from a 15.4 hectare plot to make way for a road linking to Kuala Lumpur Airport.[47] In 2010, following a 15-year legal battle, seven members of the Temuan tribe were awarded compensation of nearly $2 million. Their victory in this landmark case should have wider ramifications in the struggle for recognition of rights to customary land.[48]

The Andal Aerotropolis, in West Bengal, threatens the same loss of productive farmland as greenfield airports all over India. An article in *Asia Pacific Airports* claimed that the area, 14 sq. km, is 'largely barren/fallow farmland'.[49] In fact the site includes a large tract of arable land, hosting prosperous farmers growing rice, wheat, pulses and vegetables, and subsistence farmers cultivating fish and spinach, and tending cattle. At that stage, the scale of the development threatened to displace 19,000 villagers.[50] Sixteen agricultural labourers and sharecroppers were arrested in March 2010, when they demolished the project's temporary camps.[51]

Farmers protested throughout 2011, and succeeded in reducing the size of the aerotropolis. In May over 450 farmers refused to accept the compensation package for acquisition of the final tranche of land, and marked out their plots with bamboo poles, which they guarded around the clock.[52] Two months later the project area was reduced to 900 hectares, and plans for the areas dedicated to entertainment, residences, IT and industrial parks were modified.[53] The project's promoters thought that the final land acquisition hurdle had been cleared, but in September landowners demanding higher compensation demonstrated at the project site and blocked vehicle access.[54] There were further protests in January 2012 when 50 farmers, sharecroppers and farm labourers, claiming that they had not received compensation, uprooted a portion of barbed wire fencing and fenced off a small section of land acquired for the project with bamboo poles.[55]

Construction of a second airport for Colombo, Sri Lanka's capital on the southern tip of the island, commenced at Weerawila, on rice paddies near a bird sanctuary, before an environmental impact assessment had been conducted.[56] Protests led to the selection of new site, near the town of Mattala. The new location preserved agricultural land, but development of the airport is removing a wildlife habitat, as it consists of 20 sq. km of virgin forest and shrubland.[57] Eight sq. km of forest were cleared for airport construction in August 2010. Kumudini Hettiarachchi, a local conservationist, reported that large tracts of forest were set alight, and there was a 'massacre of anything that moves'. Mouse deer, snakes, frogs and ant eaters were surrounded by electric fencing, which should have been built in stages to enable them to leave the area.[58] One hundred elephants were relocated, and the Wildlife Department announced that a new elephant corridor would be created, with an area for passengers to observe them.[59] Visitors will have no inkling that wildlife was destroyed to enable easy access to a managed spectacle.

Removal of elephants' habitat can result in herds venturing into human settlements, trampling over people in search for food. Dr Prithviraj Fernando, an expert on Asian elephants, warned that villages near the new airport were at risk since there was a herd of 50 in the Mattala area. He pointed out that the airport was protected by an electric fence, but villages were not.[60] Herds of elephants rampaged through Mattala villages in January 2012, killing three people. Road connectivity for the airport impacted on agriculture. The Airport Expressway cutting through rice paddies in the villages of Pahala Andara Wewa and Kandhasurindugama, was half complete, and the farmers had received no compensation for the loss of their land, which was their sole or main source of income.[61]

The airport and port provide the international connectivity for industrial and tourism development of Hambantota, which the chair and managing director of the Board of Investment, Jayampathi Bandaranayake, described as 'a new mega city' and a 'new city built from scratch'.[62] Only 4 sq. km, about one-fifth of the site, is taken up by the airport. The remaining 16 sq. km are for real estate, for businesses, landscaped gardens and lakes. The airport is part of an integrated industrial complex with an oil refinery and a deep water seaport 18 km away, close to the main shipping lanes.[63]

At the beginning of 2012 the airport, with its runway big enough to accommodate the Airbus A380, was on target for inauguration by the end of the year, thanks to a $190 million loan from the Chinese government. The new airport is to be cargo-oriented in its initial stages. Tourism will follow. The first hotel, described as an 'eco-friendly paradise', is under construction.[64] In March 2012, as the airport prepared for opening, President Mahinda Rajapaksa granted free landing and parking for airlines during the first year of operations. Government-owned SriLankan Airlines offered 50 per cent off handling fees.[65]

The plan for aerotropolis development around Taoyuan, the main international airport for Taiwan's capital city Taipei, on the north-east coast, is likened to a 'fried egg'. The central cluster of the airport is the 'egg yolk'. The surrounding area, the 'egg white', is designated for aviation-related businesses, trade and exhibition complexes, light manufacturing and residential zones. The site, consisting of farmland and several towns, is 61.5 sq. km, slightly bigger than Incheon Airport. The Taoyuan County Government, in rezoning villages and farmland, anticipated that land acquisition would be the biggest barrier to the project, raising complex legal issues, and called for central government intervention.[66]

Tensions have emerged over the allocation of land for the aerotropolis. In August 2011, villages hosting 400 small factories were threatened with forced eviction for an industrial zone and housing near the Taipei Mass Rapid Transit (MRT), the rail link with Taipei. Dozens of people from Leshan village, facing expropriation of land, formed the 'MRT A7 Station Development Project Self-Help Group' and rallied in Taipei, carrying ancestral tablets which represent their rights to inherited land, and burning incense sticks.[67] Two months later the group lodged a protest with Taoyuan County Government, declaring that the pre-auctioning of land without their agreement violated the Constitution. Chairwoman Hsu Yu-hung stated that 'We will defend our homes with our blood and our lives.'[68]

The odds are stacked against the landowners, as the Taoyuan aerotropolis has high-level government support. It is one of the 'Taiwan 12' flagship public construction projects and has a $40 billion budget.[69] In 2012 Chan Shun-kuei, a lawyer, said that 'the government is contemplating the largest programme of eviction in Taiwan history'. The plan entails the expropriation of 3,211 hectares of land and demolition of 15,000 houses.[70]

Money on the Ground

Denver Airport opened in 1995, with a 138 sq. km site, the largest in the United States, bigger than the cities of Boston, Miami and San Francisco.[71] Aside from the solar energy installations, a convenience store and service station, most of the land is 'still rolling fields'. Radical change to this landscape is imminent. The aeronautical masterplan is complemented by a commercial masterplan for exploitation of real estate.[72] Denver's land gives ample room for a seventh runway, and key building projects include a 500 room hotel and conference centre and an open air plaza intended to extract revenue from the local population as well as visitors.[73]

Denver Airport has an additional, unusual source of income. There were oil and gas wells on the site when the airport opened, and, by 2010 76 wells, all on outlying areas of airport property, raised $7 million. Oil and gas revenue is dwarfed by conventional non-aeronautical income sources. Car parking brings in more than $213 million, car rental £44 million and concessions $43 million.[74] Nevertheless, when the oil price rises, Denver's earnings from its oil and gas wells go up. This helps counter any loss of income should airlines make cuts in routes serving the airport. When Patrick Heck, the airport's chief finance officer, addressed an ACI conference in London in March 2011, he raised what must have been rueful laugher when he pointed out that he was the only attendee rejoicing that the oil price exceeded $100 per barrel.[75]

Dallas/Fort Worth Airport owns 73 sq. km of land, making it the second biggest airport site in the United States, after Denver. The airport sits on top of Barnett Shale, one of the largest onshore gas fields in the United States, stretching underneath 13,000 sq. km of Texas.[76] The gas is embedded within thin layers of hard rock shale, so could only be accessed with the advent of new drilling techniques. A 52 m high oil rig was erected in the northwest of the airport site, and on 22 May 2007 the first gold drill bit burrowed into the ground. Bore wells were drilled to a vertical depth of up to 2.5 km, turned to drill horizontally, then turned again to resume downwards drilling. Almost all the airport's site was available for gas exploration, and 50 potential pad sites had been identified.[77] A land planner was hired to minimise visibility of the oil wells.[78]

Dallas/Fort Worth Airport claimed that sale of the gas lease would allow it to 'become more self-sustaining'.[79] But the new source of revenue came at a cost to citizens of Dallas and Fort Worth. The two cities, joint owners of the airport, granted the mineral rights, along with the land, to the airport, thereby forfeiting royalties from the gas. Within a few months 35 gas wells had been drilled, 15 of which were in production. The airport received an initial bonus of $186 million from the gas, and was awaiting its first royalty cheque.[80] John Terrell, vice president of real estate, said, 'Being able to find and capture natural gas on DFW is like finding money on the ground.' The airport is entitled to 25 per cent royalties on all gas produced. By July 2008, 60 wells were in production and royalties of $8.7 million had been used to renovate rest rooms, upgrade flight information display systems and for other terminal improvements.[81]

Shale gas wells proliferated in the Dallas Fort-Worth area, but it did not take long for this new energy source to become one of the most divisive issues in the United States. Supporters welcomed the prospect of weaning the country off its dependence on foreign oil. Additional revenue to local and state government eased the strain on public services, and some landowners leasing sites for drilling made instant fortunes. But opposition intensified as the environmental damage caused by the heavy industrial processes used to extract gas embedded in rock became evident. Horizontal drilling techniques were combined with hydraulic fracturing of rock formations, known as 'fracking'. Each time a well is fracked, millions of litres of water and chemicals are injected at high pressure, resulting in a heavily polluted waste water stream. Wells, pipes, compressors and storage tanks all produce air pollution, including methane which is a potent green-house gas. Emissions of smog-forming pollutants from the oil and gas sector in the Dallas–Fort Worth area now exceed the levels from motor vehicles.[82]

Exploration and drilling expanded, and by October 2010 the Barnett shale was supplying 40 per cent of all the shale gas in the United States. Dallas/Fort Worth Airport held the largest contiguous shale gas lease in the country, and airport revenue to date was $257 million.[83] By 2011, the airport anticipated that the total number of shale gas wells could be as high as 330, and that earnings over 10–15 years might be as high as $1 billion. The airport achieved its goal of hiding the gas wells; people driving around the airport will not see a single one.[84]

Shale Gas Hotspots

By 2010, minor airports across Texas located above Barnett Shale reported substantial incomes from on-site gas wells. Denton Airport had received $8.5 million in shale gas royalties.[85] Spinks had raised $27.6 million which funded expansion of the apron. Arlington earned $10.6 million and Cleburne and Grand Prairie each raked in over $1 million. All the gas income funded airport upgrade and expansion.[86] By 2012, Dallas/Fort Worth Airport's total earnings from shale gas reached $293.4 million, and were projected to be $10 million per year for the next decade.[87]

Fracking became even more controversial when evidence that it might cause earthquakes emerged. Seismologists traced the epicentre of eleven minor quakes between 2008 and 2009, in an area of Dallas–Fort Worth where no quakes were previously recorded, to a wastewater reinjection well just south of Dallas/Fort Worth Airport. The quakes occurred over a period when each day 1.43 million litres of brine and sand were injected.[88]

Fracking techniques honed in Dallas are being copied all over the United States, in particular above the Marcellus shale formation, the country's biggest gas field, extending underneath eastern Ohio, West Virginia, Pennsylvania and southern New York. Airports sitting above shale gas deposits, and owning substantial tracts of undeveloped land, are prime sites for new wells. In October 2010 airport managers converged at Elmira Corning Airport in Chemung County, New York, for the first ever Airports Natural Gas Conference, discussing drilling techniques and legal issues.[89] As fracking activity intensified, Elmira Corning Airport personnel noticed an increase in the number of passengers wearing cowboy hats, and thought this influx from Texas might be due to the shale gas rush. An audit of car license plates confirmed that one-fifth of passenger throughput was associated with the industry.[90] Pollution soon became apparent. In February 2011, nine households north of the airport site issued New York's first suit against a gas-drilling operation, alleging that their drinking water had been contaminated.[91]

Denver Airport has hired a consultant to explore options for shale gas drilling.[92] The airport sits atop the western edge of the Niobrara formation, a band of shale 2,000 m deep under north-east Colorado and parts of Wyoming, Nebraska and Kansas, estimated to hold the equivalent of more than 1 billion barrels of oil.[93] Nearby Front Range Airport has already received $985 for signing a lease for shale drilling, and hopes for royalties of 20 per cent, which would obviate the need for $1 million per year in assistance from Adams County.[94]

The film *Gasland* explores the shale gas industry in Colorado, Wyoming, Utah, Texas and Pennsylvania, revealing the devastating impact on health and the environment. Air and water contamination is suspected of causing health problems, predominantly neurological, gastrointestinal and dermatological disorders. Some householders' water supply is so heavily polluted with gas that they can set it alight as it pours from the faucet. Aerial shots show how the accumulation of small-scale infrastructure has transformed the landscape, leaving it pockmarked with wells, storage tanks and ponds containing used fracking fluid.[95]

Shale gas extraction and pollution is most intensive in the state of Pennsylvania, where in 2010 alone the Department of Environmental Protection issued 750 violation notices. Bradford County, in north-east Pennsylvania, is the most fracked place on the planet. Flares from newly completed wells light up the night sky, and shale gas drilling areas are blighted by pollution from wells, pipelines, generators and compressor stations. Enormous trucks carry heavyweight equipment along small rural roads, frequently groaning with loads which exceed legal limits. Speed violations and accidents with trucks overturning are common. Property values have plummeted and several families have abandoned their homes, suspecting that fracking has caused serious health problems including heart problems and cancer. Methane released by fracking percolates into rivers. When residents of Sugar Run community discovered bubbles in the Susquehanna River, they set them alight with a click of a lighter, sending flames shooting along the riverbank.[96]

Bradford County Airport is situated in the Susquehanna River Valley, and shale drilling has increased traffic, boosting hangar rental and fuel sales.[97] Other Pennsylvania airports are cashing in directly on the shale boom by leasing land for drilling. Bradford Regional Airport has earned $323,000 from 32 shallow oil and gas wells since 2003. Now the airport is set to become a shale gas hotspot. Drilling is under way to access newly discovered Marcellus Shale deposits under the northern portion of the airport site.[98] Pittsburgh Airport is so under-used that only 15 per cent of its gates are occupied. In 2012, the owners, Allegheny County, opened up airport land for shale gas extraction to reduce airline costs.[99] Proceeds from gas 1.6 km beneath 3,700 hectares of land could amount to $95 million. Some members of Allegheny County argued that a proportion of this revenue should benefit local taxpayers. They put the case that the county contributed to airport construction, owns the airport land and purchased the mineral rights. But the entirety of the gas earnings will go towards improving airport facilities, and to reducing fees for airlines and the airport's debt of over $400 million. FAA rules are on the airport's side, stipulating that all revenue generated on airport property must be used for aviation-related expenses.[100]

Concerns over the risk of explosions from Pennsylvania shale gas production proved well founded. After a blow-out at Clearfield County, on 3 June 2010, gas and wastewater spewed into the air for 16 hours. Four days later drillers pierced a pocket of methane underneath a farm near Moundsville, West Virginia.

Seven workers suffered burns and the 15 m high flare burned for four days.[101] In Charleston, the West Virginia state capital, Yeager Airport sits atop the Huron Shale formation, which is shallower and easier to tap than the Marcellus formation. The airport is anticipated to receive annual royalties of $50,000 from four wells, on 300 hectares of land, plus over 22,600 cu. m of free gas.[102]

12

How Aviation
Keeps Growing

The Importance of Non-Aeronautical Revenue

When the world was plunged into economic crisis in autumn 2008, the contraction in travel and trade impacted on aviation. By February 2009 2,300 planes, 11 per cent of the global fleet, were in storage, the highest number since the immediate aftermath of 9/11, when all planes flying over the United States were grounded. Most of the idle planes were parked in the California and Arizona deserts, where the hot, dry atmosphere minimises corrosion.[1] When the full-year results were compiled, Giovanni Bisignani, chief executive officer of IATA, stated that '2009 goes into the history books as the worst year the industry has ever seen'. The decline was the biggest in the post-war era. Globally, passenger traffic was down 3.5 per cent, and freight fell 10.1 per cent.[2]

The financial crisis evolved into a global economic downturn, but aviation quickly resumed its growth path. ACI reported growth in passenger numbers and cargo volumes in all world regions in 2010. Global passenger growth was 6.6 per cent; the number of passengers exceeded 5 billion for the first time. Air cargo bounced back, hitting record volumes of 92 million tonnes, a rise of 15.3 per cent for the year.[3] Growth continued in 2011. Air passenger numbers increased 5.3 per cent, reaching

5.44 billion. Cargo volumes were in excess of 93 million tonnes.[4]

Airports' non-aeronautical revenue proved remarkably robust. 2009 saw a decline of only 1.5 per cent worldwide. Announcing the figures, ACI director general Angela Gittens underlined the importance of non-aeronautical revenues to airport finances:

> During the downturn the diversification of airport revenues cushioned the impact of lower passenger and freight volumes. Non-aeronautical revenues critically determine the financial viability of an airport as they tend to generate higher profit margins than aeronautical activities, which are typically cost-recovery only or operate at a deficit.[5]

Contraction in revenue from car parking and advertising was balanced by growth in other sectors. Retail grew by 2 per cent, food and beverages by 7 per cent, car rental by 9 per cent, real estate by 10 per cent.[6] Airports' non-aeronautical revenues resumed a growth path in 2010. ACI reported a global increase of 7 per cent to $47.337 billion.[7]

An 'airport-only' holiday package, launched in February 2013, takes maximisation of non-aeronautical revenue to its logical conclusion. A 48-hour tour takes in gardens, museums, ice-skating and butterfly sanctuaries at Incheon, Changi, Hong Kong and Taipei.[8] Taking a series of short-haul flights for no other reason than to sample the delights of airport terminals will no doubt appeal to a niche market of aviation enthusiasts. But growth of tourism in aerotropolis-style developments, outside the airport fence, is of greater significance. Travellers spend more time and money on airport land, largely unaware that they are still inside the airport system. Airports that have recently announced new aerotropolis-style projects on real estate include Qatar, Stockholm, Vienna, Copenhagen, Cairo, Miami, Soekarno-Hatta in Jakarta, Tocumen in Panama and the Caribbean island of Curacao.

If aerotropolis developments proliferate as planned, the tourism generated will resemble the cruise ship industry. Gigantic ships carrying thousands of holidaymakers call in at a string of destinations, but passenger spending is limited to excursions. Boarding, food and drink, entertainment – the mainstays of the tourism business – are part of an all-inclusive package provided on the boat. Trade with coastal communities is minimal. Unlike cruise ship passengers, on the boat out at sea much of the time, air travellers are not physically confined to airport-owned land. But a full-blown aerotropolis covers a large area and offers a more comprehensive range of facilities than a cruise liner.

The Oil Price

The oil price is a critical factor in airlines' financial viability. Jet fuel prices and oil prices are closely correlated. Oil price volatility has intensified since the economic downturn, but remains on an upward trajectory. Yet we cannot assume that the rising oil price will rein in aviation growth, within the narrow window of opportunity for reducing emissions, from all industrial sectors, to avert catastrophic climate change. Oil supplies are finite. But new oil discoveries and extraction methods depress the oil price and slow the upward trend.

Efforts to constrain aviation have to contend with the industry's continued growth in spite of rising oil prices. IATA reported that in 2008 the world's airlines, hit by an unprecedented oil price spike in the middle of the year, made heavy losses of over $26 billion. Rising fuel prices throughout the year contributed to a $4.6 billion loss in 2009. However, the global airline industry was back in the black by 2010, making profits of $15.8 billion. A halving of profits in 2011, to $7.9 billion, was mainly because of higher fuel prices.[9] Airlines are sensitive to the oil price, but have a long track record of being resilient to it.

John Kasarda tracked air passenger and cargo data against jet fuel prices between 1987 and 2008, and found no evidence that higher fuel prices curbed aviation growth. In fact, he discovered a positive correlation, the statistics showing that 'higher jet fuel prices and greater volumes of passengers and cargo have moved along together'.[10]

Profit margins are another indicator of airlines' economic viability, but periods of wafer-thin and negative margins are not unprecedented. Airlines weathered negative profit margins throughout the recessions of the late 1970s and early 1980s, and in the early 1990s. Indeed, the reduction in airlines' profit margins after the oil price spike of mid-2008 was short-lived in comparison with, and only marginally steeper than, the loss-making period between 2000 and 2006.[11] The early years of the new millennium saw the airline industry hit by a series of external shocks: the bursting of the dotcom bubble of 2000 caused a stock market crash, the 9/11 terrorist attacks led to an escalation in security costs, and the 2003 SARS (severe acute respiratory syndrome) outbreak grounded many flights in Asia.

Higher oil prices squeeze airlines' profit margins, but the effect on aviation growth is not straightforward. Economic growth stimulates demand for air services, and the relationship between the oil price and economic growth is complex. A high oil price can either stimulate or depress economic activity. Airbus alludes to this in its forecast, projecting aviation growth between 2011 and 2030:

> Ironically from aviation's perspective, crude oil prices and economic activity are closely correlated: strong and developing economic activity increases demand for oil, which has a positive impact on crude oil prices. Conversely, an exogenous increase of crude oil prices has a negative impact on economies.[12]

A high oil price is not an unmitigated disaster for airlines, but the challenge to the balance sheet is undeniable. Between 2001 and 2011 the proportion of airlines' operational costs attributed to fuel more than more than doubled, rising from 13 per cent to 30 per cent.[13] Flexibility in cost structures helps airlines accommodate increasing fuel costs. As a short-term measure, slapping on a surcharge passes on the some of the cost. In the longer term, airlines reduce other costs. IATA reported that from 2004 to 2010 the airline industry increased labour productivity by 67 per cent, which translates to lower staffing levels. Other cost-reduction measures included improved fuel efficiency and a 10 per cent cut in sales and marketing costs. Furthermore, campaigns to reduce external costs saved $6.5 billion in tax reductions and $17.5 billion in airport and navigation charges.[14] Airports are able to reduce charges to airlines because of growth in non-aeronautical revenues.

A majority of the world's airlines are, to some degree, insulated from rising fuel costs by 'hedging' programmes. By purchasing fuel at a capped price in a forward contract, airlines shift exposure to future fuel prices to companies or investors that are willing to take the risk for the profit opportunity. Emirates' hedging strategy reduced its fuel bill by over $1 billion between 2000 and 2007.[15] Dallas-based Southwest Airlines is renowned for its hedging strategy. Savings of $3.5 billion between 1999 and 2008 tipped the balance sheet from loss to profit.[16] However, hedging can backfire on airlines. If the oil price goes down, they are locked into paying higher than market prices. When the global economy plunged into recession in autumn 2008 the oil price tumbled, falling below $50 per barrel for the first time since May 2005. Several carriers made losses on their hedging programmes. Cathay Pacific lost $994 million, Air China $994 million and Emirates $428 million. Hedging stalwart Southwest Airlines lost $117 million.

As the oil price resumed its upward trajectory, airlines' fuel-hedging programmes were more successful in smoothing price volatility.[17] IATA stated that 'the fuel hedging experiences of airlines in 2011 was much better than it was in 2008'.[18] The majority of the world's airlines hedged between 21 and 40 per cent of their fuel purchasing in 2012.[19] Complex derivative instruments enable airlines to pass on the inherent risks of fuel hedging to other parties, but this bodes ill for the wider economy. Derivatives, largely unregulated and not reflecting the true market price of underlying assets, were a factor in financial crisis of 2007–08. We are still stuck in the economic downturn that followed.

Forecasts and the Future

Worldwide, government aviation expansion policies, and airport masterplans, base traffic projections on the presumption of future growth and forecasts by Airbus and Boeing.[20] Packed with statistics, charts and diagrams, the aircraft manufacturers' forecasts predict aviation growth over the coming two decades. The increase in passenger number and cargo volumes is supposedly driven by demand, as if governments, providing airport capacity, along with road links, a raft of subsidies and allocation of land for non-aeronautical revenue, have no control over it. The forecasts are the framework for 'predict and provide' planning. Growth rates are extrapolated into the future, and the government provides capacity so the growth can take place.

Traffic forecasts are based on the premise that aviation growth and economic growth are mutually reinforcing. Economic growth stimulates aviation growth as people have more money to spend. Aviation's impact on the economy is less straightforward. Undoubtedly, aviation expansion increases the profits of major corporations – aircraft manufacturers, airlines, construction, concrete and security firms, oil companies, international hotel consortia and global retail chains selling global brands. Constructing an airport boosts economic activity in the short term, even if it ends up under-utilised. The predominance of government funding for airport construction means that firms get paid, even if the project turns out to be a white elephant.

It may well be the case that aviation expansion is an overall contributor to economic growth. But we need to decouple economic activity from consumption of resources. As an energy-intensive industry, aviation must be constrained. Taking a wider view, economic growth is the wrong metric. Centuries of narrow fixation on increasing productivity and accumulating capital have widened inequalities, left a bottom billion in poverty and hunger, and driven the overconsumption of resources that underlies the environmental crisis.

Campaigners opposing aviation expansion are united in calling for an end to short-haul flights, replacing these journeys with surface transport. Carbon emissions, per kilometre, are higher from short-haul flights, as the extra fuel burn required for take-off and ascent to cruising altitude forms a higher proportion of emissions. Dr Christian N. Jardine devised a model to determine the emissions of flights of different lengths. It showed that flights under 2,000 km are the least efficient: the shorter the distance, the higher the emissions. Once long-haul flights exceed 4,000 km there is a decrease in fuel efficiency as more fuel must be carried to cover the distance, but the differential is slight compared with the higher fuel consumption of short-haul flights.[21]

For all the aviation industry's promotion of its pivotal role in the glamour of international travel and the dynamism of globalised business, the world's largest air passenger traffic flows are domestic and short-haul flights. Airbus's 2011 statistics show US domestic traffic as the world's largest passenger flow, at over 900 billion revenue passenger kilometres (RPK). Traffic within Western Europe ranked second at 560 billion RPK.

Airbus's forecast anticipates that, over the next 20 years, the highest growth rates will be seen in domestic traffic flows. Domestic US traffic is expected to reach more than 1,400 billion RPK, accounting for 10.4 per cent of global traffic. Domestic traffic within China is anticipated to more than quadruple, to equal that of the United States and share the position of the largest passenger traffic flow in the world. Traffic within Western Europe is expected to almost double to over 1,000 billion RPK. Indian domestic traffic is projected to show the highest growth rate of all, increasing sevenfold to more than 380 billion RPK.[22]

Yet there is widespread scepticism over the feasibility of domestic capacity expansion. Leading industry analysts question the viability of India's plans for greenfield airports to provide air links for minor cities.[23] China's goal of 82 new airports by 2015, the majority for shuttle services, is certainly not driven by evidence of demand. Existing airports are losing domestic passengers to high-speed rail, and over three-quarters operate at a deficit.[24] Europe already has a surfeit of runways that are of sufficient length to handle the larger aircraft used for long-haul flights. Forty-eight per cent of long-haul-length runways at secondary airports are not used for long-haul flights.[25] A recent HACAN report reveals that Heathrow's runways are clogged up with short-haul flights. The airport clings to its status as an international hub, but between a fifth and a quarter of flights serve domestic or nearby European countries. Of the top ten destinations just one, New York, is long haul.[26]

Aviation expansion is driven by powerful industries, supported by governments. Passengers are eagerly reaping the benefits of fast long-distance travel – excitement, novelty, business opportunities and maintaining relationships. This is only possible because they pay little of the true costs, but I believe personal responsibility is also important, and that everyone who does fly has a duty to make a concerted effort to minimise the number of flights they take. The severity of environmental damage necessitates compromise and sacrifice. Virtual communication has its limitations, but can substitute for some air travel. Business meetings and conferences in airport venues are prime candidates for replacement with videoconferencing. Live projections of plays, concerts and operas are high quality, and very different from watching a performance on the screen of a personal electronic device.

Engagement in action for change shapes the future as much as individual behaviour. Local groups opposing airport expansion have joined forces, forming Airport Watch in the United Kingdom and Aviation Justice in the United States.[27] Plane Stupid, in the United Kingdom and now also Germany, combines direct action with an incisive, gloriously irreverent critique of the industry.[28] In Europe, there is solidarity between campaigns in several countries. John Stewart said, 'Wherever a new runway or new airport is planned in Western Europe it is meeting with well-organised and well-informed opposition'. Plans for new airports in Italy, in Siena and Viterbo, have been defeated. A third runway at Munich Airport has been 'stopped in its tracks' by the scale of opposition and a decisive referendum vote against the project.[29] The multifaceted nature of the movement against aviation expansion is its key strength. Tackling the seemingly unstoppable laying of concrete is possible.

Appendix: NGOs working to address the environmental and economic impacts of aviation expansion

International

ICSA (International Coalition for Sustainable Aviation): www.icsa-aviation.org/

Europe

European Union Against Aircraft Nuisances: www.uecna.eu/
Transport and Environment: www.transportenvironment.org/browse/transport-mode/aviation

United Kingdom

Airport Watch: www.airportwatch.org.uk
Aviation Environment Federation: www.aef.org.uk
Plane Stupid: www.planestupid.com

United States

Aviation Justice: http://aviationjustice.org/

Notes

Websites were accessed 27 March 2013, except where specified.

Introduction

1   Camille Allaz, *The History of Air Cargo and Airmail*, Christopher Foyle Publishing in association with International Air Cargo Association, 2004, pp. 21–2.
2   ACI, 'ACI releases its 2011 World Airport Traffic Report: airport passenger traffic remains strong as cargo traffic weakens', 27 August 2012, www.aci.aero/News/Releases/Most-Recent/2012/08/27/ACI-Releases-its-2011-World-Airport-Traffic-Report-Airport-Passenger-Traffic-Remains-Strong-as-Cargo-Traffic-Weakens
3   Boeing, 'Current market outlook 2012–2031', 2012, www.boeing.com/commercial/cmo/pdf/Boeing_Current_Market_Outlook_2012.pdf; Airbus, *Navigating the Future: Global market forecast 2012–2031*, 2012, www.airbus.com/company/market/forecast/?eID=dam_frontend_push&docID=25773
4   Boeing, 'Current market outlook 2012–2031'.

1 The future of flight

1   ACI, 'World's busiest airports by passenger traffic', http://en.wikipedia.org/wiki/World's_busiest_airports_by_passenger_traffic
2   ACI, 'World's busiest airports by international passenger traffic', http://en.wikipedia.org/wiki/World%27s_busiest_airports_by_international_passenger_traffic
3   Knowatlanta.com, 'Your gateway to the world', www.knowatlanta.com/about_atlanta/airport
4   Zac Goldsmith, 'A third runway at Heathrow would be an off-the-scale betrayal', *Guardian*, 7 September 2012, www.guardian.co.uk/commentisfree/2012/sep/07/third-runway-heathrow-betrayal
5   Andrew Parker, 'Four-runway Heathrow is in panel's options', *Financial Times*, 1 February 2013, www.ft.com/cms/s/0/c3c23bea-6c7b-11e2-b774-00144feab49a.html#axzz2LT3suWXW
6   ACI, 'World's busiest airports by passenger traffic'.

7   Greg Lindsay and John D. Kasarda, *Aerotropolis: The way we'll live next*, Allen Lane, 2011, p. 168.

8   Ivan Gale, 'Fresh delay for Dubai's Maktoum airport', *The National*, 10 February 2011, www.thenational.ae/business/aviation/fresh-delay-for-dubais-maktoum-airport

9   Airport-technology.com, 'Dubai International Airport (DXB, OMDB)', www.airport-technology.com/projects/dubai/

10 *Airport Cities*, 'Al Naboodah, "Laing O'Rourke does a great job"', issue 21, p. 22, www.lnnnews.com/AC/ac21.pdf (accessed 20 January 2009).

11 ACI, 'World's busiest airports by passenger traffic'.

12 Aude Lagorce, 'The airport with an X factor', Market Watch, 24 June 2008, http://articles.marketwatch.com/2008-06-24/news/30700174_1_dubai-world-central-new-airport-new-dubai

13 Ivan Gale, 'Fresh delay for Dubai's Maktoum airport'.

14 ACI, 'World's busiest airports by cargo traffic', http://en.wikipedia.org/wiki/World%27s_busiest_airports_by_cargo_traffic

15 Amana Pipelines, 'Amana Pipelines to construct staging facility and fuel farm at Al Maktoum International Airport', 12 June 2006, www.amanapipelines.com/News_Details.aspx?id=44 (accessed 31 January 2011).

16 Hugh Tomlinson, 'Mall emptied as Dubai Aquarium starts to leak', *The Times*, 26 February 2010, www.timesonline.co.uk/tol/news/world/middle_east/article7041417.ece

17 Amana Holdings, 'Staging facility and fuel farms for Dubai Department of Civil Aviation at Al Maktoum Intl Airport', 30 November 2009, www.amanaholdings.com/ProjectDetails.aspx?id=1528 (accessed 31 January 2011).

18 Nadia Saleem, 'Al Maktoum International airport receives first flight', Gulfnews.com, 21 June 2010, http://gulfnews.com/business/aviation/al-maktoum-international-airport-receives-first-flight-1.644057

19 Alex McWhirter, 'Emirates brings Airbus A345 flagship to Heathrow and Hamburg', *Business Traveller,* 8 March 2007, www.businesstraveller.com/news/emirates-brings-airbus-a345-flagship-to-heathro

20 *Middle East Logistics*, 'Emirates unveils London's newest landmark', 24 July 2008, www.middleastlogistics.com/topnews.asp?id=21853

21 Mark Caswell, 'Emirates launches A380 model at LHR', *Business Traveller*, 24 July 2008, www.businesstraveller.com/news/emirates-launches-a380-model-at-lhr

22 Wendy Leung, 'Large model airplane headed for London', *Inland Valley Daily Bulletin*, 15 June 2008, www.dailybulletin.com/news/ci_9597665

23 *Passenger Terminal Today*, 'California firm builds A380 model for

Heathrow', 18 June 2008, www.passengerterminaltoday.com/news. php?NewsID=6228 (accessed 19 June 2008).

24 John Adams, 'Concorde crash', 2006, http://john-adams.co.uk/ wp-content/uploads/2006/Concorde%20crash.pdf

25 *GreenAir*, 'New carbon efficient eco retirement home unveiled for Concorde at Manchester Airport', 26 February 2009, www.green aironline.com/news.php?viewStory=386

26 Joe Lynam, 'Are the skies turning green?', BBC News, 19 July 2006, http://news.bbc.co.uk/1/hi/business/5195964.stm

27 Adams, 'Concorde crash'.

28 Julian Coman and David Harrison, 'The key question: has Concorde flown too far?', *Telegraph*, 19 June 2001, www.telegraph.co.uk/ news/worldnews/europe/france/1350970/The-key-question-has-Concorde-flown-too-far.html

29 Nicola Clark, 'French court convicts continental in Concorde disaster', *New York Times*, 6 December 2010, www.nytimes.com/2010/12/07/ world/europe/07concorde.html

30 BBC News, 'Heathrow Concorde model removed', 30 March 2007, http://news.bbc.co.uk/1/hi/england/london/6509667.stm

31 Balint 01, 'Supersonic business jet plans', *Airline World*, 10 March 2008, http://airlineworld.wordpress.com/2008/03/10/ supersonic-business-jet-plans/

32 Thomas Black, 'Billionaire joins boomless supersonic-jet quest', Bloomberg, 28 November 2012, www.bloomberg.com/news/2012-11-27/billionaire-joins-quest-for-boomless-supersonic-jets.html

33 John Strickland, 'Four decades of a flying giant', BBC News, 10 February 2009, http://news.bbc.co.uk/1/hi/magazine/7880808.stm

34 Boeing, 'Boeing freighters – leading the air cargo industry', www. boeing.com/commercial/freighters/index.html

35 Globalsecurity.org, 'Antonov-An-225 Mriya (Cossack)', www. globalsecurity.org/military/world/russia/an-225.htm

36 Paul Eisenstein, 'Extreme machines: Antonov-An-225 is the world's biggest plane', *Popular Mechanics*, January 2003, www.popular mechanics.com/science/extreme_machines/1280771.html

37 Memphis Airport, 'World's largest plane flies a heavy load out of Memphis', August 2007, www.memphisairport.org/notes/ mem_2007_aug_an-225.htm

38 Aerospace-technology.com, 'Antonov-An-124 Long-Range Heavy Transport Aircraft, Russia', www.aerospace-technology.com/projects/ antonov/

39 *Payload Asia*, 'Booming Polet faces fleet dilemma', 1 August 2007, www. payloadasia.com/article/booming-polet-faces-fleet-dilemma/940

40 Space-travel.com, 'Hot Bird 10 delivered for multi-payload Ariane 5

February liftoff', 12 January 2009, www.space-travel.com/reports/
Hot_Bird_10_Delivered_For_Multi_Payload_Ariane_5_February_
Liftoff_999.html

41 Ian Sample, 'Oil: the final warning', *New Scientist*, 25 June 2008,
www.science.org.au/nova/newscientist/046ns_001.htm

42 David S. Lee, 'Aviation and climate change: impacts and trends',
Transport and Environment, 7 February 2012, www.transportenviron
ment.org/sites/default/files/media/David_Lee_presentation.pdf

43 AEF, 'Aviation now contributes 4.9% of climate change worldwide',
21 May 2009, www.aef.org.uk/?p=479

44 George Monbiot, *Heat: How to Stop the Planet Burning*, Penguin,
2007, pp. 173–85.

45 Anirvan Chatterjee, 'Last flight', 29 July 2009, www.yearofnoflying.
com/2009/07/last-flight.html

46 Aviation Justice, http://aviationjustice.org/

47 John   Leahy,   Airbus   global   market   forecast   2010–2029,
www.airbus.com/company/market/gmf2010/?eID=dam_
frontend_push&docID=14868

48 Airbus, *Delivering the Future: Market forecast 2011–2030*, p. 6,
www.eads.com/dms/eads/int/en/investor-relations/documents/2011/
Presentations/2011-2030_Airbus_full_book_delivering_the_future.
pdf

49 Sally Cairns and Carey Newson, *Predict and Decide: Aviation, climate
change and UK policy*, Environmental Change Institute, September
2006, www.eci.ox.ac.uk/research/energy/downloads/predictand
decide.pdf

50 George Monbiot, *Heat: How to stop the planet burning*, p. 177.

51 Stefan Gössling, Jean-Paul Ceron, Ghislain Dubois and Michael C.
Hall, 'Hypermobile travellers', pp. 131–47 in Stefan Gössling and
Paul Upham, *Climate Change and Aviation,* Earthscan, 2009.

52 Charles Starmer-Smith, 'Airbus A380 "not as green as it's painted"',
Telegraph, 27 October 2007, www.telegraph.co.uk/travel/738647/
Airbus-A380-not-as-green-as-its-painted.html

53 Chuck Collins, Sarah Anderson, Dedrick Muhammad, Sam Bollier
and Robert Weissman, *High Flyers: How private jet travel is straining
the system, warming the planet, and costing you money*, Institute for
Policy Studies and Essential Action, June 2008, www.ips-dc.org/
files/228/HighFlyersReport.pdf; Cait Weston, 'Examples of rough
estimates of "bizjet" emissions', AEF, December 2008, www.aef.org.
uk/uploads/BizjetEmissions.doc

54 Albawaba, 'Business jet industry looks to 2012 for growth',
9   October   2011,   wwwalbawaba.com/business-jet-industry
-looks-2012-growth-395907

55 Jettogether.com, 'The future of private jet travel', 10 April 2013, www.
    dotwnews.com/on-trend/the-future-of-private-jet-travel (accessed
    11 April 2013).
56 DEFRA, '2008 Guidelines to DEFRA's GHG conversion factors:
    methodology paper for transport emission factors', www.defra.gov.
    uk/environment/business/reporting/pdf/passenger-transport.pdf
    (accessed 12 November 2009).
57 Roger Turney, 'Carbon admissions', *Air Cargo World*, August 2008,
    www.aircargoworld.com/regions/euro_0808.htm (accessed 22
    February 2011).
58 Stefan Gössling and Paul Upham, *Climate Change and Aviation*, pp.
    8–9.
59 AEF, 'What's wrong with the ETS?', May 2009, www.aef.org.uk/
    uploads/What_s_wrong_with_aviation_ETS.pdf
60 Kirsty McGregor, 'Political storm continues to rage over EU ETS',
    Flightglobal, 21 February 2012, www.flightglobal.com/news/articles/
    in-focus-political-storm-continues-to-rage-over-eu-ets-368551/
61 WWF, 'US aviation ETS Prohibition Act "largely irrelevant", say
    environmental groups', 29 November 2012, www.wwf.eu/?206890/
    US-aviation-ETS-Prohibition-Act-largely-irrelevant-say-environ
    mental-groups
62 IATA, 'Halving emissions by 2050 – aviation brings its targets
    to Copenhagen', 8 December 2009, www.iata.org/pressroom/pr/
    Pages/2009-12-08-01.aspx
63 Stefan Gössling and Paul Upham, *Climate Change and Aviation*, p. 8.
64 Paul Steele, '5th Aviation & Environment Summit: Summit Commu-
    niqué', ATAG (Air Transport Action Group), September 2010, www.
    enviro.aero/Content/Upload/File/AES2010_SummitCommunique.
    pdf
65 Airport International , 'Air traffic control improvements could lower
    emissions', 1 February 2010, www.airport-int.com/news/air_traffic_
    control_improvements_could_lower_emissions.html
66 Paul Steele, '5th Aviation & Environment Summit: Summit
    communiqué'.
67 Boeing, 'Long-term market', www.boeing.com/commercial/cmo/
    index.html
68 *Economist*, 'The Dreamliner dreams on', 27 July 2009, www.
    economist.com/blogs/gulliver/2009/07/the_dreamliner_dreams_on
69 BBC News, 'Boeing halts 787 Dreamliner test flights', 10 November
    2010, www.bbc.co.uk/news/business-11728915
70 BBC News, 'Boeing's Dreamliner completes first commercial flight',
    26 October 2011, www.bbc.co.uk/news/business-15456914
71 Jon Ostrower, Andy Pasztor and Yoree Koh, 'Boeing Dreamliners are

grounded world-wide', *Wall Street Journal*, 17 January 2013, http://online.wsj.com/article/SB1000142412788732378370457824621346 1653662.html

72 Jon Ostrower and Hiroyuki Kachi, 'Boeing's Dreamliner returns to commercial service', *Wall Street Journal*, 28 April 2013, http://online.wsj.com/article/SB10001424127887323789704578448751119295 708.html (accessed 28 April 2013).

73 Stephen Trimble, 'Boeing, FAA say 787s in no catastrophic danger from battery overheating', *Flight International*, 29 April 2013, www.flightglobal.com/news/articles/boeing-faa-say-787s-in-no-catastrophic-danger-from-battery-overheating-385145/ (accessed 29 April 2013).

74 Bennett Daviss, 'Green sky thinking', *New Scientist*, 24 February 2007.

75 Jimmy Lee Shreeve, 'Airships: Colonel Blimps' eco-flight credentials', *Telegraph*, 20 June 2008, www.telegraph.co.uk/earth/greenerliving/3344952/Airships-Colonel-Blimps-eco-flight-credentials.html

76 Michael Fitzpatrick, 'Future of flight: fuel for thought', *Independent*, 17 May 2011, www.independent.co.uk/news/science/future-of-flight-fuel-for-thought-2284963.html

77 William Matthews, 'Global observer takes off', *Defense-News*, 23 August 2010, www.defensenews.com/story.php?i=4753382&c=FEA&s=TEC

78 BBC News, 'Solar plane prototype in first test flight', 7 April 2010, http://news.bbc.co.uk/1/hi/8607149.stm

79 Lori Zimmer, 'Solar impulse sun-powered plane successfully completes first international flight', Inhabitat, 14 May 2011, http://inhabitat.com/solar-impulse-sun-powered-plane-successfully-completes-first-international-flight/

80 Adina Solomon, 'Solar-powered aircraft heading to U.S.', *Air Cargo World*, 21 February 2013, www.aircargoworld.com/Air-Cargo-News/2013/02/solar-powered-aircraft-heading-to-u-s/2112372

81 BBC News, '"Eternal" solar plane's records are confirmed', 10 December 2010, www.bbc.co.uk/news/science-environment-12074162

82 John Gillie, 'Boeing 747-8 freighter sets record for weight', *News Tribune*, 24 August 2010, www.thenewstribune.com/2010/08/24/1312293/748-freighter-sets-record-for.html (accessed 24 December 2010).

83 Max Kingsley-Jones, 'Airbus poised to start building new higher weight A380 variant', *Flight International*, 18 May 2010, www.flightglobal.com/articles/2010/05/18/341926/airbus-poised-to-start-building-new-higher-weight-a380.html

2 Feeding the Fuel Tanks

1   AEF, 'Aviation and climate change: can alternative fuel save the day?' October 2008, www.aef.org.uk/uploads/Alternative_fuels_article. pdf
2   GreenAir, 'South Africa's Sasol claims world's first commercial aircraft flight to be fully fuelled with synthetic jet fuel', 23 September 2010, www.greenaironline.com/news.php?viewStory=1095
3   Qatar Airways, 'Word's first commercial passenger flight powered by fuel made from natural gas lands in Qatar', 12 October 2009, www.qatarairways.com/global/en/newsroom/archive/press-release-12Oct09-2.html (accessed 19 January 2010).
4   AMEinfo, 'Qatar Airways leads search for alternative jet fuels', 14 November 2012, www.ameinfo.com/qatar-airways-leads-search-alternative-jet-318998
5   AEF, 'Aviation and climate change: can alternative fuel save the day?'
6   David Strahan, 'Green fuel for the airline industry', *New Scientist*, 13 August 2008, www.science.org.au/nova/newscientist/039ns_005. htm
7   Aditya Chakrabortty, 'Secret report: biofuel caused food crisis', *Guardian*, 3 July 2008, www.guardian.co.uk/environment/2008/jul/03/biofuels.renewableenergy
8   Jim Lane, 'Biofuels mandates around the world', *BiofuelsDigest*, 22 November 2012, www.biofuelsdigest.com/bdigest/2012/11/22/biofuels-mandates-around-the-world-2012/
9   Ryan Tracy, 'U.S. corn-ethanol producers: curb imports from Brazil', *Wall Street Journal*, 30 January 2013, http://online.wsj.com/article/SB10001424127887324610504578273842341906004.html
10 Rachel Smolker, 'A "sustainable" military?', Huffpost, 12 April 2012, www.huffingtonpost.com/rachel-smolker/military-biofuels_b_2239137.html
11 Ruth Kelly et al., 'The hunger grains', Oxfam, September 2012, www. oxfam.org/sites/www.oxfam.org/files/bp161-the-hunger-grains-170912-en.pdf
12 Valentina Pop, 'EU to limit controversial biofuels from 2020', euobeserver.com, 17 October 2012, http://euobserver.com/environment/117557
13 GreenAir, 'EU to contribute 10 million euros towards ITAKA supply chain project to develop European sustainable aviation fuels', 19 December 2012, www.greenaironline.com/news. php?viewStory=1634
14 GreenAir, 'Successful Air New Zealand jatropha biofuel test flight

hailed as a commercial aviation milestone', 6 January 2009, www.greenaironline.com/news.php?viewStory=343

15 FoE Europe, 'Losing the plot', December 2009, www.foeeurope.org/agrofuels/jatropha_in_india.pdf

16 FoE International, 'The jatropha trap?' May 2010, pp. 7–8, www.unece.lsu.edu/biofuels/documents/2010Aug/bf10_02.pdf

17 Servaas van den Bosch, 'Jatropha: from buzz to bust in Namibia', AlertNet, 1 June 2010, www.alertnet.org/db/an_art/60167/2010/05/1-124301-1.htm (accessed 8 June 2010).

18 Nick Wadhams, 'How a biofuel "miracle" ruined Kenyan farmers', *Time*, 4 October 2009, www.time.com/time/world/article/0,8599,1927538,00.html

19 ActionAid, Birdlife International, Nature Kenya, RSPB, 'Jatropha biofuels in Dakatcha, Kenya – the climate consequences', 10 March 2011, www.actionaid.org.uk/doc_lib/dakatcha_biofuels_report_march_10_2011_-_final_tr1_and_2_mc.pdf

20 Emmanuel K. Dogbevi, 'Scanfuel's Ghana jatropha plantation wipes out settlements, farms', *Ghana Business News*, 23 February 2010, www.ghanabusinessnews.com/2010/02/23/scanfuel%e2%80%99s-ghana-jatropha-plantation-wipes-out-settlements-farms/

21 FoE, 'Jatropha: wonder crop? Experience from Swaziland', May 2009, www.foe.co.uk/resource/reports/jatropha_wonder_crop.pdf

22 FoE International, 'Jatropha: money doesn't grow on trees', December 2010, p. 12, www.foei.org/en/resources/publications/pdfs/2011/jatropha-money-doesnt-grow-on-trees

23 Jon R. Luoma, 'Hailed as a miracle biofuel, jatropha falls short of hype', *Guardian*, 5 May 2009, www.guardian.co.uk/environment/2009/may/05/jatropha-biofuels-food-crops

24 Geert Ritsema, 'Biokerosene: take-off in the wrong direction', Milieudefensie and FoE Netherlands, February 2012, http://milieudefensie.nl/publicaties/rapporten/biokerosene-take-off-in-the-wrong-direction

25 Andreas Becker and Sam Edmonds, 'Lufthansa suspends biofuel test flights', *DW*, 12 January 2012, www.dw.de/lufthansa-suspends-biofuel-test-flights/a-15661617

26 Gary Pinnell, 'County still waiting for biofuels', *Highlands Today*, 21 March 2010, http://www2.highlandstoday.com/content/2010/mar/21/la-county-still-waiting-for-biofuels/ (accessed 25 March 2010).

27 David Biello, 'First passenger flight powered by biofuel – but are the petroleum alternatives ready to take off?' *Scientific American*, 3 December 2009, www.scientificamerican.com/article.cfm?id=are-jet-biofuels-ready-for-takeoff

28 RenewableEnergyWorld.com, 'Camelina biofuel powers US

Navy F/A-18 test flight', 26 April 2010, www.renew ableenergyworld.com/rea/news/article/2010/04 camelina- biofuel-powers-us-navy-fa-18-test-flight

29 *Currents*, 'From seed to supersonic', Winter 2011, http://climate solutions.org/programs/aviation-biofuels-initiative/ seed-to-supersonic

30 Businesswire.com, 'Camelina-based biofuel breaks sound barrier on U.S. Air Force F-22 Raptor test flight', 21 March 2011, www.businesswire.com/news/home/20110321006869/en/ Camelina-Based-Biofuel-Breaks-Sound-Barrier-U.S.-Air

31 Marketwire, 'AltAir fuels partners with USDA to produce camelina sativa', 26 July 2011, www.environmental-expert.com/news/ altair-fuels-partners-with-usda-to-spur-camelina-growth-249521/

32 Naval Air Systems Command, 'NAVAIR's biofuel efforts energize Green Strike Group during RIMPAC exercise', 18 July 2012, www.navair.navy.mil/index.cfm?fuseaction=home. PrintNewsStory&id=5067

33 Carin Hall, 'Senate supports U.S. military, business with biofuel vote', Energydigital.com, 30 November 2012, www.energy digital.com/green_technology/senate-supports-us-military-business-with-biofuel-vote

34 Gabe Starosta, 'The Air Force's fuel problem', Airforce-magazine. com, July 2012, www.airforce-magazine.com/MagazineArchive/ Pages/2012/July%202012/0712fuel.aspx

35 Sustainable Oils, 'Three new camelina varieties released', www. susoils.com/camelina/varieties.php

36 US Census Bureau, *Statistical Abstract of the United States: 2012*, p. 536, www.census.gov/prod/2011pubs/12statab/agricult.pdf

37 Andrew Brandess, Catherine Keske and Can Erbil, 'Gold-of-pleasure', US Association for Energy Economics, 2011, http://dialogue.usaee.org/index.php?option= com_content&view=article&id=132&Itemid=364

38 Biofuelwatch, 'Aviation biofuels in 2011', www.biofuelwatch.org.uk/ docs/aviation_biofuels.pdf

39 Oilprice.com, 'A look at US military energy consumption', 8 June 2011, http://oilprice.com/Energy/Energy-General/A-Look-At-US-Mili-tary-Energy-Consumption.html

40 Smolker, 'A "sustainable" military?'

41 Julie Ingwersen, 'In aftermath of drought, U.S. corn movement turns upside down', Reuters, 29 October 2012, www. reuters.com/article/2012/10/29/us-usa-drought-corn-id USBRE89S06Y20121029

42 Smolker, 'A "sustainable" military?'

43 David Biello, 'Air algae: U.S. biofuel flight relies on weeds and pond scum', *Scientific American*, 7 January 2009, www.scientificamerican.com/article.cfm?id=air-algae-us-biofuel-flight-on-weeds-and-pond-scum

44 Damian Kahya and Richard Anderson, 'Algae fuel firms face moment of truth', BBC News, 30 November 2011, www.bbc.co.uk/news/business-15947205

45 www.enviro.aero, 'JAL flight brings aviation one step closer to using biofuel', 30 January 2009, www.enviro.aero/Aviationindustry environmentalnews.aspx?NID=316

46 *Flightglobal*, 'Airframers step up biofuel efforts ahead of Farnborough', 12 July 2010, www.flightglobal.com/articles/2010/07/12/343776/farnborough-airframers-step-up-biofuel-efforts-ahead-of.html

47 *GreenAir*, 'EADS undertakes first aircraft flight powered by algae-derived biofuel and signs Brazilian production venture', 7 June 2010, www.greenaironline.com/news.php?viewStory=843

48 *GreenAir*, 'Airbus and EADS join Chinese venture to develop algae-based jet fuels, with demo flight planned for 2013', 12 November 2012, www.greenaironline.com/news.php?viewStory=1623

49 Katie Howell, 'Is algae worse than corn for biofuels?', *Scientific American*, 22 January 2010, www.scientificamerican.com/article.cfm?id=algae-biofuel-growth-environmental-impact

50 Richard Coltharp, 'Growing green in the desert', *Las Cruces Bulletin*, 31 August 2012, www.mveda.com/blog/2012/08/growing-green-in-the-desert/

51 Solazyme, 'Solazyme completes MH 60S Seahawk helicopter test flight on a 50/50 blend of algal derived SolajetHRJ-5 jet fuel', 20 June 2011, www.solazyme.com/media/2011-06-20

52 David Louie, 'Aviation companies use local biofuel', Abc, 8 November 2011, http://abclocal.go.com/kgo/story?section=news/business&id=8424255

53 David Biello, 'Bio-jet fuel struggles to balance profit with sustainability', *Scientific American*, 5 December 2011, www.scientificamerican.com/article.cfm?id=bio-jet-fuel-struggles-to

54 Biofuelwatch, 'Biofuels for aviation: more future land grabbing and deforestation for agrofuels to justify today's airport expansion?', Biofuelwatch, June 2009, www.biofuelwatch.org.uk/docs/aviation_biofuels_article.pdf

55 Katie Fehrenbacher, 'For algae fuel, 2013 could be a make-or-break year', *Business Week*, 18 January 2013, www.businessweek.com/articles/2013-01-18/for-algae-fuel-2013-could-be-a-make-or-break-year

56 GreenAir, 'Alaska Air prepares for a series of used cooking oil biofuel

flights using Boeing and Bombardier aircraft', 8 November 2011, www.greenaironline.com/news.php?viewStory=1556

57 FoE, 'Thomson Airways launches biofuel flights', 6 October 2011, www.foe.co.uk/resource/press_releases/thomson_biofuels_06102011.html

58 Dominic Gates, 'Alaska Air starts test of biofuel-powered flights', *Seattle Times*, 8 November 2011, http://seattletimes.nwsource.com/html/businesstechnology/2016719598_alaska09.html

59 Lukas Ross, *Eco-Skies: The Global Rush for Aviation Biofuel*, Oakland Institute, pp. 8–9, www.oaklandinstitute.org/sites/oaklandinstitute.org/files/OI_Report_Eco-Skies.pdf

60 Jim Lane, 'Jet stream: *Biofuels Digest* special report on aviation biofuels', *BiofuelsDigest*, 3 March 2010, www.biofuels.digest.com/bdigest/2010/03/03/jet-stream-biofuels-digest-special-report-on-aviation-biofuels/

61 *Helsingin Sanomat*, 'Finnair postpones introduction of biofuel', 31 January 2011, www.hs.fi/english/article/Finnair+postpones+introduction+of+biofuel/1135263446292

62 *BusinessGreen*, 'Virgin Australia to tap native eucalyptus trees for jet biofuels', 6 June 2011, www.businessgreen.com/bg/news/2086052/virgin-australia-tap-native-eucalyptus-trees-jet-biofuels

63 *Wall Street Journal*, 'The cellulosic ethanol debacle', 14 December 2011, http://online.wsj.com/article/SB10001424052970204012004577072470158115782.html

64 Kevin Bullis, 'To survive, some biofuels companies give up on biofuels', *MIT Technology Review*, 11 December 2011, www.technologyreview.com/energy/39371/

65 Green Car Congress, 'LanzaTech receives $3M contract from FAA for alcohol-to-jet project; one of 8 awards worth total of $7.7M', 1 December 2011, www.greencarcongress.com/2011/12/faa-20111201.html

66 Bruce Dorminey, 'Flying on woody biomass and camelina: consortium seeks biofuel answers', RenewableEnergyWorld.com, 21 August 2012, www.renewableenergyworld.com/rea/news/article/2012/08/flying-on-woody-biomass-and-camelina-consortium-seeks-biofuel-answers

67 Almuth Ernsting, 'Plantation expansion and forest degradation for wood bioenergy in Europe', p. 5 in Global Forest Coalition, 'Wood based bioenergy: the green lie', May 2010, www.globalforestcoalition.org/wp-content/uploads/2010/10/briefing-paper-bioenergy_final_1.pdf

68 Smolker, 'A "sustainable" military?'

69 Embraer, 'Azul Brazilian Airlines makes demonstration flight

with renewable jet fuel produced from Brazilian sugarcane', 19 June 2012, www.embraer.com/en-US/ImprensaEventos/Press-releases/noticias/Pages/Azul-Linhas-Aereas-realiza-voo-experimental-bem-sucedido-com-biocombustivel.aspx

70 Byogy, 'Byogy reaches significant milestones in delivering renewable jet fuel derived from ethanol', 14 March 2012, http://byogy.com/pdf/Byogy%20Release%203-15-2012%20distribution%20copy.pdf

71 Mark Harden, 'Air Force tests jet using Gevo biofuel', *Denver Business Journal*, 3 July 2012, www.bizjournals.com/denver/news/2012/07/03/air-force-tests-jet-using-gevo-biofuel.html

72 Justin Doom, 'Gevo gets patent for system that missed goal at Minnesota plant', *Business Week*, 9 October 2012, www.businessweek.com/news/2012-10-09/gevo-gets-patent-for-system-that-missed-goal-at-minnesota-plant

73 ASDNews, 'First solely-biofuel jet flight raises clean travel hopes', 8 November 2012, www.asdnews.com/news-46032/First_solely-biofuel_jet_flight_raises_clean_travel_hopes.htm

74 Barb Glen, 'Alta. firm targets more carinata acres', *Western Producer*, 21 December 2012, www.producer.com/2012/12/alta-firm-targets-more-carinata-acres%E2%80%A9/

75 IATA, 'Fact sheet: alternative fuels', December 2012, www.iata.org/pressroom/facts_figure s/fact_sheets/pages/alt-fuels.aspx

76 European Commission, '2 million tons per year: a performing biofuels supply chain for EU aviation', June 2011, http://ec.europa.eu/energy/technology/initiatives/doc/20110622_biofuels_flight_path_technical_paper.pdf

77 Megan Kuhn, 'Salicornia producer preps for delayed Interjet biofuel demo', *Flightglobal*, 29 January 2010, www.flightglobal.com/articles/2010/01/29/337830/salicornia-producer-preps-for-delayed-interjet-biofuel.html

78 FoE Europe, 'Flying in the face of the facts', June 2011, www.foeeurope.org/publications/2011/FoEE_Flying_in_the_face_of_facts_June2011.pdf

79 IATA, 'Fact sheet: alternative fuels'.

3 Local Environmental Impacts

1 Debi Wagner, *Over My Head*, Trafford Publishing, 2011, p. xi.
2 Wagner, *Over My Head*, pp. xii–xv.
3 Wagner, *Over My Head*, p. xi.
4 Wagner, *Over My Head*, pp. 161–6.
5 Wagner, *Over My Head*, pp. 161–4.
6 Wagner, *Over My Head*, pp. 162–3.

7   Wagner, *Over My Head*, p. 165.

8   Morgan Bettex, 'MIT study finds aircraft emissions at cruise altitude contribute to 8,000 premature deaths per year worldwide', *GreenAir*, 8 October 2010, www.greenaironline.com/news.php?viewStory=947

9   John Stewart with Arline L. Bronzaft, Francis McManus, Nigel Rodgers and Val Weedon, *Why Noise Matters*, Earthscan, 2011.

10 Stewart et al., *Why Noise Matters*, pp. 102–4.

11 Marcus Berry, 'Swiss study links aircraft noise to heart attacks', Swisster.ch, 5 October 2010, www.swisster.ch/guide/health/swiss-health-topic/swiss-study-links-aircraft-noise-heart-attacks.html (accessed 18 October 2010).

12 James Randerson, 'Night flight noise linked to hypertension', *Guardian*, 13 February 2008, www.guardian.co.uk/science/2008/feb/13/medicalresearch.health

13 Advertising Standards Authority, 'ASA adjudication on Boeing United Kingdom Ltd', 9 January 2008, www.asa.org.uk/ASA-action/Adjudications/2008/1/Boeing-United-Kingdom-Ltd/TF_ADJ_43767.aspx

14 Stewart et al., *Why Noise Matters*, p. 104.

15 Aviation Safety Network, http://aviation-safety.net/database/record.php?id=20120402-0

16 Dan Coombs, 'Heathrow Airport fined for causing death of hundreds of fish', *Uxbridge Gazette*, 17 May 2010, www.uxbridge-gazette.co.uk/west-london-news/local-uxbridge-news/2010/05/17/heathrow-airport-fined-for-causing-death-of-hundreds-of-fish-113046-26463113/

17 EPA, *Source Water Protection Practices Bulletin*, August 2010, www.epa.gov/safewater/sourcewater/pubs/fs_swpp_deicingair.pdf

18 Associated Press, 'Portland airport's de-icing system harms fish', 17 October 2006, www.msnbc.msn.com/id/15308715/ns/travel-news/t/portland-airports-de-icing-system-harms-fish/

19 Northwest Public Radio, 'Portland International deals with de-icing waste', 19 January 2012, http://nwpublicmedia.typepad.com/nwpr_news/2012/01/portland-international-deals-with-de-icing-waste.html

20 John Howell, 'Airport, DEM have agreement on chemical runoff into brook', *Warwick Beacon*, 29 December 2011, www.warwickonline.com/stories/Airport-DEM-have-agreement-on-chemical-runoff-into-brook,66267

21 Rhode Island Airport Corporation, 'RIDEM and RIAC reach agreement', 21 December 2011, www.pvdairport.com/main.aspx?guid=5efd8a43-da73-4fac-bcce-7c1a1f7fc9fc

22 Monica Dias, 'Cincinnati Airport pollution spreads 3 miles',

Cincinnati Post, 9 May 2001, http://archives.californiaaviation.org/airport/msg14924.html

23 Brenna R. Kelly and Dan Klepal, 'Silent streams', *Cincinnati Enquirer*, 7 March 2004, www.enquirer.com/editions/2004/03/07/loc_kycreeks07.html

24 Tom Valtin, 'Water sentinels stop toxic antifreeze runoff', Sierra Club, February 2005, www.sierraclub.org/planet/200502/antifreeze.asp

25 Don Chapman, Jason Sundrup and Kevin Flynn, 'Deicing fluid and stormwater management at Cincinnati/Northern Kentucky International Airport', Airports Council International Deicing Management Conference, 8 July 2009, http://74.209.241.69/static/entransit/Chapman.pdf

26 Ken Kolker, 'New airport plan: dump de-icer in river', Wood TV, 9 September 2011, www.woodtv.com/dpp/news/local/kent_county/New-airport-plan%3A-Dump-de-icer-in-river

27 Andrea Gusty, 'Airport's deicing pollutant likely "stressing aquatic life" in Cook Inlet', KTVA, 2 February 2011, www.ktva.com/news/eye-team-investigates/Airports-Deicing-Pollutant-Likely-Stressing-Aquatic-Life-in-Cook-Inlet-115140004.html

28 Alaska Center for the Environment, 'De-icing at the Anchorage Airport', http://akcenter.org/sustainable-communities/airport-issues/de-icing-at-the-anchorage-airport/?searchterm=glycol

29 Carroll McCormick, 'Infrared deicing: giving glycol a run for its money', *Wings*, www.wingsmagazine.com/content/view/1325/38/

30 Brad Sewell, 'Proposed JFK expansion would harm Jamaica Bay', NRDC, 18 March 2011, http://switchboard.nrdc.org/blogs/bsewell/proposed_jfk_expansion_would_h.html

31 *Crain's New York Business*, 'JFK deicing's toll on Jamaica Bay', 12 January 2011, www.airportbusiness.com/web/online/Top-News-Headlines/JFK-deicings-toll-on-Jamaica-Bay/1$14779

32 K. Manikandan and T. Madhavan, 'Subways in Chennai flooded, suburbs inundated', *The Hindu*, 10 November 2005, www.hindu.com/2005/11/10/stories/2005111005360600.htm

33 T. S. Shankar, 'Rain delays flights, airport flooded', *The Hindu*, 4 December 2005, www.hindu.com/2005/12/04/stories/2005120407940600.htm

34 K. Manikandan, 'Airport wall collapses', *The Hindu,* 8 December 2005, www.hindu.com/2005/12/08/stories/2005120814880400.htm

35 V. Ayyappan, 'Airport wall floods surrounding areas', Save People from Chennai Airport Expansion, 30 November 2008, http://chennaiairportexpansionaffectedpeople.blogspot.com/2008/11/airport-wall-floods-surrounding-areas.html

36 *Times of India*, 'Chennai weather: 50 houses flooded in Nandambakkam', 28 November 2011, http://articles.times ofindia.indiatimes.com/2011-11-28/chennai/30449925_ 1_secondary-runway-adyar-river-water-level

37 Vaishnavi C. Sekhar, 'How the airport ate up Mithi river', *Times of India*, 7 August 2005, http://articles.timesofindia.indiatimes.com/2005-08-07/mumbai/ 27836981_1_mithi-river-kranti-nagar-runway

38 Nidhi Jamwal, 'Navi Mumbai airport: a silent conspiracy', *Down To Earth*, 3 July 2010, www.downtoearth.org.in/node/1497

39 Nidhi Jamwal, 'Open floodgates', *Down To Earth*, 31 May 2006, www.downtoearth.org.in/node/7807

40 Sharad Vyas, 'Changing Mithi's course will help check floods: IIT', *Times of India*, 22 April 2009, http://articles.timesofindia.indiatimes.com/2009-04-22/mumbai/ 28034044_1_iit-b-technology-bombay-mial

41 Debabrata Das, 'Mumbai airport runway won't be hit by flooding this year: MIAL', *Hindu Business Line*, 10 May 2011, www.thehindu businessline.com/todays-paper/tp-economy/article2032936.ece

42 Soubhik Mitra, 'Mithi river less likely to flood Mumbai airport this monsoon', *Hindustan Times*, 3 May 2012, www.hindustantimes. com/India-news/Mumbai/Mithi-river-less-likely-to-flood-Mumbai-airport-this-monsoon/Article1-849825.aspx

43 Jamwal, 'Navi Mumbai airport: a silent conspiracy'.

44 Kalpana Sharma, 'Did Mumbai learn nothing from 2005?', Info Change India, July 2010, http://infochangeindia.org/Urban-India/ Cityscapes/Did-Mumbai-learn-nothing-from-2005.html

45 Jamwal, 'Navi Mumbai airport: a silent conspiracy'.

46 DNAIndia, 'Jairam Ramesh counters Praful Patel's charge on Navi Mumbai airport project', 6 July 2010, www.dnaindia.com/india/ report_jairam-ramesh-counters-praful-patel-s-charge-on-navi-mumbai-airport-project_1406215

47 Sandeep Ashar, 'Another green nod for airport in Navi Mumbai', *Times of India*, 11 May 2012, http://articles.timesofindia. indiatimes.com/2012-05-11/mumbai/31668531_1_airport-site-navi-mumbai-international-airport-airport-work

48 Suvarnabhumi Airport, 'Flood dyke sinking, in need of repair', 20 July 2008, www.airportsuvarnabhumi.com/flood-dyke-sinking-in-need-of-repair/

49 AsiaViews, 'Airport blamed for longer floods', 21 December 2010, www.asiaviews.org/index.php?option=com_content&view= article&id=25119:reportalias6294&catid=2:regional-news-a-special-reports&Itemid=9

50 *Bangkok Post*, 'Flood prevention at Suvarnabhumi', 27 October

2010, www.bangkokpost.com/breakingnews/203460/flood-prevention-measures-at-airport (accessed 10 November 2010).

51 James Hookway, 'Thai airport offers a flood refuge', *Wall Street Journal*, 1 November 2011, http://online.wsj.com/article/SB100014 2405297020370750457700969269780610.html

52 BBC News, 'Bangkok's Don Muang airport reopens after floods', 6 March 2012, www.bbc.co.uk/news/world-asia-17267833

53 Hila Bouzaglou, 'Airport fuel spill: how it happened', *Mail and Guardian Online*, 12 December 2006, www.mg.co.za/article/2006-12-12-airport-fuel-spill-how-it-happened

54 Today'sTMJ4.com, 'Pipeline leaking fuel at Mitchell International Airport reportedly fixed', 23 February 2012, www.todaystmj4.com/news/local/140222953.html

55 Trevor Yearwood, 'Shell out time!' *Daily Nation*, www.gcmonitor.org/article.php?id=464

56 NATIONews.com, 'Shell, farmers reach deal', 1 August 2010, www.nationnews.com/articles/view/Shell-farmers-reach-deal/

57 Noel Gries, 'Fuel leak being cleaned up at New York's JFK Airport', *Energy Pipeline News*, 30 March 2009, http://energypipelinenews.blogspot.com/search/label/JFK%20Airport

58 Environment Agency, 'Company fined for Heathrow groundwater pollution', October 2010, www.environment-agency.gov.uk/news/123720.aspx (accessed 12 October 2010).

59 US Department of the Interior's (DOI) Natural Resource Damage Assessment and Restoration Program (NRDA Restoration Program), 'Final damage assessment and restoration plan for the July 2007 Jet A fuel discharge into Turkey Creek in Walker County, Texas', April 2009, http://restoration.doi.gov/Case_Docs/Restoraton_Docs/plans/TX_Explorer_Pipeline_Turkey_Creek_RP_04-09.pdf (accessed 24 June 2010).

60 Sharon Udasin, 'Tractor causes 1.5-million-liter jet fuel spill in Negev', Jpost.com, 30 June 2011, www.jpost.com/Sci-Tech/Article.aspx?id=227219

61 Tracey Hancock, 'Fuel system commissioning underway', *Engineering News*, 26 March 2010, http://www.engineeringnews.co.za/article/king-shaka-fuelled-for-takeoff-2010-03-26

62 Airport-technology.com, 'King Shaka International Airport, Durban, South Africa', www.airport-technology.com/projects/king-shaka/; Buddy Naidu and Simpiwe Piliso, 'Airport in cover-up of serious fuel line leaks', *Sunday Times Live*, 9 May 2010, www.timeslive.co.za/sundaytimes/article440294.ece/Airport-in-cover-up-of-serious-fuel-line-leaks

63 Robert Brauchle, 'Drum jet fuel leak cleanup slated', Watertown-

dailytimes.com, 13 May 2010, www.watertowndailytimes.com/
article/20100513/NEWS03/305139955/-1//NEWS03

64 Koat.com, 'New test checks water near KAFB fuel leak', 30 August
2010, www.koat.com/news/24820219/detail.html (accessed 23
September 2010).

65 Jeri Clausing, 'Kirtland jet fuel spill may reach 24M gallons', *Air
Force Times*, 23 May 2012, www.airforcetimes.com/news/2012/05/
ap-kirtland-jet-fuel-spill-may-reach-24-million-gallons-052312/

66 *Washington Times*, '2 convicted in JFK airport explosion plot', 2
August 2010, www.washingtontimes.com/news/2010/August/2/ny-
jury-convicts-2-jfk-airport-tank-blast-plot/ (accessed 24 September
2010).

67 *Popular Mechanics*, 'JFK terror plot reality check: why jet fuel pipelines
are tough targets', www.popularmechanics.com/science/4217760

68 *Bangkok Post*, 'Oil depot hit in grenade attack', 22 April 2010, www.
bangkokpost.com/news/politics/36403/oil-depot-hit-in-grenade-
attack (accessed 24 September 2010).

69 Chris Green, 'Final cost of Buncefield fire could hit £1bn', *Independent*, 12 December 2008, www.independent.co.uk/news/uk/
home-news/final-cost-of-buncefield-fire-could-hit-1631bn-1063051.
html (accessed 7 September 2010).

70 Buncefield Investigation, *The Buncefield Incident 11 December 2005:
The final report of the Major Incident Investigation Board*, Vol. 1, 2008,
p. 27, www.buncefieldinvestigation.gov.uk/reports/volume1.pdf

71 Buncefield Investigation, *Control of Major Hazards Directive: Major
Accident: Short Report – amended, 10 July 2006*, www.buncefield
investigation.gov.uk/reports/rep080306.pdf

72 Buncefield Investigation, *Buncefield Incident final report*, Vol. 1, p. 27.

73 Paul Lewis and Terry Macalister, 'Buncefield fire: Oil storage firm
found guilty of safety breaches', *Guardian*, 18 June 2010, www.
guardian.co.uk/uk/2010/jun/18/buncefield-fire-oil-company-guilty

74 Paul Haste, 'Total stands accused over worker death', *Morning Star*,
30 June 2010, www.morningstaronline.co.uk/news/content/view/
full/92204

75 Dennis Rivera, 'Feds probe cause of Puerto Rico fuel depot fire',
Msnbc.com, 25 October 2009, www.msnbc.msn.com/id/33472140

76 Reuters, 'Fuel leak caused Puerto Rican depot blast – FBI', 30
October 2009, www.alertnet.org/thenews/newsdesk/N30416826.
htm

77 Expressindia.com, 'IOC Jaipur depot still blazing', 3 July 2009,
www.expressindia.com/latest-news/IOC-Jaipur-depot-still-blazing-
fuel-worth-140150-cr-gutted/535071/

78 GCCapitalIdeas.com, 'Explosions and fire at oil storage depot, Jaipur,

India', 30 October 2009, www.gccapitalideas.com/2009/10/30/explosions-and-fire-at-oil-storage-depot-jaipur-india/

79 Apurva, 'Indian Oil GM, 8 others held for Jaipur depot fire that killed 11', Indianexpress.com, 3 July 2010, www.indianexpress.com/news/indian-oil-gm-8-others-held-for-jaipur-depo/641758/

80 Peter Holley and Michelle Mondo, 'South Side refinery fire leaves mess', MySA, 6 May 2010, www.mysanantonio.com/news/Fire_burning_on_South_Side.html (accessed 2 November 2010).

81 Jordan Guinn, 'A pipeline under Lodi', Lodinews.com, 21 September 2010, www.lodinews.com/news/article_2aaba1d1-eacd-5c59-b25b-3fd64ee045f9.html

82 Sfist, 'Explosion in Walnut Creek', 10 November 2004, http://sfist.com/2004/11/10/explosion_in_walnut_creek.php

83 Frank Mortimer, 'Halo over Foxboro', *Foxboro Reporter*, 8 July 2010, www.foxbororeporter.com/articles/2010/07/12/news/7626692.txt

84 *Times of India*, 'Four from state killed in Erode bus accident', 8 November 2011, http://timesofindia.indiatimes.com/city/bangalore/Four-from-state-killed-in-Erode-bus-accident/articleshow/10650370.cms

4 Threats to Wildlife and Farmland

1 Animal Welfare Institute, 'Bird strikes on aircraft – what's the risk?' Winter 2010, www.awionline.org/ht/display/ContentDetails/i/19142/pid/19130 (accessed 15 February 2011).

2 Animal Welfare Institute, 'Bird strikes on aircraft'.

3 CBSNews.com, 'FAA: bird strikes way up at big airports', 24 April 2009, www.cbsnews.com/stories/2009/04/24/national/main4966084.shtml

4 Associated Press, 'Bird–plane strike incidents may pass 10,000, a first', Fox News, 12 January 2010, www.foxnews.com/story/0,2933,582817,00.html

5 Verena Dobnik, 'Bird strikes still a concern at New York airports', USAToday.com, 30 June 2010, http://travel.usatoday.com/flights/2010-06-30-new-york-airport-geese_N.htm

6 Airportbusiness.com, 'The goose menace at JFK', 6 July 2010, www.airportbusiness.com/online/article.jsp?siteSection=1&id=37787 (accessed 19 July 2010).

7 Isolde Raftery, '400 park geese die, for human fliers' sake', *New York Times*, 13 July 2010, www.nytimes.com/2010/07/13/nyregion/13geese.html

8 Vera Chinese, 'USDA bird-strike prevention plan would cull half-dozen bird species in Jamaica Bay', *New York Daily News*,

26 May 2012, www.nydailynews.com/new-york/usda-bird-strike-prevention-plan-cull-half-dozen-bird-species-jamaica-bay-article-1.1085167

9 Jason Sweeney, 'Birds killed to protect planes at Oakland airport', *Oakland Tribune*, 31 December 2009, www.insidebayarea.com/dailyreview/localnews/ci_14096374

10 Port of Oakland, 'Millions will be touched by art at Oakland International Airport', www.portofoakland.com/portnyou/publicar.asp (accessed 10 September 2010).

11 Philadelphia Airport, 'Artwork premieres in the New International Terminal A-West', 13 June 2003, www.phl.org/news/030613.html (accessed 22 February 2011).

12 Philadelphia Airport, 'Art and exhibitions – current', www.phl.org/art_current.html (accessed 22 February 2011).

13 Linda Lloyd, 'Philadelphia airport efforts minimize bird damage', Airportbusiness.com, 12 January 2011, www.airportbusiness.com/web/online/Top-News-Headlines/Philadelphia-airport-efforts-minimize-bird-damage/1$27523 (accessed 7 March 2011).

14 Tampa Airport, 'Public art programme', www.tampaairport.com/about/guest_services/public_art/index.asp#rotating

15 Myfoxtampabay.com, 'Protecting planes from bird strikes', 14 June 2009, www.myfoxtampabay.com/dpp/news/local/Protecting_planes_bird_strikes_061309 (accessed 17 May 2010).

16 Bill Read, 'Airport bird dispersal systems', *Airport Suppliers*, 13 September 2010, www.airport-suppliers.com/supplier/Scarecrow_BioAcoustic_Systems_Ltd/press_release/Air port_Bird_Dispersal_Systems/

17 NZExporter, 'NZ grass which makes bird sick wins DuPont award', 23 May 2011, http://nzexporter.co.nz/2011/05/nz-grass-which-makes-bird-sick-wins-dupont-award/ (accessed 25 May 2011).

18 Bird Radar Blog, 'FAA airport circular on avian radars for birdstrikes released', 27 November 2010, www.birdradar.com/?p=282 (accessed 2 February 2011).

19 Janine Erasmus, 'Airport flips the birds', Iafrica.com, 10 April 2010, http://travel.iafrica.com/flights/2356160.htm

20 Airports Company South Africa, 'King Shaka International Airport's new bird control dog', 26 March 2012, https://www.ewt.org.za/FORYOU/LatestNews/tabid/85/EntryId/65/Default.aspx (accessed 4 April 2012).

21 Stop Expansion of Manchester Airport, stopmanchesterairport.blogspot.com/

22 Ken Peters, 'Protest with a bite', Thespec.com, 12 October 2010, www.thespec.com/news/local/article/266408--protest-with-a-bite

23 Hans-Martin Niemeier, *Expanding Airport Capacity under Constraints in Large Urban Areas: The German Experience*, International Transport Forum/OECD, 2013, p. 15. www.internationaltransportforum.org/jtrc/DiscussionPapers/DP201304.pdf

24 Airport-technology.com, 'Frankfurt International Airport (FRA/EDDF), Germany', www.airport-technology.com/projects/frankfurt/ (accessed 8 July 2010); *The Local,* 'Frankfurt airport expansion approved', 21 August 2009, www.thelocal.de/money/20090821-21409.html

25 Airport Watch, 'Frankfurt Airport', www.airportwatch.org.uk/?page_id=7420

26 Airport Watch, 'Large demonstration in Paris against building of airport at Nantes', www.airportwatch.org.uk/?p=4694

27 John Stewart, 'Nantes – the French Heathrow?' *Airport Watch Bulletin*, July 2011, www.aef.org.uk/downloads/AirportWatch_bulletin_July2011.pdf

28 Airport Watch, 'Nantes Airport news', www.airportwatch.org.uk/?page_id=6149

29 Land Over Landings, www.landoverlandings.com

30 Pinaki Roy and Pankaj Karmakar, 'Major wetland to vanish for airport', *Daily Star*, 29 December 2010, www.thedailystar.net/newDesign/news-details.php?nid=167921 (accessed 1 March 2011).

31 *Daily Star,* 'Locals protest construction of airport in Munshiganj', 27 December 2010, www.thedailystar.net/newDesign/latest_news.php?nid=27627 (accessed 1 March 2011).

32 BBC News, 'Bangladesh: clashes over Dhaka airport plans', 31 January 2011, www.bbc.co.uk/news/world-south-asia-12325667

33 Bdnews24.com, '3 sites being considered for airport', 22 April 2011, www.bdnews24.com/details.php?cid=2&id=193761

34 Stephan Hauser, 'Field of dreams – filled with concrete', *Tokyo Journal*, February 2000, www.tokyo.to/backissues/feb00/tj0200p6,7,8,9/index.html

35 House of Japan, 'Narita runway to open fully', 24 February 2011, www.houseofjapan.com/local/narita-runway-to-open-fully

36 Hiroshi Matsubara, 'Runway now in land holdouts' backyard', *Japan Times*, 28 May 2002, http://search.japantimes.co.jp/cgi-bin/nn20020528b7.html

37 House of Japan, 'Narita runway to open fully'.

38 Daniel P. Aldrich, *Site Fights: Divisive facilities and civil society in Japan and the West*, Cornell University Press, May 2010, pp. 81–3.

39 Overseas Coastal Area Development Institute of Japan, 'Design-build procurement scheme for the expansion of the Tokyo International Airport', www.ocdi.or.jp/en/en-pdf/Haneda1-2.pdf

40 Philippa Fogarty, 'Anger simmers over Okinawa base burden', BBC News, 8 October 2010, www.bbc.co.uk/news/world-asia-pacific-11404406

41 Isabel Reynolds, 'Japan PM says finalizing plan to end U.S. base row', Reuters, 27 April 2010, www.reuters.com/article/2010/04/27/us-japan-politics-usa-idUSTRE63Q0OI20100427

42 Anjuli Bhargava, 'Connectivity tops new Hyderabad airport agenda', *Business Standard*, 13 February 2008, www.business-standard.com/india/storypage.php?autono=313583 (accessed 20 August 2010).

43 R. Uma Maheshwari, 'Losing ground', *Frontline*, 2010, http://hindu.com/fline/fl2702/stories/20100129270209700.htm

44 Divya Gandhi, 'No compensation for these airport-displaced tillers', *The Hindu*, 19 April 2009, www.hindu.com/2009/04/19/stories/2009041950310100.htm

45 *The Hindu*, 'Police open fire in air to control agitating farmers', 16 February 2009, www.hindu.com/2009/02/16/stories/2009021653330600.htm

46 *The Hindu*, 'Farmers protest against land acquisition', 26 March 2009, www.hindu.com/2009/03/26/stories/2009032653380400.htm

47 *The Hindu*, 'Farmers stage protest, seek end to Bellary airport plan', 4 July 2009, www.hindu.com/2009/07/04/stories/2009070453640300.htm

48 *The Hindu*, 'Farmers draw carts to register protest against airport construction', 25 July 2009, www.thehindu.com/todays-paper/tp-national/tp-karnataka/article238063.ece

49 Habib Beary, 'Mining lobby behind Bellary airport project', *Sakal Times*, 15 March 2010, www.sakaaltimes.com/SakaalTimes-Beta/20100315/5362194312632836334.htm (accessed 16 March 2010).

50 *The Hindu*, 'Farm workers seek to cultivate land acquired for Bellary airport', 4 April 2012, www.thehindu.com/todays-paper/tp-national/tp-karnataka/article3278995.ece

51 *Financial Express*, 'Govt thumbs up to 12 greenfield airports', 24 March 2010, www.financialexpress.com/news/govt-thumbs-up-to-12-greenfield-airports/594899/

52 Subodh Varma, 'Superpower? 230 million Indians go hungry daily', *Times of India*, 15 January 2012, http://articles.timesofindia.indiatimes.com/2012-01-15/india/30629637_1_anganwadi-workers-ghi-number-of-hungry-people

53 *The Hindu*, 'Airport project for Aranmula gets approval', 2 September 2010, www.thehindu.com/news/states/kerala/article609578.ece

54 *Times of India*, 'Airport developer wants police protection', 12 February 2012, http://articles.timesofindia.indiatimes.com/2012-02-12/

kochi/31051676_1_police-protection-petition-airport-developer; *The Hindu*, 'BJP-BJYM activists lock airport company office in Aranmula', 9 January 2012, www.thehindu.com/news/states/kerala/article2788238.ece

55 Radhakrishnan Kuttoor, 'MoEF urged to cancel clearance for airport project', *The Hindu*, 19 February 2012, www.thehindu.com/news/states/kerala/article2910150.ece

56 *Times of India*, 'Kerala cabinet panel to study land acquisitions', 25 May 2012, http://timesofindia.indiatimes.com/city/thiruvananthapuram/Kerala-cabinet-panel-to-study-land-acquisitions/articleshow/13462249.cms

57 Movement against SEZ in Tamil Nadu, 'Villagers oppose land acquisition for green field airport', 17 October 2010, http://tnantisez.wordpress.com/2010/10/17/sez_bulletin_oct_2010/

58 Sumana Narayanan, 'Call to ground airport plan', *Down to Earth*, 15 September 2010, www.downtoearth.org.in/node/1856

59 Government of Tamil Nadu, *Tamil Nadu Vision 2023: Strategic plan for infrastructure development*, March 2012, p. 25, www.thehindu.com/multimedia/archive/00991/Vision_Tamil_Nadu_2_991204a.pdf

60 *Times of India*, 'Pipeline from Manali to supply fuel to airport', 5 July 2009, http://timesofindia.indiatimes.com/city/chennai/Pipeline-from-Manali-to-supply-fuel-to-airport/articleshow/4738881.cms

61 *Navhind Times*, 'Chandel villagers oppose land acquisition for Mopa airport', 6 December 2010, www.navhindtimes.in/goa-news/chandel-villagers-oppose-land-acquisition-mopa-airport

62 *Times of India*, 'Villagers chase away officials who went to value Mopa airport land', 12 May 2011, http://articles. timesofindia.indiatimes.com/2011-05-12/goa/29536009_1_mopa-airport-m-k-vasta-sandip-kambli

63 Oneindia news, 'Farmers protest against acquisition of land for international airport in Kushinagar', 5 July 2009, http://news.oneindia.in/2009/07/05/farmersprotest-against-acquisition-of-land-for-internationa.html

64 Tarannum Manjul, 'Farmers' protests may drive away Maitreya Buddha project to Bihar', *Indian Express*, 24 August 2010, www.expressindia.com/latest-news/farmers-protests-may-drive-away-maitreya-buddha-project-to-bihar/664116/

65 Tarannum Manjul, 'As farmers protest, Maya scales down Maitreya Buddha project', *Indian Express*, 26 May 2011, www.indianexpress.com/news/as-farmers-protest-maya-scales-down-maitreya-buddha-project/795471/

66 Deepa Jainani, 'UP govt to revive Kushinagar airport project',

Financial Express, 19 April 2012, www.financialexpress.com/news/up-govt-to-revive-kushinagar-airport-project/938508/0

67 CAPA, 'Indian airlines turn their attention to regional market', 11 October 2011, http://centreforaviation.com/analysis/indian-airlines-turn-their-attention-to-regional-market-60302

68 CAPA, 'India: the world's fastest growing domestic aviation market', 9 November 2011, http://centreforaviation.com/analysis/india---the-worlds-fastest-growing-domestic-market-62124

69 Jay Menon, 'India's commercial air transport sector beset by myriad problems', *Aviation Daily,* 18 February 2013, http://www.aviationweek.com/Article.aspx?id=/article-xml/avd_02_18_2013_p04-01-545015.xml

70 CAPA, 'India under-prepared for massive airport capacity challenge', 8 August 2012, http://centreforaviation.com/analysis/capa-report-india-requires-usd40bn-investment-in-50-greenfield-airports-by-2025-79925

71 *Cargo News Asia,* 'Breather for airlines as India approves air fuel import', 8 February 2012, www.cargonewsasia.com/secured/article.aspx?id=15&article=27666

5 Green Garnish

1 Auckland Airport, 'Auckland Airport – continuous improvement drives energy efficiency', December 2010, www.aucklandairport.co.nz/Social-Responsibility/~/media/Files/Community/Earth-check/EEC1623%20Auckland%20Airport%20CStudy%205_0%20WEB.ashx

2 Government of South Australia, 'Renewable energy in South Australia', 2 February 2011, www.climatechange.sa.gov.au/index.php?page=renewable-energy-in-sa (accessed 11 March 2011).

3 Solamon, 'BVI's biggest solar power project going up at King Airport: more to come', 4 April 2011, www.solamonenergy.com/bvis-biggest-solar-power-project-going-up-at-king-airport-more-to-come

4 Brit Liggett, 'Düsseldorf Airport installs one of the largest solar arrays in Germany', *Inhabitat,* 29 November 2011, http://inhabitat.com/dusseldorf-airport-installs-one-of-the-largest-solar-arrays-in-germany/

5 *Passenger Terminal Today,* 'Dubai Airports reduces CO_2 emissions by 72,000 tonnes', 28 March 2012, www.passengerterminaltoday.com/viewnews.php?NewsID=37820

6 Harriet Baskas, 'Solar-powered airports? It could happen', *USA Today,* 28 April 2009, www.usatoday.com/travel/columnist/baskas/2009-04-28-solar-powered-airports_N.htm

7   Brad McAllister, 'Solar ambitions', *Airport Business*, 2011, www.airportbusiness.com/print/Airport-Business-Magazine/Solar-Ambitions/1$43476 (accessed 15 April 2011).

8   Heather Clancy, 'Denver Airport uses more solar power than any other in U.S.', Smartplanet.com, www.smartplanet.com/blog/business-brains/denver-airport-uses-more-solar-power-than-any-other-in-us/18704

9   RenewableEnergyWorld.com, '1.6-MW sharp solar array at Denver International Airport goes online', 5 March 2010, www.renewableenergyworld.com/rea/news/article/2010/03/1-6-mw-solar-system-completed-at-denver-airport

10 Chattanooga Airport, www.chattairport.com/www

11 Chattanooga Airport, *Masterplan Update*, July 2010, www.chattairport.com/downloads/Master_Plan_Final_vers_1.0.pdf

12 San Francisco International Airport, *2011 Environmental Sustainability Report*, December 2011, p. 29, www.flysfo.com/downloads/reports/SFO_2011_Environmental_Sustainability_Report.pdf

13 Businesswire.com, 'Fitch affirms San Francisco Airport (SFO Fuel Co.), CA special facil revs at 'BBB+'; outlook stable', 3 May 2012, www.businesswire.com/news/home/20120503007009/en/Fitch-Affirms-San-Francisco-Airport-SFO-Fuel

14 *Passenger Terminal Today*, 'Solar panels installed at Schiphol', 18 July 2012, www.passengerterminaltoday.com/viewnews.php?NewsID=41206

15 Schiphol, 'Aircraft fuel supply AEO-certified', 24 February 2012, www.schiphol.nl/B2B/Cargo/CargoNews2/AircraftFuelSupplyAE-Ocertified.htm

16 Joe Bates, 'Energy on tap', *Airport World*, 15 April 2011, www.airport-world.com/home/item/458-energy-on-tap

17 Environmental Leader, 'Orly Airport taps into geothermal', 6 April 2008, www.environmentalleader.com/2008/04/06/orly-airport-taps-into-geothermal/

18 Hong Kong Airport, 'Hong Kong International Airport, our green airport, annual report 2009', p. 3, www.hongkongairport.com/eng/pdf/media/publication/report/09_10/e_full.pdf

19 Walter Brooks, 'Boston Airport installs its own wind farm', Capecodtoday.com, 5 March 2008, www.capecodtoday.com/blogs/index.php/2008/03/05/boston_airport_installs_its_own_wind_far?blog=53 (accessed 3 March 2010).

20 *Airport Watch Bulletin*, 'EMA wind turbines to produce a tiny amount of the airport's electricity', May 2011, p. 7, www.aef.org.uk/downloads/AirportWatch_bulletin_July2011.pdf

21 BBC News, 'East Midlands Airport objects to farmer's turbine plan', 25 May 2011, www.bbc.co.uk/news/uk-england-13543225

22 David Bartlett, 'Giant wind turbine "a threat to JLA air safety" transport', *Airport Business*, 22 April 2011, www.airportbusiness. com/web/online/Top-News-Headlines/Giant-wind-turbine-a-threat-to-JLA-air-safety-transport/1$44307 (accessed 27 May 2011).

23 RenewableUK, www.bwea.com/aviation/index.html (accessed 11 June 2012).

24 Northeastern University, 'East Boston walking tour', www. northeastern.edu/urbanstudiesminor/wp-content/uploads/ East-Boston-Immigrant-History-tour.pdf

25 Kamelia Angelova, 'Photos: the Boston neighborhood that was demolished to make way for Logan Airport', *Business Insider*, 29 September 2011, www.businessinsider.com/ east-boston-neptune-road-1970s-2011-9

26 Jeremy S. Bluhm, 'Peaceful Earth Day ends with conflict at airport', *Harvard Crimson*, 23 April 1970, www.thecrimson.com/ article/1970/4/23/peaceful-earth-day-ends-with-conflict/

27 Katherine Gregor, 'The First Earth Day, 1970', *Austin Chronicle*, 23 April 2010, www.austinchronicle.com/news/2010-04-23/1018735/

28 Dina Cappiello, 'Earth Day becomes victim of corporate takeover', *Houston Chronicle*, 22 April 2003, www.chron.com/news/ houston-texas/article/Earth-Day-becomes-victim-of-corporate-take-over-2118315.php

29 Massport, 'Massachusetts Port Authority along with the City of Boston announce first cab incentive program to encourage the use of hybrid and alternate fuel vehicles', 23 April 2007, www.massport. com/news-room/News/MassachusettsPortAuthorityAnnounceFirst-CabIncentiveProgram.aspx

30 Massport, 'Massport celebrates Earth Day with recycling, wildflowers and green asphalt', 22 April 2009, www.massport.com/about/press_ news_Earth_Day20091.html (accessed 14 June 2010).

31 Massport, 'Boston Logan celebrates Earth Day' 20 April 2011, www.massport.com/news-room/News/BostonLoganCelebrate-sEarthDay2011.aspx

32 *Transport Weekly*, 'Denver International Airport to celebrate Earth Day', 21 April 2009, www.transportweekly.com/pages/en/news/ articles/60418/

33 B.TownBlog, 'Sea-Tac Airport hosting Earth Day Fair Wed. 4/22', 21 April 2009, http:// b- townblog.com/2009/04/21/ sea-tac-airport-hosting-earth-day-fair-wed-422/

34 Joel Siegfried, 'San Diego Airport and e-cars embrace Earth Day', examiner.com, 19 April 2010, www.examiner.com/article/ san-diego-airport-and-e-cars-embrace-earth-day

35 Philadelphia Parking Authority, 'Earth Day award: congrats

to Joe!' May 2005, http://philapark.org/2012/05/earth-day-award-congrats-to-joe/
36 Wvgazette.com, 'Glenville State baseball team spruces up Yeager Airport', 20 April 2012, www.sundaygazettemail.com/News/201204200193
37 Amy Schneider, 'Airport marks Earth Day', Atlanta Airport, May 2005, www.atlanta-airport.com/HJN/2012/05/business5.htm
38 Energy Alternatives India (EIA), 'Coimbatore airport to use bio degradable bags', 23 April 2012, www.eai.in/360/actionbar/news/4722 (accessed 1 August 2012).
39 Nomankhan78, 'Earth Day 2011 at Karachi Airport', 24 April 2011, www.youtube.com/watch?v=BFybEWKlb3s
40 Riga Airport, 'Earth Day celebrations at the airport', *Newsletter* April–June 2011, www.riga-airport.com/en/main/newsroom/newsletter/2011/april-june-2011/earth-day-celebrations-at-the-airport
41 Sarina Houston, 'How airlines are celebrating Earth Day', About.com, 19 April 2012, http://aviation.about.com/b/2012/04/19/how-airlines-are-celebrating-earth-day.htm
42 Laura M, 'Celebrate Earth Day with the Nature Conservancy & Delta', Delta, 1 April 2012, http://blog.delta.com/2012/04/01/celebrate-earth-day-with-the-nature-conservancy-delta-2/
43 *Khaleej Times*, 'Abu Dhabi airport joins Earth Hour 2010', 26 March 2010, www.khaleejtimes.com/DisplayArticle09.asp?xfile=data/theuae/2010/March/theuae_March735.xml&section=theuae
44 Changi Airport, 'Earth Hour takes off at Changi Airport for the third consecutive year', 24 March 2011, www.changiairport.com/our-business/airport-news/earth-hour-takes-off-at-changi-airport
45 Los Angeles World Airports, 'LAX gateway pylons to go dark in support of International Earth Hour, Saturday, March 31', www.lawa.org/welcome_LAWA.aspx?id=1866
46 Auckland Airport, 'Auckland Airport marks World Environment Day', 5 June 2008, www.auckland-airport.co.nz/Corporate/NewsAndMedia/AllMediaReleases/World-Environment-Day.aspx
47 Malaysia Airports, 'KLIA continues pursuit of environmental excellence with 'Walk The Environment' campaign', 14 June 2008, www.malaysiaairports.com.my/index.php/news-archieve/year-2008/164-klia-continues-pursuit-of-environmental-excellence-with-walk-the-environment-campaign-jun142008.html
48 Association of Private Airport Operators (APAO), *Newsletter*, June 2012, www.apaoindia.com/wp-content/uploads/2012/06/APAO-Monthly-Newsletter-June-2012.pdf
49 *Times of India*, 'World Environment Day in Etawah', http://time-

sofindia.indiatimes.com/topic/World-Environment-Day-in-Etawah/news/

50 NDTV, 'World Environment Day: Sanjay Gandhi Zoological Park declared plastic free zone', 6 June 2012, www.ndtv.com/article/cities/world-environment-day-sanjay-gandhi-zoological-park-declared-plastic-free-zone-227897

51 Nuance Group, 'Walkthrough concepts driving sales', *Pulse*, April 2009, www.moodiereport.com/pdf/Nuance_Pulse_3_Apr09_en.pdf

52 John Rimmer, 'Hyderabad seizes the moment', *Moodie Report*, Oct.–Nov. 2011, http://edition.pagesuite-professional.co.uk/launch.aspx?referral=other&pnum=41&refresh=6Mf013ZnmB04&EID=effef60e-0e49-425a-bfb5-bcd592603871&skip=&p=41

53 Frankfurt Airport, 'Mediafacts 2012', www.media-frankfurt.de/news.html?&L=1 (accessed 18 January 2012).

54 Ben Flanagan, 'Motorola says Dubai advert is longest ever', *The National*, 1 June 2012, www.thenational.ae/thenationalconversation/industry-insights/media/motorola-says-dubai-advert-is-longest-ever

55 Jeff Gonzales, 'Denver International Airport's new digital-advertising deal', Digital Signage Blog, 23 July 2012, www.deploid.com/blog/denver-international-airports-new-digital-advertising-deal/

56 Naresh Kumar, 'Digital advertising mirrors at Chicago's O'Hare Airport', PSFK, 2 February 2011, www.psfk.com/2011/02/digital-advertising-mirrors-at-chicago%E2%80%99s-o%E2%80%99hare-airport.html

57 Laurie Segall, 'Ads that analyze and target you personally', CNNMoney, 21 April 2011, http://money.cnn.com/2011/04/14/technology/immersive_labs_targeted_ads/index.htm

58 Denver International Airport, 'Public art', www.flydenver.com/publicart (accessed 18 June 2010).

59 Fly2Houston.com, 'Hobby Airport unveils new original artwork, 25 March 2010, www.fly2houston.com/0/3903169/0/83280D83284/

60 Mark Chivers, 'Evolution not revolution', *Global Airport Cities*, Autumn 2006, http://insightgrp.co.uk/pdfs_web/Magazines/GAPC/GAC_autumn_06_3.6mb.pdf (accessed 15 February 2008).

61 Robin Stone, 'Secret gardens', *Airport World*, 8 July 2010, www.airport-world.com/home/item/54-secret-gardens

62 Middle East Logistics, 'Planters adds the interior landscaping of recently opened Terminal 3 at Dubai International Airport', 23 December 2008, www.middleastlogistics.com/topnews.asp?id=22295 (accessed 13 February 2009); Emily Meredith, 'Bringing life to malls through landscaping', *Khaleej Times*, 22 January 2009, www.araburban.org/AUDI/English/Right_en/03ArabCitiesNews_en/ACN3101090130GG.htm (accessed 13 February 2009).

63 Surnender Sharma, 'Greener pastures for Delhi airport', Mid-day. com, 13 May 2010, www.mid-day.com/news/2010/may/130510-Greener-pastures-Delhi-International-Airport-T3-terminal.htm

64 DNAIndia, 'Finally, a swanky airport to welcome the world', 4 July 2010, www.dnaindia.com/india/report_finally-a-swanky-airport-to-welcome-the-world_1404625

65 Constructionupdate.com, 'Delhi International Airport Integrated Passenger Terminal 3 Terminal boom', August 2009, www.construc-tionupdate.com/products/projectsinfo/2009/August-10-16/006. html (accessed 12 October 2010).

66 Future Green Studio, 'Vertical gardens at Chennai International Airport', 12 March 2012, http://futuregreenstudio.com/studio/news/2012/mar/12/vertical-gardens-chennai-international-airport/

67 WebEcoist, 'Surprising green nature park inside Amster-dam's airport', http://webecoist.momtastic.com/2011/07/03/surprising-green-nature-park-inside-amsterdams-airport/

68 *Scoop*, 'Christchurch Airport gives passengers an experience of the South Island', 8 October 2010, www.scoop.co.nz/stories/BU1010/S00225/airport-gives-passengers-an-experience-of-s-island.htm

69 *Atlanta Journal-Constitution*, 'Atlanta city council approves nearly $4 million airport art project', 16 July 2012, www.ajc.com/news/atlanta/atlanta-city-council-approves-1479012.html (accessed 16 July 2012).

70 Katie Johnston Chase, 'Logan is first with scanners', Boston.com, 6 March 2010, http://articles.boston.com/2010-03-06/ business/2929 7466_1_full-body-scanners-tsa-worker-logan-inter national-airport

71 Leischen Stelter, 'Logan Airport leads technology charge, but "inte-gration is unwieldy"', *Security Director News*, 19 October 2010, www.securitydirectornews.com/?p=article&id=sd201010qkYVtx

72 *InformationAge*, 'Gatwick unveils "iris at a distance" biometric security', 11 October 2011, www.information-age.com/it-manage ment/outsourcing-and-supplier-management/1662618/gatwick-unveils-%E2%80%98iris-at-a-distance%E2%80%99-biometric-security

73 Charlie Leocha, 'New iris scanning system scans 30 passengers per minute at a distance', *Consumer Traveller*, 26 April 2010, www.consumertraveler.com/today/new-iris-scanning-system-scans-30-passengers-per-minute-at-a-distance/

74 Airport-technology.com, 'Acquris – airport surveillance cameras', www.airport-technology.com/contractors/security/acquris/ (accessed 6 August 2010).

75 John Naughton, 'Airport scanning technology is a transparent victory for terrorism', *Guardian*, 15 July 2012, www.guardian.co.uk/technology/2012/jul/15/internet-privacy

6 Air Cargo

1   Alfred Romann, 'Keeping trade flowing', www.chinadailyapac.com, 22 March 2013, www.chinadailyapac.com/article/keeping-trade-flowing

2   *Port of Hong Kong Handbook and Directory 2012*, www.mardep.gov. hk/en/publication/pdf/porthk.pdf

3   Azfreight.com, 'Air freight – tomorrow's world', 24 June 2010, www. azfreight.com/cfm/news_detail.cfm?id=2111&site_id=15 (accessed 15 July 2010).

4   Dubaicityguide, 'HH Sheikh Ahmed Bin Saeed Al Maktoum inaugurates Dubai logistics corridor', 11 October 2010, www.dubaicity guide.com/site/news/news-details.asp?newsid=31325

5   Andy Ashby, 'River feeds Aerotropolis concept', *Business Journals*, 17 May 2010, www.bizjournals.com/birmingham/ othercities/memphis/stories/2010/05/17/story1.html? b=1274068800%5E3347591&s=industry&i=logistics_ transportation

6   Samsung, 'SHI produces world's largest container ships', 11 July 2005, www.shi.samsung.co.kr/Eng/pr/news_view. aspx?Seq=448&mac=1139b7e21745aeeb14fa127566017d78

7   *Supply Chain Digest*, 'Global logistics news: just as world trade slows, here come the megaships', 17 February 2009, www.scdigest.com/ assets/On_Target/09-02-17-3.php (accessed 9 September 2009).

8   Damian Brett, 'Maersk set to order 18,000teu containerships', *International Freighting Weekly*, 29 November 2010, www.ifw-net.com/ freightpubs/ifw/index/maersk-set-to-order-18000teu-container-ships/20017829580.htm?source=ezine (accessed 22 February 2011).

9   BBC News, 'New Burma port "to become trade corridor"', 5 May 2011, www.bbc.co.uk/news/world-asia-pacific-12490521

10 Dr Alun Anderson, 'Can we keep up with Arctic change?' *Culture and Conflict Review*, 22 April 2011, www.nps.edu/Programs/CCS/ WebJournal/Article.aspx?ArticleID=76 (accessed 7 June 2011).

11 Boeing, *World Air Cargo Forecast 2012–2013*, www.boeing.com/ commercial/cargo/wacf.pdf

12 ACI, 'ACI releases its 2011 World Airport Traffic Report: airport passenger traffic remains strong as cargo traffic weakens'.

13 Pierre David and Richard Stewart, *International Logistics: The Management of International Trade Operations*, Cengage Learning, 2010, p. 291.

14 Daniel Michaels, 'Gunmen waylay jet, swipe diamond trove', *Wall Street Journal*, 19 February 2013, http://online.wsj.com/article/SB10 001424127887323495104578313523821463276.html

15 Dawn.com, 'Dazzle Park to boost gems export', 9 February 2013, http://dawn.com/2013/02/09/dazzle-park-to-boost-gems-export/

16 Camille Allaz, *The History of Air Cargo and Airmail,* Christopher Foyle/International Air Cargo Association, 2004, p. 128.

17 MergeGlobal, 'End of an era?' August 2008, www.mergeglobal.com/ (accessed 26 February 2010).

18 James Wilsdon, 'Dot-com ethics: e-business and sustainability', ch. in *Digital Futures: Living in a dot-com world*, Earthscan, 2001, pp. 72–3.

19 Rupert Neate, 'iPhone 5 demand leads to "huge" increase in air freight costs', *Guardian*, 11 October 2012, www.guardian.co.uk/technology/2012/oct/11/apple-iphone5-demand-huge-increase-air-freight-costs

20 *Manila Bulletin*, 'Etihad crystal cargo carries Picasso masterpieces', 6 June 2006, www.mb.com.ph/issues/2008/06/06/20080606126618.html (accessed 14 July 2008); *CargoTalk India*, 'Etihad to start Sydney, Dublin Service', March 2007, p. 10, www.cargotalk.in/pdfs/march07.pdf (accessed 18 May 2008).

21 *Payload Asia*, 'Terracotta army moves by UPS 747-400', June 2008, www.payloadasia.com/morenews-2-s-Gateways-6-2008-Payload-Asia.html (accessed 23 June 2008).

22 *Cargolux Newsletter,* December 2008, www.cargolux.com/Press/newsletterPDF/dec.08.pdf (accessed 17 November 2009).

23 *International Freighting Weekly*, 'Ice skating rink delivered by freighter', 29 June 2007, www.ifw-net.com/freightpubs/ifw/airarticle.htm?artid=1182561242962 (accessed 14 November 2007).

24 Soman Baby, 'Formula One entourage arrives', *Gulf Daily News*, 10 April 2007, www.gulf-daily-news.com/1yr_arc_Articles.asp?Article=178543&Sn=BNEW&IssueID=30021&date=4-10-2007

25 TIACA, 'Liège handles 500 horses', 6 October 2010, www.tiaca.org/tiaca/NewsBot.asp?MODE=VIEW&ID=9769&SnID=2084318152

26 TIACA, 'Liège handles 500 horses', p. 327.

27 KLM Royal Dutch Airlines, 'Animal transport', May 2009, http://corporate.klm.com/en/topics/school-reports/animal-transport (accessed 31 March 2010).

28 Russian Aviation, 'AirBridgeCargo has performed its first cross-polar flight', 7 March 2012, www.ruaviation.com/news/2012/3/7/834/

29 Samantha Bomkamp, 'Paws up: All-pet airline hits skies', Breitbart, 14 July 2009, www.breitbart.com/article.php?id=D99ECQSG0&show_article=1 (accessed 16 March 2010).

30 BBC News, 'Airline fined for shredding squirrels', 21 March 2001, http://news.bbc.co.uk/1/hi/world/europe/1232935.stm

31 Rüdiger Kasper, 'Perishables around the world', Kuehne+Nagel, Cool Logistics 2010 Conference, 22 September 2010, www.

coollogisticsconference.com/downloads/Ruediger%20Kasper_2981.pdf

32 Frankfurt Airport, 'Perishable Center', www.frankfurt-airport.com/content/frankfurt_airport/en/business_location/cargo_hub/perishable_center.html

33 *Cargolux Newsletter,* May 2009, www.cargolux.com/Press/news letterPDF/NewsletterCVMay09.pdf (accessed 11 November 2011).

34 Skycargo.com, 'Cool chain solutions', 2012, www.skycargo.com/english/Images/Emirates%20SkyCargo%20Cool%20Chain%20Leaflet.pdf

35 Khalifa Alzaffin, 'Dubai Flower Centre well placed to serve perishables cargo sector', *Zawya*, 19 January 2007, https://www.zawya.com/printstory.cfm?storyid=ZAWYA200701191422 23&l=142200070119 (accessed 27 April 2009).

36 Schiphol Group, 'The importance of cargo', March 2013, https://www.google.co.uk/url?sa=t&rct=j&q=&esrc=s&source=web&cd=2&ved=0CEMQFjAB&url=http%3A%2F%2Fwww.schiphol.nl%2Fweb%2Ffile%3Fuuid%3Dfc5c5d91-a500-4065-b6d6-f32f89a6d7c0%26owner%3D7ccedf61-a8f4-4180-b5b0-849e8def7d3e&ei=C6RHUeO_Lu754QTjhYDICQ&usg=AFQjCNHswhpsgoQUnUPyqE6DJgdrboaw1w&sig2=_g5Al4GVBgR-HT5aBRTNDw&bvm=bv.43828540,d.bGE

37 John McQuaid, 'The secrets behind your flowers', *Smithsonian Magazine*, February 2011, www.smithsonianmag.com/people-places/The-Secrets-Behind-Your-Flowers.html

38 Beatrice Gachenge, 'Kenya's 2012 flower export earnings seen lower', Reuters, 21 March 2012, www.reuters.com/article/2012/03/21/ozabs-kenya-flowers-idAFJOE82K06W20120321

39 Kenya Flower Council, 'The flower industry in Kenya', www.kenyaflowercouncil.org/floricultureinkenya.php (accessed 22 March 2013).

40 Chris Lewis, 'Africa – high costs hold back growth', *International Freighting Weekly*, 30 May 2008, www.ifw-net.com/freightpubs/ifw/featuresarticle.htm?artid=1212105947399 (accessed 2 June 2008).

41 George Omondi, 'Eldoret Airport buzzes after years of slow trade', *Business Daily*, 11 February 2008, http://allafrica.com/stories/200802111076.html

42 Solomon Mburu, 'Kenya: storage facility set up at Eldoret Airport', Allafrica.com, 10 June 2008, http://allafrica.com/stories/200806101203.html

43 Food and Water Watch and Council of Canadians, 'Lake Naivasha withering under the assault of international flower vendors', January 2008, www.canadians.org/water/documents/NaivashaReport08.pdf

44 Jeremy Hance, 'Kenya's pain: famine, drought, government ambiv-
    alence cripples once stable nation', Mongabay.com, 17 September
    2009, http://news.mongabay.com/2009/0917-hance_kenyapain.
    html

45 Allafrica.com, 'Flower farmers scale down production amid
    water scarcity', 17 September 2009, http://allafrica.com/
    stories/200909180575.html

46 Manfred Singh, 'The "pride of Africa" is set to shine brighter',
    Payload Asia, November 2009, www.payloadasia.com/
    article-4419-theprideofafricaissettoshinebrighter-asia.html

47 Kenya Airways, 'Kenya Airways to acquire cargo freighter', 23
    February 2011, www.kenya-airways.com/home/about_kenya_
    airways/press_releases/current_press_releases/default.aspx
    ?colm=&cid=3638 (accessed 4 July 2011).

48 Joshua Masinde, 'Kenya to increase US flower exports', *Daily
    Nation*, 5 January 2013, www.nation.co.ke/business/news/Kenya-to-
    increase-US-flower-exports-/-/1006/1658464/-/lxnsc7/-/index.
    html

49 Airport Business, 'Houston launches new air cargo facility at
    Intercontinental Airport for perishable imports', 18 August
    2009, www.airportbusiness.com/online/article.jsp?site
    Section=1&id=30290&pageNum=2 (accessed 4 September 2009).

50 Trammell Crow, 'International Air CargoCentre II', http://marketing.
    trammellcrow.com/Cynthia/Houston%20Marketing%20Brochure.
    pdf

51 Jenalia Moreno, 'Flower trade hasn't blossomed at Bush airport',
    Houston Chronicle, 11 February 2011, www.chron.com/disp/story.
    mpl/business/7423972.html

52 Miami Airport, 'Cargo hub 2012–2013', www.miami-airport.com/
    pdfdoc/MIA_Cargo_Brochure.pdf

53 Jo Erickson, 'Reflecting on the real cost of Valentine's Day: GMOs
    and pesticides with love', Mint Press News, 14 February 2013, www.
    mintpress.net/reflecting-on-the-real-cost-of-valentines-day-gmos-
    pesticides-with-love/

54 Anna Morser and Simon McRae, *Growing Pains,* War on Want,
    March 2007, www.waronwant.org/attachments/Growing%20Pains.
    pdf

55 Erickson, 'Reflecting on the real cost of Valentine's Day'.

56 Rex A. Harrison (ed.), *Colombia: A country study*, Library of Congress,
    p. 156, http://lcweb2.loc.gov/frd/cs/pdf/CS_Colombia.pdf

57 *Cargolux Newsletter*, August 2010, www.cargolux.com/Press/
    newsletterPDF/NewsletterAug.pdf (accessed 11 November 2011).

58 *Passenger Terminal Today*, 'Patel: India will have 400 airports in

10 years', 23 February 2009, www.passengerterminaltoday.com/news.php?NewsID=10882 (accessed 24 February 2009).

59 Dwayne Ramakrishnan, 'Hunger in India: the crisis worsens', *EconomyWatch*, 13 November 2009, www.economywatch.com/economy-business-and-finance-news/hunger-in-india-the-crisis-worsens-13-11.html

60 *New Delhi News*, 'Cochin Airport to have largest perishable cargo center in India', 3 February 2009, www.newdelhinews.net/story/462093

61 *Business Standard*, 'Perishable cargo complex at Cochin intl airport', 2 February 2009, www.business-standard.com/india/news/perishable-cargo-complex-at-cochin-intl-airport/347659/

62 Ratan Kr Paul, 'AAI set to offer modern infrastructure for cargo operations across India', *Cargo Talk India*, December 2009, www.aai.aero/misc/Cargo_Talk.pdf

63 *The Hindu*, 'Air freight subsidy for North East perishables', 22 June 2006, www.hindu.com/2006/06/22/stories/2006062204431700.htm

64 Government of India Ministry of Commerce and Industry, *Annual Report 2008–2009*, ch. 13, Trade promotion initiatives in the North East Region', http://commerce.nic.in/publications/anualreport_chapter13-2008-09.asp

65 BBC News, 'Flashback 1984: portrait of a famine', 6 April 2000, http://news.bbc.co.uk/1/hi/world/africa/703958.stm

66 Aschale Dagnachew Siyoum, Dorothea Hilhorst and Gerrit-Jan Van Uffelen, 'Food aid and dependency syndrome in Ethiopia: local perceptions', *Journal of Humanitarian Assistance*, 27 November 2012, http://sites.tufts.edu/jha/archives/1754

67 Andrew Rice, 'Is there such a thing as agro-imperialism', *New York Times*, 16 November 2009, www.nytimes.com/2009/11/22/magazine/22land-t.html

68 René Lefort, 'The great Ethiopian land-grab: feudalism, leninism, neo-liberalism ... plus ça change', Open Democracy, 31 December 2011, www.opendemocracy.net/ren%C3%A9-lefort/great- ethiopian-land-grab-feudalism-leninism-neo-liberalism -plus-%C3%A7-change

69 Tsegaye Tadesse, 'Ethiopia 2009 oilseed, pulse exports to jump-trade', Reuters, 26 February 2009, http://in.reuters.com/article/domesticNews/idINLQ55781820090226

70 *Addis Times,* 'Ethiopia inaugurates international airport at Humera', 27 July 2009, www.addistimes.com/ethiopia/3143-ethiopia-inaugurates-international-airport-at-humera.html (accessed 12 March 2013).

71 African Development Bank, 'Ethiopia's economic growth

performance: current situation and challenges', 17 September 2010, www.afdb.org/fileadmin/uploads/afdb/Documents/Publications/ECON%20Brief_Ethiopias%20Economic%20growth.pdf

72 Mahlet Mesfin, 'Meles Zenawi blossoms through flower sector rise', Allafrica.com, 2 September 2012, http://allafrica.com/stories/201209060932.html

73 Catherine Riungu, 'Flower farming slowly wilting', Allafrica.com, 30 August 2010, http://allafrica.com/stories/201008300271.html

74 Rolien Wiersinga and André de Jager, 'Business opportunities in the Ethiopian fruit and vegetable sector', February 2009, http://edepot.wur.nl/12

75 Elias Meseret, 'Ethiopia – flower companies plea for help to cope with slowdown', Nazret.com, 30 March 2009, http://nazret.com/blog/index.php?title=ethiopia_flower_companies_plea_for_help_

76 CBC News, 'Ethiopia appeals for urgent food aid', 22 October 2009, www.cbc.ca/world/story/2009/10/22/drought-ethiopia-africa.html

77 *Aircargo News*, 'Peter Conway interviews Tewolde Gebremariam', November 2009, www.aircargonews.net/Content/Records.aspx?ID=163 (accessed 15 November 2009).

78 DireTube, 'Ethiopia secures $216 million from export of horti-culture, floriculture products', 14 August 2010, www.diretube.com/ethiopian-news/ethiopia-secures-216m-from-export-of-horticulture-floriculture-products-video_cb758d6e9.html

79 Reuters, 'Ethiopia, U.N. launch food appeal for 2.8 million people', 7 February 2011, www.reuters.com/article/2011/02/07/us-ethiopia-foodaid-idUSTRE7164XF20110207

80 Ethionet, 'PM inaugurates 'hortiflora' trade exhibition', 13 March 2011, http://ethionetblog.blogspot.com/2011/03/pm-inaugu-rates-hortiflora-trade.html

81 EHPEA, 'Exporting fruit and vegetables from Ethiopia', 15 March 2011, www.ehpea.org/documents/FV%20Main%20Document.pdf (accessed 24 October 2011).

82 Yonas Abiye, 'Ethiopia appeals for 398 mln USD in emergency food aid', Egeza.com, 11 July 2011, www.ezega.com/News/NewsDetails.aspx?Page=heads&NewsID=2972

83 *Aircargo News*, 'Ethiopian to buy four 777Fs', 5 September 2011, www.aircargonews.net/news/single-view/news/ethiopian-to-buy-four-777fs.html

84 Ethiopia Investor, 'Ethiopian receives first B777 freighter', 25 September 2012, www.ethiopiainvestor.com/index.php?view=article&catid=1%3Alatest-news&id=3556%3Aethiopian-receives-first-b777-freighter&option=com_content

85 Ethiopia Investor, 'New B777 freighter aircraft for horticulture

export', 31 July 2012, http://ethiopiainvestor.com/index.php?
option=com_content&view=article&id=3410:new-b777-freighter-
aircraft-for-horticulture-export&catid=69:archives

86 *Daily Monitor*, 'Ethiopia suspends forex reserves', 16 August 2012,
www.monitor.co.ug/News/World/Ethiopia+suspends+forex+re-
serves/-/688340/1480392/-/in2lmbz/-/index.html

87 Allafrica.com, 'Ethiopian inaugurates new perishable cold
cargo storage facility', 10 March 2013, http://allafrica.com/
stories/201303110110.html

88 Freshplaza.com, 'Celtic Cooling build large cold store for Ethiopian
Airlines Enterprise', 17 August 2012, www.freshplaza.com/news_
detail.asp?id=99720

89 Ethiopia Investor, 'Ethiopian receives first B777 freighter'.

7 Industrial Cargo

1 Lufthansa, 'Airfreight in Germany', http://konzern.lufthansa.com/
en/themen/100-years-of-airfreight/history.html

2 MergeGlobal, 'End of an era?' August 2008, p. 36, www.mergeglobal.
com/ (accessed 26 February 2010).

3 John D. Kasarda, 'Designing an aerotropolis to provide Michigan's
competitive advantage', Taubman College, University of Michigan,
20 January 2006, p. 9, www.tcaup.umich.edu/charrette/2006/
aerotropolis06_kasarda.pdf

4 Mike Flanagan, 'Do consumer concerns threaten fast fashion?'
Juststyle.com, 28 August 2007, www.just-style.com/comment/
do-consumer-concerns-threaten-fast-fashion_id98337.aspx

5 Camille Allaz, *The History of Air Cargo and Airmail*, Christopher
Foyle/International Air Cargo Association, 2004, p. 128.

6 Allaz, *The History of Air Cargo and Airmail*, p. 136.

7 Allaz, *The History of Air Cargo and Airmail*, p. 264.

8 'Keeping the car makers rolling', *Cargo Matters Swiss World-
Cargo Magazine*, Issue 1, 2009 www.swissworldcargo.com/web/
EN/pressroom/publications/Documents/CM_MAGAZINE_
0208_240409%20FIN2.pdf

9 Remo Hanselmann, 'Converting to air freight', *Cargo Matters*,
April 2005, p. 13, www.swissworldcargo.com/web/EN/pressroom/
publications/Documents/CargoMatters_1_2005.pdf

10 Lara L. Sorinski, 'Air cargo saves the bacon', *World Trade Magazine*,
1 September 2004, www.worldtrademag.com/CDA/Articles/Air_
Sea_InlandPorts/609e938c89af7010VgnVCM100000f932a8c0____
(accessed 20 May 2009).

11 John Owstrower, 'Fourth and final Dreamlifter enters

service', *Flightglobal*, 17 February 2010, www.flightglobal.comarticles/2010/02/17/338460/fourth-and-final-dreamlifter-enters-service.html

12 Dominic Gates, 'Boeing 787: parts from around the world will be swiftly integrated', *Seattle Times,* 11 September 2005, http://seattletimes.nwsource.com/html/businesstechnology/2002486348_787global11.html

13 Lesley Wayne, 'Boeing reinvents supply chain', *World Trade Magazine,* April 2007, www.worldtrademag.com (accessed 12 May 2007).

14 Airbus, 'Supporting the Airbus production system', www.airbus.com/innovation/proven-concepts/in-manufacturing/transport/

15 India Strategic, 'India's first aviation SEZ opened in Belgaum', November 2009, www.indiastrategic.in/topstories415.htm

16 *Times of India,* 'Boeing MRO to start by 2013, says Keskar', 26 May 2011, http://articles.timesofindia.indiatimes.com/2011-05-26/nagpur/29585974_1_dreamliners-boeing-mro-boeing-s-india

17 Alex Hawkes, 'Cargolux breaks weight record', Arabian business.com, 19 September 2007, www.arabianbusiness.com/500598-cargolux-breaks-weight-record

18 Aviation Tribune, 'Cargolux Celebrates its 25th Boeing 747 Freighter', 14 March 2013, http://aviationtribune.com/airlines/europe/item/467-cargolux-celebrates-its-25th-boeing-747-freighter

19 Volga-Dnepr, 'Charter operations', 2009, www.volga-dnepr.com/eng/charter/; Volga-Dnepr, 'Volga-Dnepr Airlines delivered glasswork equipment', 11 December 2008, www.volga-dnepr.com/eng/presscentre/releases/?id=5352

20 Ashwini Phadnis, 'Panalpina airlifts bogies to China', *Hindu Business Line,* 23 December 2002, www.thehindubusinessline.com/2002/12/23/stories/2002122300240600.htm

21 Allaz, *The History of Air Cargo and Airmail,* p. 335.

22 Volga-Dnepr, 'Dutch, Italian and UK governments charter AN-124s to rush relief aid to victims of Hurricane Katrina', October www.jamierochepr.co.uk/newsletters/volga-dnepr/october2005/content_1.php

23 *Transportweekly,* 'Eight An-124 flights for Haiti', 24 February 2010, www.transportweekly.com/pages/en/news/articles/69584/

24 Janet Nodar, 'Antonov An-225 carries equipment for Haiti relief', *Journal of Commerce,* 24 February 2010, www.joc.com/air-expedited/antonov-225-carries-equipment-haiti-relief

25 Volga-Dnepr, 'Volga-Dnepr charity flight is first international civil flight to Sendai after earthquake and flood', Big News, April/May 2011, www.volga-dnepr.com/rus/files/2011/38april_may2011.pdf

26 M. J. Subiria Arauz, 'Concrete pumper leaves Hartsfield-Jackson

for Japan', *Clayton News Daily*, 15 April 2011, www.news-daily.com/news/2011/apr/15/concrete-pumper-leaves-hartsfield-jackson-for/

27 Mohammed H. Zayer, 'Saudi Aramco oil spill approach, prevention, and readiness', International Oil Spill Conference, www.iosc.org/papers_posters/01959.pdf (accessed 24 October 2011).

28 Ray Tyson, 'Air cargo climbs', February 1990, *Alaska Business Monthly*, http://findarticles.com/p/articles/mi_hb5261/is_n2_v6/ai_n28592481/ (accessed 24 October 2011).

29 US Air Force, '436th Airlift Wing history', www.dover.af.mil/library/factsheets/factsheet_print.asp?fsID=4050&page=1 (accessed 24 October 2011).

30 Julian Borger and John Vidal, 'Katrina oil spills may be among worst on record', *Guardian*, 16 September 2005, www.guardian.co.uk/environment/2005/sep/16/usnews.hurricanekatrina

31 Glasgow Prestwick Airport, 17 May 2006, http://www.gpia.co.uk/AirFreight/news/default.asp (accessed 7 November 2007).

32 Foxnews.com, '2 years later: what's latest on Gulf oil spill?' 19 April 2012, www.foxnews.com/us/2012/04/19/2-years-later-what-latest-on-gulf-oil-spill/

33 Chapman Freeborn, 'Skimmer boats to aid Gulf of Mexico oil spill response', 7 July 2010, www.chapman-freeborn.com/en/news/?article=46

34 Steve Phillips, 'Planes flying oil spill clean-up mission from Stennis International Airport', WLOX, 27 April 2010, www.wlox.com/global/story.asp?s=12386067

35 David Adam, 'BP oil spill: death and devastation – and it's just the start', *Guardian*, 31 May 2010, www.guardian.co.uk/environment/2010/may/31/bp-oil-spill-death-impact

36 Allaz, *The History of Air Cargo and Airmail*, p. 131.

37 Graham Chandler, 'Flying the friendly skies', 2006, http://gchandler.ehclients.com/index.php/graham/farnorth2_aviation/flying_the_friendly_skies/

38 Carolyn Heinze, 'Super-sizing', *Air Cargo World*, July 2008, www.aircargoworld.com/features/0708_3.htm (accessed 1 July 2008).

39 Matt Price, '11 million litres a day: the tar sands' leaking legacy', Environmental Defence, December 2008, http://environmentaldefence.ca/sites/default/files/report_files/TailingsReport_FinalDec8.pdf

40 CBCNews, 'Syncrude says duck death toll was 3 times original estimate', 31 March 2009, www.cbc.ca/news/canada/edmonton/story/2009/03/31/edm-syncrude-ducks.html

41 Edmonton Airport, 'Gateway for Canada's Northwest, Edmonton

Airport's Annual Report 2004', 2004, pp. 16–17, http://corporate.
flyeia.com/media/7791/52.pdf

42 Heinze, 'Super-sizing'.

43 Polet Airlines, 'Houston takes delivery of its "Christmas Tree" early',
October 2003, www.poletairlines.com/english/press/xmastree.htm
(accessed 22 July 2010).

44 Polet Airlines, 'Charter operations', Volga-Dnepr, 2009, www.volga-
dnepr.com/eng/charter/

45 Ruslan International, 'Oil & gas production and exploration', www.
ruslanint.com/GALLERY?ID=24

46 Steve Wilhelm, 'Antonov 225, largest flying aircraft, visits Moses
Lake', *Puget Sound Business Journal*, 13 March 2012, www.bizjournals.
com/seattle/news/2012/03/13/antonov-225-largest-aircraft-ever.html

47 Clarice Azuatalam, 'Air cargo bus lands in Rivers', *The Nation*,
19 March 2012, www.thenationonlineng.net/2011/index.php/
news/40264-air-cargo-bus-lands-in-rivers.html

48 Kansas.com, 'Antonov An-225, the world's biggest cargo plane,
in Wichita today', 2 April 2012, http://blogs.kansas.com/
aviation/2012/04/02/antonov-an-225-the-worlds-biggest-cargo-
plane-in-wichita-today/ (accessed 5 April 2012).

49 Cargolux, 'Africa connections', 2007, www.cargolux.com/ftp/press/
Flyers/pdfs/Africa-aug07.pdf (accessed 8 November 2007).

50 Arabianbusiness.com, 'Perishable priority', 1 January 2007, www.
arabianbusiness.com/5931-perishable-priority-?ln=en

51 *Cargolux Newsletter*, December 2008, p. 3, www.cargolux.com/Press/
newsletterPDF/dec.08.pdf (accessed 17 November 2009).

52 Cargolux, 'Baku's black gold', *Cargolines*, 2004, pp. 16–17, www.
cargolux.com/ftp/press/Cargolines/pdfs/Cargolines_Internet.pdf

53 Baku-Ceyhan Campaign www.bakuceyhan.org.uk/

54 *Cargolux Newsletter*, December 2008, pp. 2–4.

55 Freightnet, 'Cargolux introduces a second destination in Kazakhstan',
21 November 2007, www.freightnet.com/release/1134.htm

56 Nariman Gizitdinov, 'Biggest find in decades becomes $39 billion
cautionary tale', Bloomberg, 17 November 2011, www.bloomberg.
com/news/2011-11-16/biggest-oil-find-in-decades-becomes-39-
billion-cautionary-tale.html

57 FoE, *Kashagan Oil Field Development*, December 2007, www.foe
europe.org/publications/2007/KashaganReport.pdf

58 Volga-Dnepr, 'AN-124 lands on Sakhalin Island for first time', January
2011, www.volga-dnepr.com/rus/files/2011/36januare2011.pdf

59 Lynden, 'Projects team arranges air charter of lifeboats to Russia',
27 March 2012, http://info.lynden.com/blog/bid/82526/
Projects-team-arranges-air-charter-of-lifeboats-to-Russia

60 Sakhalin Energy, 'Molikpaq Platform (PA-A)', www.sakhalinenergy. ru/en/project.asp?p=paa_platform

61 Rose Bridger, 'Sakhalin oil workers swept away', 31 January 2012, www.rosebridger.com/2012/01/sakhalin-oil-workers-swept-away. html

62 Stanley Mamu, LNG Watch, http://lngwatchpng.blogspot.co.uk/

63 Andrew Alphonse, 'Stupid Tari Airport LO's', Network54, 30 October 2011, www.network54.com/Forum/159830/thread/ 1319947285/1320880326/Stupid+Tari+Airport+LO%27s

64 Andrew Alphonse, 'Protest disrupts work on LNG airport', Post-Courier, 12 September 2011, www.postcourier.com.pg/20110912/ news10.htm

65 PNG LNG, 'Komo Airstrip Resettlement Action Plan', November 2010, http://pnglng.com/media/pdfs/committment/Komo%20 Airstrip%20RAP%20PGHU-EH-SPZZZ-42001_Rev%201%20 FINAL.pdf

66 Blair Price, 'Yet to be harmless', PNGIndustryNews.net, 29 February 2013, www.pngindustrynews.net/storyview.asp?storyid= 3200845

67 Australian Pipeliner, 'Massive projects, massive attendance at Brisbane', October 2010, http://pipeliner.com.au/news/massive_ projects_massive_attendance_at_brisbane/043568/#

68 Bill Ogilvie, 'EPC4 PROJECTCBI Clough JV Contractor Workshop – April 20th–23rd', PNG LNG, 26 November 2010, www.pnglng. com/pnglng/uploads/media/EPC4%20CBI%20Clough%20JV%20 Presenter%20Bill%20Ogilvie.pdf (accessed 14 May 2012).

69 Stanley Mamu, LNG Watch.

70 Blair Price, 'Yet to be harmless'.

71 Lord Sempill, 'New Guinea's Goldfields', Flight International, 18 April 1935, www.flightglobal.com/pdfarchive/view/1935/1935%20 -%200889.html; Allaz, The History of Air Cargo and Airmail, p. 134.

72 Malum Nalu, 'Bulolo reopens for business', Islands Business, July 2011, www.islandsbusiness.com/2011/7/aviation/bulolo-reopens-for-business/

73 Indigenous Peoples Issues and Resources, 'Watut River Community riots against Newcrest and Harmony', 4 June 2011, http:// indigenouspeoplesissues.com/index.php?option=com_content &view=article&id=10780:papua-new-guinea-watut-river-community-riots-against-newcrest-and-harmony&catid= 28&Itemid=61

74 Allaz, The History of Air Cargo and Airmail, p. 137.

75 Harry Winston Inc, 'Mining diamonds in the arctic north', 2011, www.diavik.ca/index_ouroperations.asp

76 Mining Technology, 'Minry Diamond Mine, Russia', www.mining-technology.com/projects/minry-diamond/

77 Elliot Blair Smith, Eltaf Najafizada and James Rupert, 'Afghan mineral wealth: no easy road for westerners', Bloomberg, 17 June 2010, www.businessweek.com/magazine/content/10_26/b4184011396010.htm

78 *Aircargo News*, 'Airfreight demand grows in Afghanistan', 6 July 2010, www.aircargonews.net/news/single-view/news/airfreight-demand-grows-in-afghanistan.html

79 Richard Weitz, 'Is China freeloading off the U.S. Military's work in Afghanistan and Iraq?', Huffington Post, 15 August 2011, www.huffingtonpost.com/2011/08/15/china-military-afghanistan-iraq_n_927342.html

80 Allaz, *The History of Air Cargo and Airmail,* pp. 225–6.

81 Emirates SkyCargo, 'Service expanding in Africa and Russia', 2006, www.skycargo.com/mediacentre/newsletter/2006/2006_Issue1/issue1details.asp (accessed 16 April 2008).

82 Payload Asia, 'Astral Aviation links the world to the "rest of Africa"', April 2011, www.payloadasia.com/article-6253-astralaviationlinks theworldtotherestofafrica-PayloadAsia.html

8 Arms, Aid and Accidents

1 Hugh Griffiths and Mark Bromley, 'Air transport and destabilizing commodity flows', SIPRI, May 2009, p. 10, http://books.sipri.org/files/PP/SIPRIPP24.pdf

2 Griffiths and Bromley, 'Air transport and destabilizing commodity flows', pp. 1–29.

3 *Aircargo News*, 'Seized Il-76 tracked back to Kazakhstan', 26 January 2010, www.aircargonews.net/news/single-view/news/seized-il-76-tracked-back-to-kazakhstan.html

4 Griffiths and Bromley, 'Air transport and destabilizing commodity flows', pp. 39–45.

5 IATA, 'Safety in Africa – united approach', April 2011, www.iata.org/publications/airlines-international/april-2011/pages/safety.aspx

6 Andy Sambidge, 'MENA's air crash record worsens in 2011, says IATA', Arabiansupplychain.com, 7 March 2012, www.arabian supplychain.com/article-7231-menas-air-crash-record-worsens-in-2011-says-iata/

7 European Commission, 'List of airlines banned within the EU', 23 November 2011, http://ec.europa.eu/transport/air-ban/doc/list_en.pdf

8 Terminal U, 'EU using airline blacklist to block African carriers

competing in Europe, says African Airlines group', 21 July 2011, www.terminalu.com/travel-news/eu-using-airline-blacklist-to-block-african-carriers-competing-in-europe-says-african-airlines-group/12592/

9 Tim Hepher, 'IATA says EU's airline safety bans hinder Africa', Reuters, 10 June 2012, www.reuters.com/article/2012/06/10/uk-iata-africa-safety-idUSLNE85900G20120610

10 Simon Hradecky, 'Crash: Aerolift AN12 at Luxor on Feb 20th 2009, engine fire', *Aviation Herald*, 20 February 2009, http://avherald.com/h?article=41552e2f

11 Adrian Stuijt, 'US military locates crashed Russian plane deep in Ugandan lake', *Digital Journal*, 26 March 2009, www.digitaljournal.com/article/269876

12 ASN, http://aviation-safety.net/database/dblist.php?Type=314

13 Alex Lennane, 'Flying in the face of a ban', *International Freighting Weekly*, 10 February 2010, www.ifw-net.com/freightpubs/ifw/index-article.htm?artid=20017747400 (accessed 21 December 2010).

14 ASN, http://aviation-safety.net/database/record.php?id=20050203-0

15 ASN, http://aviation-safety.net/database/record.php?id=20050602-0

16 Nichola Mandil, 'Juba Air Cargo crashes killing two airport's guards', GOSS Mission-USA, 8 November 2008, www.gossmission.org/goss/index.php?option=com_contentandtask=viewandid=289andItemid=192

17 Sam Jones, '120 feared killed in Sudan plane crash', *Guardian*, 11 June 2008, www.guardian.co.uk/world/2008/jun/11/sudan.jordan

18 Al Jazeera, 'Cargo airplane crashes in Khartoum', 30 June 2008, http://english.aljazeera.net/news/africa/2008/06/2008630111410905359.html

19 ASN, http://aviation-safety.net/database/record.php?id=20050909-1

20 ASN, http://aviation-safety.net/database/record.php?id=20090826-0

21 Damian Brett, 'Mystery surrounds victims of cargo aircraft crash in Congo', *International Freighting Weekly*, 22 March 2011, www.ifw-net.com/freightpubs/ifw/index/mystery-surrounds-victims-of-cargo-aircraft-crash-in-congo/20017858674.htm (accessed 24 March 2011).

22 ASN, http://aviation-safety.net/database/record.php?id=20121130-0

23 David Learmont, 'Kinshasa sees repeat of ground carnage after crash', *Flight International*, 5 October 2010, www.flightglobal.com/articles/2007/10/05/217951/kinshasa-sees-repeat-of-ground-carnage-after-crash.html

24 ASN, http://aviation-safety.net/database/record.php?id=19960606-2

25 ASN, http://aviation-safety.net/database/record.php?id=20030508-0

26 ASN, http://aviation-safety.net/database/record.php?id=20031129-0

27 CBC News, 'Death toll rises in Kinshasa plane crash', 4 October 2007, www.cbc.ca/world/story/2007/10/04/congo-crash.html?ref=rss

28 BBC News, 'Fatal UN plane crash at DR Congo's Kinshasa airport', 4 April 2011, www.bbc.co.uk/news/world-africa-12962210

29 1001crash.com, 'TRACEP – Antonov AN-28 Bukavu, Congo', 3 August 2006, www.1001crash.com/index-page-description-accident-Traset_AN28-lg-2-crash-134.html

30 ASN, http://aviation-safety.net/database/record.php?id=20101021-0

31 ASN, http://aviation-safety.net/database/record.php?id=20120130-0

32 ASN, http://aviation-safety.net/database/record.php?id=20120212-0

33 ASN, http://aviation-safety.net/database/record.php?id=20080901-1

34 Airdisaster.info, 'LET410 crash in DRC', 15 February 2011, www.airdisaster.info/forums/viewtopic.php?f=6andp=52651

35 ASN, http://aviation-safety.net/database/record.php?id=20070215-1

36 ASN, http://aviation-safety.net/database/record.php?id=20070517-0

37 Nicholas Garrett, *Walikale: Artisanal cassiterite mining and trade in North Kivu implications for poverty reduction and security, communities and small scale mining (CASM)*, 1 June 2008, pp. 33–4, www.artisanalmining.org/userfiles/file/CASM_WalikaleBooklet.pdf

38 ASN, http://aviation-safety.net/database/record.php?id=20070907-0

39 ASN, http://aviation-safety.net/database/record.php?id=20080415-0

40 ASN, http://aviation-safety.net/database/record.php?id=20091119-0

41 David Barouski, 'Transcript of David Barouski's 10/19/08 presentation for Congo Week in Chicago, IL.', 18 November 2008, www.zcommunications.org/transcript-of-david-barouskis-10-19-08-presentation-for-congo-week-in-chicago-il-by-david-barouski

42 Ruben de Koning, 'Artisanal mining and postconflict reconstruction in the Democratic Republic of the Congo', SIPRI, October 2009, p. 10, http://books.sipri.org/files/misc/SIPRIBP0910b.pdf

43 Gerson Lehrman Group, 'Mining ban in Democratic Republic of Congo – industry impact and future prospects', 1 March 2011, www.glgroup.com/News/Mining-Ban-in-Democratic-Republic-of-Congo--Industry-Impact--Future-Prospects-52762.html

44 Michael J. Kavanagh, 'Two pilots kidnapped in main Congolese tin-mining area, UN says', *Business Week*, 2 September 2010, www.businessweek.com/news/2010-09-02/two-pilots-kidnapped-in-main-congolese-tin-mining-area-un-says.html (accessed 13 December 2010).

45 Damien Fruchart, 'United Nations arms embargoes, their impact on arms flows and target behaviour, case study: Rwanda, 1994–present', SIPRI, 2007, pp. 13–14, http://books.sipri.org/files/misc/UNAE/SIPRI07UNAERwa.pdf

46 Camille Allaz, *The History of Air Cargo and Airmail,* Christopher Foyle/International Air Cargo Association, 2004, p. 12.

47 Allaz, *The History of Air Cargo and Airmail,* p. 18.

48 Allaz, *The History of Air Cargo and Airmail,* p. 35.

49 Allaz, *The History of Air Cargo and Airmail,* pp. 21–2.

50 Allaz, *The History of Air Cargo and Airmail,* pp. 32–3.

51 Allaz, *The History of Air Cargo and Airmail,* p. 151.

52 Robert W. Moorman, 'Cargo's hot market', *Air Cargo World,* November 2006, www.aircargoworld.com/features/1106_2.htm (accessed 8 July 2008).

53 *Air Cargo World,* 'Pentagon hands air $3.6 billion', 21 September 2007, www.aircargoworld.com/break_news/09212007a.htm (accessed 7 November 2007).

54 Evergreen Aviation, www.evergreenaviation.com/EIA/services.html

55 Michael Fabey, 'Cargo's defense posture', *Air Cargo World,* June 2008, www.aircargoworld.com/features/0608_4.htm (accessed 15 August 2009).

56 Erik Holmes, 'Charleston AFB delivers 2,000th MRAP to Iraq', *AirForceTimes,* 10 March 2008, www.airforcetimes.com/news/2008/03/airforce_mrap_charleston_030708w/

57 Erik Holmes, 'MRAPs going to Iraq on Russian cargo plane', *ArmyTimes,* 26 October 2007, www.armytimes.com/news/2007/10/airforce_MRAP_russian_071026w/

58 Allaz, *The History of Air Cargo and Airmail,* p. 335.

59 Aviaglobus, 'The return of the "prodigal son" from Hainan Island', August 2001, www.poletairlines.com/english/press/prodigal_son.htm (accessed 15 April 2011).

60 Evergreen Aviation, 'Evergreen humanitarian and relief services', www.ehrsi.org/

61 Alex Hawkes, 'Heavy metal', *Arabian Business,* 1 April 2007, www.arabianbusiness.com/heavy-metal-147053.html

62 HeavyLift Cargo Airlines, http://heavyliftcargo.com/belfastcap.htm

63 Stephen Grey, *Ghost Plane: The inside story of the CIA's secret rendition programme,* C. Hurst, 2006, pp. 16–17.

64 Grey, *Ghost Plane,* p. 207.

65 Glasgow Prestwick Airport, 'Specialist capabilities', www.gpia.co.uk/AirFreight/specialist/default.asp (accessed 7 November 2007).

66 Ian Cobain and Ben Quinn, 'How US firms profited from torture flights', *Guardian,* 31 August 2011, www.guardian.co.uk/world/2011/aug/31/us-firms-torture-flights-rendition

67 Mark Urban, 'The nature of President Obama's rendition programme', BBC News, 9 September 2011, www.bbc.co.uk/news/world-14862161

9 Concrete and Overcapacity

1 Matt Phillips, 'Airport projects approved to receive stimulus money', *Wall Street Journal*, 31 March 2009, http://blogs.wsj.com/middleseat/2009/03/31/airport-projects-approved-to-receive-stimulus-money/

2 Michael Grabell, 'Tiny airports take off with stimulus', ProPublica, 13 July 2009, www.propublica.org/article/tiny-airports-take-off-with-stimulus-713

3 Carolyn D. Leonnig, 'Murtha's earmarks keep airport aloft', *Washington Post*, 19 April 2009, www.washingtonpost.com/wp-dyn/content/article/2009/04/18/AR2009041802128.html

4 Scott Whitlock, 'ABC's Jonathan Karl hits stimulus waste; derides Murtha Airport as a "ghost town"', NewsBusters, 18 September 2009, http://newsbusters.org/blogs/scott-whitlock/2009/09/18/abc-s-jonathan-karl-hits-stimulus-waste-derides-murtha...

5 FAA, 'Pavement design and construction', 10 September 2012, www.faa.gov/airports/engineering/pavement_design/

6 CAPA, 'US airport bond issues to rise as AIP grants reduce', 15 August 2012, http://centreforaviation.com/analysis/us-airport-bond-issues-to-rise-as-aip-grants-reduce-80196 (accessed 5 September 2012).

7 Associated Press, 'House panel boosts rural air service subsidies', 19 June 2012, http://wap.yahoo.com/w/legobpengine/news/house-panel-boosts-rural-air-subsidies-195808972.html

8 Joe Brancatelli, 'The odd case of taxpayer subsidies to small airports', *Business Journals*, 27 July 2011, www.bizjournals.com/bizjournals/blog/seat2B/2011/07/budget-fight-hits-faa-and-essential-air-service.html

9 Associated Press, 'House panel boosts rural air service subsidies'.

10 Jim Glab, 'Flying on private jets', Executivetravelmagazine.com, May/June 2011, http://www.executivetravelmagazine.com/articles/flying-on-private-jets

11 Mark Maremont and Tom McGinty, 'Corporate jet set: leisure vs. business', *Wall Street Journal*, 16 June 2011, http://online.wsj.com/article/SB10001424052748703551304576260871791710428.html

12 Glab, 'Flying on private jets'.

13 Richard Rubin and Andrew Zajac, 'Corporate jet tax gets six Obama mentions, $3 billion estimate', Bloomberg, 1 July 2011, www.bloomberg.com/news/2011-06-29/jet-tax-break-cited-six-times-by-obama-would-cut-debt-by-about-3-billion.html

14 Hal Herring, 'The Panhandle paradox', MillerMccune, 17 August 2009, http://halherring.com/files/PDF/CoastalDev/panhandle paradox.pdf

15 Jason Koertge, 'Main runway is *paved* at new airport', PCBDaily, 2 February 2009, http://pcbdaily.com/main-runway-is-paved-at-new-airport-video

16 Leah Stratmann, 'Airport construction dumps tons of mud in estuary', *Defuniak Herald*, 15 May 2009, http://defuniakherald.com/?p=979

17 Herring, 'The Panhandle paradox'.

18 Linda Young, 'Lawmakers should halt airport boondoggle', Tampa Bay Online, 14 April 2008, www2.tbo.com/content/2008/apr/14/na-lawmakers-should-halt-airport-boondoggle/ (accessed 16 August 2010).

19 CWN, 'Conservationists and pilots file suit against FAA's $331-million Florida Panhandle "airport to nowhere"', 14 November 2006, www.cleanwaternetwork-fl.org/content/disp_article.php?f=issues/111406-FAAsuitdefenders.html (accessed 10 June 2009).

20 PRNewswire, 'Northwest Florida Beaches International Airport, designed as country's first LEED(R) certified airport, to start passenger and freight service', May 2010, www.prnewswire.com/news-releases/northwest-florida-beaches-international-airport-designed-as-countrys-first-leedr-certified-airport-to-start-passenger-and-freight-service-may-2010-78152507.html

21 Leah Stratmann, 'Lawsuit looming to stop airport construction', *Defuniak Herald*, 3 July 2009, http://defuniakherald.com/?p=1091

22 Herring, 'The Panhandle paradox'.

23 CWN, 'Conservationists and pilots file suit against FAA's $331-million Florida Panhandle "airport to nowhere"'.

24 St Joe Company, *Annual Report 2009*, March 2010, http://files.shareholder.com/downloads/JOE/2391197492x0x363618/95D1E17F-F82E-4847-B7F3-203D214601F9/2009AnnualReport.pdf

25 Herring, 'The Panhandle paradox'.

26 Craig Pittman and Kris Hundley, 'New Panhandle airport will be first in U.S. since 9/11', *Tampa Bay Times,* 17 August 2007, www.sptimes.com/2007/08/17/State/New_Panhandle_airport.shtml

27 Pat Kelly, 'Airport vegetation provides "good impression" to travelers, officials say', Newsherald.com, 2 November 2011, www.newsherald.com/articles/say-98040-bay-travelers.html (accessed 11 November 2011).

28 J. Michael Brown, 'Defense contractor to move operations to new airport site', WMBBNews, 7 September 2011, www.wmbb.com/story/15405731/defense-contractor-announces

29 Wjhg.com, 'Airport authority discusses ground transportation, damaged wetland issues', 15 September 2010, www.wjhg.com/home/headlines/103000164.html

30 Dailymotion, 'Storm water runoff problems still exists at Northwest

Florida Beaches Airport', 23 February 2012, www.dailymotion.com/video/xp036n_storm-water-runoff-problems-still-exists-at-north-west-florida-beaches-airport_news

31 J. Terrence Brunner, *The 'Action' at O'Hare: The corruption of the public policy process leading to O'Hare expansion*, December 2004, www.areco.org/pdf/Brunner%20Report.pdf

32 Bethany Jaeger, 'Chris Kelly pleads guilty to O'Hare scheme – updated upon his death', Illinois Issues Blog, http://illinoisissuesblog.blogspot.com/2009/09/chris-kelly-pleads-guilty-to-ohare.html

33 Ray Gibson, 'Guilty plea in Azteca fraud case', *Chicago Tribune*, 3 December 2010, http://articles.chicagotribune.com/2010-12-03/news/ct-met-ohare-fraud-plea-20101203_1_thomas-masen-aurora-venegas-azteca-supply

34 Julie Johnsson and Jon Hilkevitch, 'City of Chicago to pay United Airlines $163 million to move cargo facility', *Chicago Tribune*, 22 January 2009, http://articles.chicagotribune.com/2009-01-22/news/0901211020_1_o-hare-modernization-program-runway-united-spokeswoman-jean-medina

35 *Passenger Terminal Today*, 'Bensenville president slams O'Hare expansion', 20 February 2009, www.passengerterminaltoday.com/news.php?NewsID=10855 (accessed 21 February 2009).

36 City of Chicago, 'City receives first competitive grant from Federal Stimulus Program', 30 March 2009, http://mayor.cityofchicago.org/mayor/en/press_room/press_releases/2009/march_2009/city_receives_first.print.html (accessed 10 June 2010).

37 Dick Durbin, 'Mayor Daley, Secretary LaHood, Senator Durbin and Governor Quinn announce $410 million in funding for O'Hare Modernization Program', 6 April 2010, http://durbin.senate.gov/public/index.cfm/pressreleases?ID=525891d0-9d28-4948-9018-ed058431caa4

38 Karen E. Pride, 'Rescued trees branch out at O'Hare International Airport', City of Chicago, 22 April 2010, www.cityofchicago.org/city/en/depts/doa/provdrs/sai/news/2010/apr/trees_planted_forearthday.html (accessed 15 June 2010).

39 Robert Powers, 'Victims of the revolution', 3 June 2010, http://achicagosojourn.blogspot.com/2010/06/victims-of-revolution.html

40 Eve Rodriguez, 'City of Chicago regains title and possession of St. Johanne's cemetery', City of Chicago, 26 January 2011, www.ohare.com/PDF/News/012611_CDA%20News%20Release_SJC_FINAL.pdf

41 Jon Hilkevitch and Julie Johnsson, 'Funding plan for O'Hare expansion draws another downgrade', *Chicago Tribune*, 12 January

2011, http://articles.chicagotribune.com/2011-01-12/business/
ct-biz-0113-ohare-bonds-20110112_1_major-credit-rating-agency-
airport-debt-fitch-ratings

42 Jon Hilkevitch, 'Chicago, airlines sign deal for one more O'Hare
runway', *Chicago Tribune,* 14 March 2011, http://articles.
chicagotribune.com/2011-03-14/news/ct-met-ohare-deal-
20110314_1_o-hare-runway-lahood-airline-lawsuit

43 Brunner, *The 'Action' at O'Hare,* p. 32.

44 Eno Center for Transportation, *Lessons Learned From the Chicago
O'Hare Modernization Program,* October 2011, https://enotrans-
.r.worldssl.net/wp-content/uploads/wpsc/downloadables/
Chicago-paper.pdf

45 City of Chicago, 'O'Hare Modernization Program', http://www.city-
ofchicago.org/city/en/depts/doa/provdrs/omp.html

46 ACI, 'World's busiest airports by passenger traffic', http://en.wiki-
pedia.org/wiki/World%27s_busiest_airports_by_passenger_traffic

47 NorthShore Greens, 'Shut This Airport Nightmare Down', 1
May 2010, http://northshoregreens.org/2010/05/shut-this-
airport-nightmare-down/

48 CBSChicago.com, 'Cash-Strapped Ill. government moving ahead
with Peotone land buys', 7 April 2011, http://chicago.cbslocal.
com/2011/04/07/cash-strapped-ill-government-moving-ahead-
with-peotone-land-buys/

49 Steven Malanga, 'Airfields of dreams', *City Journal,* 22 April 2012,
www.city-journal.org/2012/22_4_airports.html

50 David Nicklaus, 'MidAmerica has its lemonade stand', Stltoday.
com, 24 August 2010, www.stltoday.com/business/columns/
david-nicklaus/nicklaus-midamerica-has-its-lemonade-stand/article_
d394c921-d3d6-54d1-9915-1d15d506d7cc.html

51 Will Buss, 'Business is looking up at MidAmerica Airport', BND.
com, 12 November 2012, www.bnd.com/2012/11/12/2392283/
business-is-looking-up-at-midamerica.html (accessed 22 November
2012).

52 Melinda Roth, 'Terminal illness', RFT, 16 December 1998, www.
riverfronttimes.com/1998-12-16/news/terminal-illness/

53 J. Desy Schoenewies, '56 houses, starting October 9, 2007', http://
56housesleft.wordpress.com/about/

54 Associated Press, 'Aerotropolis: economic boon or boondoggle',
4 September 2011, www.newstribune.com/news/2011/sep/04/
aerotropolis-boon-or-boondoggle/

55 Tim Logan, 'MidAmerica goes international for incoming cargo
first flights', Aviationpros.com, 26 June 2007, www.aviationpros.
com/news/10387738/midamerica-goes-international-for-incoming-

cargo-first-flights-seed-corn-arrives-from-chile-for-monsanto-on-horizon-aviation-consultant-predicts-tough-competition

56 Valerie Shremp Hahn, 'South American cargo deal could help airport fly', *Airport Business*, 8 July 2008, www.airportbusiness.com/web/online/Top-News-Headlines/South-American-cargo-deal-could-help-airport-fly-Outlay-St-Clair-County-would-spend-279-million-on-equipment-at-MidAmerica/1$20453 (accessed 26 March 2010).

57 Nicklaus, 'MidAmerica has its lemonade stand'.

58 Susan Carey, 'Small airports struggle to get off ground', *Wall Street Journal*, 8 August 2011, http://online.wsj.com/article/SB100014240 53111903635604576476170691580238.html

59 Ken Leiser, 'MidAmerica airport pins latest hopes on growing business', Stltoday.com, 29 June 2012, www.stltoday.com/business/local/midamerica-airport-pins-latest-hopes-on-growing-business/article_ba951cc4-bc84-11e1-835c-001a4bcf6878.html

60 Will Buss, 'Business is looking up at MidAmerica airport'.

61 Audrey Spalding, 'China hub tax incentives more expensive than advertised', ShowMeDaily, 11 April 2011, www.showmedaily.org/2011/04/china-hub-tax-incentives-more.html

62 David Nicklaus, '"Aerotropolis" expert says St. Louis will never be one', Stltoday.com, 17 July 2011, http://www.stltoday.com/business/columns/david-nicklaus/article_a377c6bd-a005-57a2-a63d-227599165b77.html

63 Desy, 17 July 2011, http://56housesleft.wordpress.com/

64 U.S. Department of Transportation, 'Total passengers on U.S airlines and foreign airlines U.S. flights increased 1.3% in 2012 from 2011', 4 April 2013, www.rita.dot.gov/bts/press_releases/bts016_13 (accessed 27 April 2013).

65 ACI, 'Preliminary world airport traffic 2011', 27 March 2012, www.aci-africa.aero/aci/aci/file/Press%20Releases/2012/PR_2012-03-27_PreliminaryResults_2011.pdf

66 Boeing, *World Air Cargo Forecast 2012–2013*, p. 14, www.boeing.com/commercial/cargo/wacf.pdf

67 Boeing, *World Air Cargo Forecast 2012–2013*, p. 6.

10 Counting the Costs

1 G. R. Bimal, 'Comprehensive review of airport business models', ACI, www.airports.org/aci/ACIAPAC/File/Young%20Executive%20Award%2011/Paper_Cochin.pdf

2 CAPA, 'India's 2011/12 budget to support infrastructure development', 1 March 2011, http://centreforaviation.com/analysis-indian-2011-12-budget-to-support-infrastructure-development-46731

3   *Sunday Times*, 'Boeing-Airbus dogfight heats up at the WTO', 5 June 2005, www.timeslive.co.za/sundaytimes/article101387.ece (accessed 5 February 2010).

4   *Economist*, 'Trading blows', 13 August 2009, www.economist.com/node/14214813

5   Tom Miles and Tim Hepher , 'WTO upholds ruling on Boeing subsidies', Reuters, 13 March 2012, www.reuters.com/article/2012/03/13/us-wto-aircraft-idUSBRE82C01T20120313

6   Chan Sue Ling, 'Planemakers may end up with 200 'whitetails' in 2009', Bloomberg, 6 November 2008, www.bloomberg.com/apps/news?pid=newsarchive&sid=a7DWroUcpKEU

7   Timothy P. Carney, 'Sweeping Boeing's bank under the rug', Washingtonexaminer.com, 9 February 2007, http://washingtonexaminer.com/node/378361 (accessed 12 February 2007).

8   Cynthia Magnuson, 'Pew analysis shows more than 60 percent of export-import bank loan guarantees benefited single company', Pew Charitable Trusts, 9 November 2009, www.pewtrusts.org/news_room_detail.aspx?id=55965

9   AvBuyer, 'China to play a bigger role in aircraft financing says Airbus', 29 January 2010, www.avbuyer.com.cn/e/2010/39106.html (accessed 16 March 2010).

10 Timothy P. Carney, 'Boeing gets big tailwind from subsidized bank', Washingtonexaminer.com, 10 March 2010, http://washingtonexaminer.com/politics/boeing-gets-big-tailwind-subsidized-bank (accessed 16 March 2010).

11 Pilita Clark, 'Aircraft financing debate comes to a head', *Financial Times*, 16 July 2010, www.ft.com/cms/s/0/da7bc376-903a-11df-ad26-00144feab49a.html#axzz2Olp6U8BR

12 Arno Schuetze and Alexander Hübner, 'Aircraft financing costs seen close to peak', Reuters, 20 February 2012, www.reuters.com/article/2012/02/20/us-aircraft-financing-idUSTRE81J0XY20120220

13 Reuters, 'Airbus, Boeing top 1,000 deliveries in 2011', 12 January 2012, www.reuters.com/article/2012/01/12/us-airbus-idUSTRE80B20A20120112

14 Kevin Rozario, 'Shopping showdown', *Airport World,* 23 January 2012, http://airport-world.com/publications/all-online-articles/item/1311-shopping-showdown

15 Dubai Duty Free, 'About DDF', 2012, www.dubaidutyfree.com/about/about_ddf

16 AMEinfo, 'Dubai Duty Free sales up 15.69% in 2011', 3 January 2012, www.ameinfo.com/285733.html

17 David Hayes, 'Incheon Vuitton shop averaging $300,000 a day', *The*

Travel Retail Business, 2 February 2012, www.trbusiness.com/index. php?option=com_content&view=article&id=10893

18 CAPA, 'Potential for USD3.5bn of duty free, retail, F&B spend at Indian airports', 22 May 2012, http://centreforaviation.com/analysis/ capa-report-potential-for-usd35bn-of-duty-free-retail-fb-spend-at-indian-airports-74409

19 John Rimmer, 'Delhi aspires to new heights', *Moodie Report,* Oct.–Nov. 2011, pp. 12–22, http://edition.page-suite-professional.co.uk/launch.aspx?referral=other& pnum=41&refresh=6Mf013ZnmB04&EID=effef60e-0e49 -425a-bfb5-bcd592603871&skip=&p=41

20 Martin Moodie, 'Heathrow Airport unveils unprecedented summer advertising blitz', *Moodie Report*, 6 July 2011, www.moodiereport. com/document.php?c_id=1185&doc_id=27851

21 Nicole Mezzasalma, 'BAA reveals double-digit increase in Heathrow retail sales', DFNIonline.com, 24 February 2012, www.dfnionline. com/article/BAA-reveals-double-digit-increase-in-Heathrow-retail-sales-1862172.html

22 Brendon Sewill, *The Hidden Cost of Flying*, AEF, 2003, pp. 10–18.

23 IATA, *2012 Annual Review*, p. 8, www.iata.org/about/Documents/ annual-review-2012.pdf

24 Joe Dings, *Grounded: How ICAO failed to tackle aviation and climate change and what should happen now,* Transport & Environment, 2010, www.transportenvironment.org/sites/default/files/media/2010_09_ icao_grounded.pdf

25 Rose Bridger, 'Flag carriers – too big too fail', 9 September 2011, www.rosebridger.com/2011/09/flag-carriers-too-big-to-fail.html

26 Cargo News Asia, 'Croatia flag carrier to get capital boost, cut jobs', 21 November 2012, www.cargonewsasia.com/secured/article. aspx?id=15&article=29869

27 Bridger, 'Flag carriers – too big too fail'.

28 MercoPress, 'Aerolíneas receives a daily government support of over 2 million dollars', 3 February 2012, http://en.mercopress. com/2012/02/03/aerolineas-receives-a-daily-government-support-of-over-2-million-dollars

29 *Airline Leader*, 'Not all Gulf airlines are enjoying a healthy outlook', www.airlineleader.com/regional-focus/ not-all-gulf-airlines-are-enjoying-a-healthy-outlook

30 Albawaba.com, 'Bahrain: Gulf Air handed bail out to keep flying', 1 November 2012, www.albawaba.com/business/ bahrain-gulf-air-449058

31 Bridger, 'Flag carriers – too big too fail'.

32 *Sunday Leader*, 'SriLankan to turnaround in 2015', 19 August 2012,

www.thesundayleader.lk/2012/08/19/srilankan-to-turnaround-in-2015/ (accessed 24 August 2012).

33 Martin Rivers, 'PIA net debt of 123bn rupees prompts warning', *Flightglobal*, 12 September 2012, www.flightglobal.com/news/articles/pia-net-debt-of-123bn-rupees-prompts-warning-376397/

34 Tribune.com, 'New business plan: govt approves $4.5 million bailout for PIA', 1 August 2012, http://tribune.com.pk/story/416029/new-business-plan-govt-approves-4-5-million-bailout-for-pia/

35 Jay Menon, 'Air India expects huge aid package', Aviation Week, 14 March 2012, www.aviationweek.com/aw/generic/story_generic.jsp?topicName=india&id=news/awx/2012/03/14/awx_03_14_2012_p0-436065.xml&headline=Air%20India%20Expects%20Huge%20Aid%20Package (accessed 20 March 2012).

36 Karthikeyan Sundaram and Adi Narayan, 'Air India aid package adds to Kingfisher pain', *Business Week*, 13 March 2012, www.businessweek.com/news/2012-03-13air-india-aid-dwarfing-hospital-budget-adds-to-kingfisher-pain

37 BBC News, 'Government approves plan to save Air India', 12 April 2012, www.bbc.co.uk/news/world-asia-india-17686507

38 Bridger, 'Flag carriers – too big too fail'.

39 Panapress, 'New Mauritania national carrier begins operations', 28 April 2011, www.panapress.com/New-Mauritania-national-carrier-begins-operations--12-770388-28-lang2-index.html

40 Bridger, Flag carriers – too big too fail'.

41 Polity.org.za, 'DA: statement by Natasha Michael, Demcoratic Alliance shadow minister of public enterprises, calling for the privatisation of SAA', 15 February 2012, www.polity.org.za/article/da-statement-by-natasha-michael-democratic-alliance-shadow-minister-of-public-enterprises-calling-fort-he-privatisation-of-saa-15022012-2012-02-15

42 Verashni Pillay, 'Treasury grants SAA's R5-billion request', *Mail&Guardian*, 2 October 2012, http://mg.co.za/article/2012-10-02-treasury-announces-r5bn-bail-out-for-saa

43 Kyle Peterson and Matt Daily, 'American Airlines files for bank ruptcy', Reuters, 29 November 2011, www.reuters.com/article/2011/11/29/us-americanairlines-idUSTRE7AS0T220111129

44 Steven Pearlstein, 'Two can play the airline bankruptcy game', *Washington Post*, 28 April 2012, www.washingtonpost.com/business/steven-pearlstein-two-can-play-the-airline-bankruptcy-game/2012/04/27/gIQAJ239nT_story.html

45 HACAN, 'The government's support for a third runway at Heathrow

is "flawed and misleading"', 14 February 2008, www.hacan.org.uk/resources/briefings/ce.delft.press.release.and.key.points.pdf

46 Airport Watch, 'CE Delft economic study shows cost of building a new Nantes airport would exceed its benefits', 26 October 2011, www.airportwatch.org.uk/?p=4653

47 Sally Cairns and Carey Newson, *Predict and Decide: Aviation, climate change and UK policy,* Environmental Change Institute, September 2006, www.eci.ox.ac.uk/research/energy/downloads/predictanddecide.pdf

48 Victoria Johnson and Martin Cottingham, *Plane Truths: Do the economic arguments for aviation growth really fly?* New Economics Foundation & World Development Movement, September 2008, www.neweconomics.org/publications/plane-truths

49 Brendon Sewill, *Airport Jobs: False hopes, cruel hoax,* AEF, March 2009, www.aef.org.uk/uploads/Airport_jobs___false_hopes_cruel_hoax.pdf

50 Department for Transport, 'The air freight end-to-end journey, an analysis of the end-to-end journey of air freight through UK international gateways', May 2009, http://webarchive.nationalarchives.gov.uk/+/http:/www.dft.gov.uk/about/strategy/transportstrategy/tasts/userexperience/endtoendjourney.pdf

51 Jan Maurits de Jonge, 'No break in the storm', *Air Cargo World,* December 2008, www.aircargoworld.com/features/1208_1.htm (accessed 19 January 2009).

52 Sewill, *Airport Jobs.*

53 ACI, *Airport Economics Survey 2006,* p. 2, www.aci.aero/aci/aci/file/Economics(restricted)/ACI-1007-06-ECO%20Survey-H.pdf

54 ACI, 'New airport economics 2008 report', 26 December 2008, www.4hoteliers.com/4hots_nshw.php?mwi=5372

55 ACI, 'Airport economics 2009 report', 22 December 2009, www.aci-lac.aero/aci/aci/file/Press%20Releases/2009/PR_211208_Econ_Surv_2009_final.pdf

56 Chris Lo, 'Airport baggage systems go high-tech: handling with care', Airport-technology.com, 18 April 2012, www.airport-technology.com/features/featureairport-baggage-handling-systems

57 Tensator, 'Global Installations of the Tensator Virtual Assistant', www.tensator.com/uk/showroom/virtual-assistant-global-installations.aspx

58 Homeland Security Newswire, 'Manchester airport recalibrate facial recognition machines to shorten lines', 6 April 2009, www.homelandsecuritynewswire.com/manchester-airport-recalibrate-facial-recognition-machines-shorten-lines

59 Homeland Security News Wire, 'Manchester Airport biometric

gate unilaterally imprisons traveler', 2 December 2010, www.homelandsecuritynewswire.com/manchester-airport-biometric-gate-unilaterally-imprisons-traveler

60 Andrew Hough, 'Airport biometric scanners "failing to protect Britain's borders", whistleblower claims', *Telegraph*, 28 October 2010, www.telegraph.co.uk/travel/travelnews/8090820/Airport-biometric-scanners...

61 Andrew Nusca, 'In Amsterdam, a better airport baggage system (with robots)', Smartplanet.com, 21 March 2011, www.smartplanet.com/blog/smart-takes/in-amsterdam-a-better-airport-baggage-system-with-robots/14998

62 Spencer Ackerman, 'US Air Force to develop self-loading cargo robots', Wired.co.uk, 22 July 2010, www.wired.co.uk/news/archive/2010-07/22/us-air-force-cargo-robots

63 Adam Rawnsley, 'Air Force's robotic bags will pack themselves', Wired.com, 2 June 2011, www.wired.com/dangerroom/2011/06/robot-bags-pack-themselves/

64 Airport International, 'Heathrow's ULTra PRT robot taxis now in service', 12 August 2011, www.airport-int.com/news/heathrows-ultra-prt-robot-taxis-now-in-service.html

65 Steven Thompson, 'Heathrow's pod system could be rolled out to other airports', *Airport World*, 6 August 2012, www.airport-world.com/home/general-news/item/1786-heathrows-pod-system-could-be-rolled-out-to-other-airports

66 Frances Cha, 'Roving robotic scarecrows battle airport birds', 8 February 2012, http://travel.cnn.com/seoul/visit/birdstrike-robot-779434

67 Benet Wilson, 'Go shopping 24 hours a day 365 days a year at DFW Airport', *Aviation Week*, 4 September 2007, www.aviationweek.com/aw/blogs/commercial_aviation/TowersAndTarmacs/index.jsp?plckController=Blog&plckScript=blogScrip&plckElementId=blogDest&plckBlogPage=BlogViewPost&plckPostId=Blog%3A8427003a-9a63-4261-aa47-5e4b356bb224Post%3A22ff6973-460d-4541-bc8b-885ff7f21dd0 (accessed 12 January 2012).

68 *Asia Pacific Airports*, 'The shopping wall, the new way of shopping', April–June 2010, p. 33, www.insightgrp.co.uk/asia-pacific-airports-2010-02.html (accessed 24 May 2010).

69 John D. Kasarda, *The Evolution of Airport Cities and the Aerotropolis*, Aerotropolis.com, 2008, p. 4, www.aerotropolis.com/files/evolution-Chapter1.pdf

70 Elsa Baxter, 'Dubai Duty Free now the world's biggest airport retail operation', *Arabian Business*, 2 August 2009, www.arabianbusiness.com/563513-dubai-duty-free-named-as-the-worlds-biggest-retail-operation

71 Marion Dakers, 'Heathrow's retail sales are booming', City A.M., 8 March 2012, www.cityam.com/latest-news/heath row-s-retail-sales-are-booming

72 Nanette Byrnes, 'Home is where the airport is', *Business Week*, 20 August 2008, www.businessweek.com/magazine/content/07_34/b4047434.htm

73 *Las Vegas Review Journal*, 'Commissioners lower fees for airport slot machine concession', 2 February 2011, www.reviewjournal.com/business/casinos-gaming/commissioners-lower-fees-airport-slot-machine-concession

74 Tey-Marie Astudillo, '9 hidden venues at Incheon airport', CNN Travel, 23 September 2011, www.cnngo.com/seoul/visit/9-hidden-venues-incheon-airport-881594

75 Elizabeth Olson, 'When the fur doesn't fly', *New York Times*, 4 May 2011, www.nytimes.com/2011/05/05/business/05PET.html

76 Kenan-Flagler Business School, 'Aerotropolis is key to global competition', 1 September 2009, www.kenan-flagler.unc.edu/news/2009/09/aerotropolis-is-global-key.aspx

77 Kasarda, *The Evolution of Airport Cities and the Aerotropolis,* p. 19.

78 Joe Bates, 'The next step', *Global Airport Cities*, Issue 1, 2009, p. 7, www.insightgrp.co.uk/Globalairportcities.html (accessed 7 May 2009).

79 Chris Hutching, 'Christchurch airport parking and concessions up 25%', *National Business Review*, 5 March 2012, http://m.nbr.co.nz/article/christchurch-airport-parking-and-concessions-25-ck-111788

80 Rozario, 'Shopping showdown'.

81 IATA, *2012 Annual Review.*

82 Rozario, 'Shopping showdown'.

83 Kasarda, *The Evolution of Airport Cities and the Aerotropolis*, p. 3.

84 M. J. Subiria Arauz, 'Hartsfield-Jackson named world's most-efficient airport', *Clayton News Daily*, 18 August 2011, www.news-daily.com/news/2011/aug/18/airport-named-worlds-most-efficient-air/

85 Atlanta Airport, 'Hartsfield-Jackson receives Airport Revenue News' 2009 Best Concessions Management Team Award', 5 March 2009, www.atlanta-airport.com/airport/Newsroom/Press_Release_Article.aspx?id=624

86 UBC Asia Pacific Regional Office, 'Atlanta has world's most efficient airport, Korea now leads in Asia: UBC research', 24 July 2012, http://ubcapro.hk/2012/07/24/atlanta-has-worlds-most-efficient-airport-korea-now-leads-in-asia-ubc-research/

87 Dominic Welling, 'Atlanta approves $3bn array of airport concession contracts', *Airport World*, 4 January 2012, www.airport-world.

com/component/k2/item/1267-atlanta-approves-$3bn-array-of-airport-concession-contracts

88 Dominic Welling, 'Space fillers', *Airport World,* 21 October 2011, http://www.airport-world.com/home/item/1056-space-fillers

89 Denver Airport, Annual Financial Report December 31, 2010 and 2009, p. 13, http://business.flydenver.com/stats/financials/reports/2010_finrpt.pdf

90 Madeleine Heffernan and Matt O'Sullivan, 'Airport rakes in car revenue', *Brisbane Times,* 26 September 2012, www.brisbanetimes.com.au/travel/travel-news/airport-rakes-in-car-revenue-20120925-26jgd.html

91 Ian McIlwraith, 'Airports parking huge profits', *Sydney Morning Herald,* 31 March 2012, www.smh.com.au/business/airports-parking-huge-profits-20120330-1w3q7.html

92 Simon Calder and Alex Glover, 'Why it's cheaper to park a light aircraft at the airport than a car', *Independent,* 29 June 2012, www.independent.co.uk/travel/news-and-advice/why-its-cheaper-to-park-a-light-aircraft-at-the-airport-than-a-car-7897217.html

93 Chris Le Tourneur, 'Money spinners', *Global Airport Cities,* Spring 2007, p. 12, www.insightgrp.co.uk/images/stories/pdfs/Magazines/GAC/GAC-2007-01.pdf (accessed 7 March 2011).

94 Changi Airport Group, *Annual Report 2009/10,* www.changi-airportgroup.com/export/sites/caas/assets/changi_connection/Changi_Airport_Group_AR_0910_Full.pdf

95 John Rimmer, 'Hyderabad seizes the moment', *Moodie Report,* Oct.–Nov. 2011, p. 39, http://edition.pagesuite-professional.co.uk/launch.aspx?referral=other&pnum=41&refresh=6Mf013ZnmB04&EID=effef60e-0e49-425a-bfb5-bcd592603871&skip=&p=41

96 Geoff Tudor, 'Positive thinking', *Asia Pacific Airports,* December 2008, pp. 12–14, www.insightgrp.co.uk/images/stories/pdfs/Magazines/asia-pac/APA_2008-03.pdf (accessed 22 February 2011).

97 Joe Bates, 'Singing the same tune', *Global Airport Cities,* Summer 2007, pp. 14–16, http://www.insightgrp.co.uk/images/stories/pdfs/Magazines/GAC/GAC-2007-02.pdf (accessed 7 March 2011).

11   Real Estate and Revenue Streams

1   John D. Kasarda, *The Evolution of Airport Cities and the Aerotropolis,* Aerotropolis.com, 2008, p. 13, www.aerotropolis.com/files/evolutionChapter1.pdf

2   Kasarda, *The Evolution of Airport Cities and the Aerotropolis* p. 12.

3   John D. Kasarda, 'The new business model', *Global Airport Cities,* Autumn 2006, p. 7, http://insightgrp.co.uk/pdfs_web/

Magazines/GAPC/GAC_autumn_06_3.6mb.pdf (accessed 15 February 2008).

4   Schiphol Group, *Annual Report 2010*, p. 73, www.schiphol.nl/ SchipholGroup/InvestorRelations/FinancialInformation/Annual Reports.htm

5   Schiphol Group, *Annual Report 2011*, p. 53, www.schiphol.nl/ SchipholGroup/InvestorRelations/FinancialInformation/Annual Reports.htm

6   Oliver Clark, 'A walk in the park', *Global Airport Cities*, 16 March 2011, www.globalairportcities.com/a-walk-in-the-park (accessed 23 March 2011).

7   Erica Gingerich, 'Bavarian brilliance', *Global Airport Cities*, Autumn 2006, pp. 43–5, http://insightgrp.co.uk/pdfs_web/Magazines/ GAPC/GAC_autumn_06_3.6mb.pdf (accessed 15 February 2008).

8   *Global Airport Cities*, 'Frankfurt Airport', http://globalairportcities. com/frankfurt-airport.html

9   Frankfurt Airport, 'Mönchhof site', www.frankfurt-airport.com/ content/frankfurt_airport/en/business_location/real_estate_ development/moenchhof_site.html

10 Clark, 'A walk in the park'.

11 Oliver Clark, 'Three's a crowd', Airport World, 16 November 2009, www.airport-world.com/home/item/737-three%E2%80%99s -a-crowd

12 Kasarda, *The Evolution of Airport Cities and the Aerotropolis*, pp. 20–3.

13 *Passenger Terminal Today*, 'World champion', 2012, www.passenger-terminaltoday.com/features.php?BlogID=696

14 *SA Property Review*, 'Airports as economic engine rooms of the future', August 2010, www.acsa.co.za/content/property.pdf

15 Chris LeTourneur and Andrew Fayn, 'Destination retail', *Airport World*, 21 April 2011, http://airport-world.com/home/ item/459-destination-retail

16 Oliver, 'Canberra Airport plans 'dramatic' property expansion in 2011', *Global Airport Cities*, 12 January 2011, www.global airportcities.com/news/industry-news/canberra-airport-plans-dramatic-property-expansion-in-2011 (accessed 28 September 2012).

17 Joe Bates, 'The magnificent seven', *Global Airport Cities,* Spring 2007, pp. 28–9, www.insightgrp.co.uk/images/stories/pdfs/Magazines/ GAC/GAC-2007-01.pdf (accessed 7 March 2011).

18 Lana, 'Finding the X factor', *Global Airport Cities*, Issue 2, 2011, www.globalairportcities.com/page.cfm/Action=library/libID=1/ listID=8/libEntryID=619

19 Chris Le Tourneur, 'Money spinners', *Global Airport Cities*, Spring

2007, p. 14, www.insightgrp.co.uk/images/stories/pdfs/Magazines/ GAC/GAC-2007-01.pdf (accessed 7 March 2011).

20 Weeklytimesnow, 'Shopping hub for Avalon Airport', 30 August 2012, www.weeklytimesnow.com.au/article/2012/08/30/531705_ business-news.html

21 LeTourneur and Fayn, 'Destination retail'.

22 Lucy Siebert, 'Greek Odyssey', *Global Airport Cities*, Summer 2007, p. 18, www.insightgrp.co.uk/images/stories/pdfs/Magazines/GAC/ GAC-2007-02.pdf (accessed 7 March 2011).

23 *Airport World,* 'New €20 million solar park for Athens Airport', 3 October 2011, www.airport-world.com/home/general-news/ item/1041-athens-airport-opens-%E2%80%9A%C3%87%C 2%A820m-solar-park

24 Graham Dunn, 'Changing role for airports, *Flightglobal*, 24 November 2011, www.flightglobal.com/news/articles/ in-focus-changing-role-for-airports-365271/

25 *Times of India*, 'CIAL may invest in wind mill, solar energy sectors', 13 March 2012, http://articles.timesofindia.india times. com/2012-03-13/kochi/31158952_1_solar-energy-cial-md- cochin-international-airport-limited

26 *The Hindu,* 'Solar power project for airport', 23 July 2012, www. thehindu.com/news/cities/Kochi/article3672643.ece

27 Julie Sickel, 'Indianapolis International Airport solar farm awaits final approval', Indystar.com, 20 July 2012, www. indystar.com/article/20120720/BUSINESS/207200351/ Indianapolis-International-Airport-solar-farm-awaits-final-approval

28 *Global Airport Cities,* 'Denver – land use', 2012, www.globalairportcities. com/airports-and-partners/denver-international-airport/denver-land- use (accessed 1 October 2012); Brad McAllister, 'Defining a direction', Aviationpros.com, 15 March 2011, www.aviationpros.com/article/ 10240235/defining-a-direction (accessed 14 December 2011).

29 Richard Vacar, 'Entrepreneurialism takes off in Houston', *Aviation Insight*, HNTB, Winter 2007, p. 11, www.hntb.com/sites/default/ files/issues/AI-1-2007T.pdf (accessed 20 March 2008).

30 Swamplot, 'Bush airport makes hay: $20 a bale', 18 August 2008, http://swamplot.com/bush-airport-makes-hay-20-a-bale/ 2008-08-18/

31 Joelle Briggs, 'How airports make money and what's new in compliance', FAA, 17 April 2012, www.faa.gov/airports/northwest_ mountain/airports_news_events/annual_conference/2012/media/ how_airports_make_money_and_whats_new_in_compliance.pdf

32 Carla Wilson, 'New business park planned next to airport', *Victoria Times*, 20 July 2012, www.timescolonist.com/news/

business+park+planned+next+airport/6964000/story.html
(accessed 13 September 2012).

33 Nicole Nelson, 'A commitment to green for non-aeronautical
revenues', *Airport Improvement Magazine*, September 2012, www.
airportimprovement.com/content/story.php?article=00412

34 Peter Ng'etich, 'Authority's bid to help Eldoret Airport stand on its
own feet', PropertyKenya, 3 April 2007, www.propertykenya.com/
news/463613-authoritys-bid-to-help-eldoret-airport-stand-on-its-
own-feet (accessed 13 May 2009).

35 *Arusha Times*, '"Wonder plant" to be grown around Kilimanjaro
Airport', December 2006, www.arushatimes.co.tz/2006/12/local_
news_8.htm

36 Travis L. DeVault, Jerrold L. Belant, Bradley F. Blackwell, James A.
Martin, Jason A. Schmidt, L. Wes Burger Jr and James W. Patterson
Jr, 'Airports offer unrealized potential for alternative energy production', *Environmental Management*, 14 January 2012, www.aphis.usda.
gov/wildlife_damage/nwrc/publications/12pubs/devault123.pdf

37 Ritesh Gupta, 'Formula for success', *Global Airport Cities*, Autumn
2006, pp. 35–7, http://insightgrp.co.uk/pdfs_web/Magazines/
GAPC/GAC_autumn_06_3.6mb.pdf (accessed 15 February 2008).

38 Newsabahtimes.com, 'MAHB plans 'green makeover' for KLIA',
25 September 2008, www.newsabahtimes.com.my/nstweb/
fullstory/22011; Asiaone, 'KLIA sees green on its radar', 14 July
2008, www.asiaone.com/Travel/News/Story/A1Story20080714-
76585.html

39 Andrew Pentol, 'Malaysia Airports unveils new shopping experience at KLIA', DFNIonline.com, 21 December 2009, www.
dfnionline.com/article/Malaysia-Airports-unveils-new-shopping-
experience-at-KLIA-1859412.html

40 Oliver Clark, 'Environment friendly', *Asia Pacific Airports,* Oct.–Nov.
2009, p. 29, www.insightgrp.co.uk/asia-pacific-airports-2009-04.
html (accessed 19 January 2010).

41 Malaysia Airports, *Annual Report 2008*, p. 21, http://ir.chartnexus.
com/malaysiaairports/doc/ar/ar2008.pdf

42 *Passenger Terminal Today*, 'Kuala Lumpur criticised for government
subsidy', 11 November 2008, www.passengerterminaltoday.com/
news.php?NewsID=9111 (accessed 12 November 2008).

43 Malaysia Airports, *Annual Report 2010*, pp. 41 and 130, http://
ir.chartnexus.com/malaysiaairports/doc/ar/ar2010.pdf

44 Yong Yen Nie, 'MAHB expands KLIA project', *TheEdge*, 8 April
2011, www.theedgemalaysia.com/in-the-financial-daily/184767-
mahb-expands-klia-project.html

45 Robin Stone, 'Anyone for golf?', *Global Airport Cities*, Issue 1, 2008,

pp. 28–30, www.insightgrp.co.uk/images/stories/pdfs/Magazines/
GAC/GAC-2008-01.pdf (accessed 7 March 2011).

46 Kasarda, *The Evolution of Airport Cities and the Aerotropolis*, pp. 16–17.

47 Asian Indigenous and Tribal Peoples Network (AITPN), 'Orang
Asli's Rights: Malaysia's Federal Court faces acid test', 26 June 2006,
www.aitpn.org/Issues/II-03-06-Orang.pdf

48 Thestar.com, 'Orang asli community to get RM6.5mil settlement', 26
May 2010, http://thestar.com.my/news/story.asp?file=/2010/5/26/
nation/20100526103610andsec=nation

49 *Asia Pacific Airports*, 'Durgapur Airport: India's new greenfield
airport planned to open in West Bengal in 2013', December 2008, p.
40, www.insightgrp.co.uk/images/stories/pdfs/Magazines/asia-pac/
APA_2008-03.pdf (accessed 22 February 2011).

50 'Andal aerotropolis: a fact-finding report', trans. Siddhartha Mitra
Sanhati, 4 May 2010, http://sanhati.com/excerpted/2311/

51 Syagnik Bandopadhyay and Icore Ekdin, 'Recent unrest in Andal,
West Bengal: site of aerotropolis', Sanhati, 18 April 2010, http://
sanhati.com/excerpted/2277/

52 Abhijeet Chatterjee, 'Villagers protest airport city plan', *Telegraph*,
4 May 2011, www.telegraphindia.com/1110505/jsp/northeast/
story_13940241.jsp

53 Durgapur Adda, 'Aerotropolis near Durgapur crossed last hurdle', 16
July 2011, http://durgapuradda.com/news-durgapur/aerotropolis-
near-durgapur-crossed-last-hurdle.html

54 Rajesh Sen, 'Work at Andal aerotropolis near Durgapur stalled',
Durgapur Adda, 6 September 2011, http://durgapuradda.com/news
-durgapur/work-at-andal-aerotropolis-near-durgapur-stalled.html

55 *Telegraph*, 'Andal land protest', 31 January 2012, www.telegraphindia.
com/1120201/jsp/nation/story_15077593.jsp

56 *Passenger Terminal Today*, 'Green protests move Sri Lankan
airport', 29 July 2008, www.passengerterminaltoday.com/news.
php?NewsID=7110 (accessed 29 July 2008).

57 Kathryn Report, 'Hambantota Airport fueled by politics', 29
November 2009, www.thekathrynreport.com/2009/11/hambantota-
airport-fueled-by-politics.html (accessed 2 September 2010).

58 Kumudini Hettiarachchi, 'Wildlife in flight!' *Times Online*, 22 August
2010, http://sundaytimes.lk/100822/Plus/plus_01.html

59 *Sunday Observer*, 'Mattala int'l airport to breathe new life for
Hambantota', 6 March 2011, http://lankagazette.com/topstories/
mattala-intl-airport-to-breathe-new-life-for-hambantota/ (accessed
15 June 2011).

60 *Sunday Leader*, 'Mattala ripe for HEC', 17 July 2011, www.the
sundayleader.lk/2011/07/17/mattala-ripe-for-hec/

61 Nirmala Kannangara, 'Mattala Airport expressway disturbs the way of life', *Sunday Leader*, 22 January 2012, www.thesundayleader.lk/2012/01/22/mattala-airport-expressway-disturbs-the-way-of-life/

62 *Lanka Gazette*, 'Hambantota: the catalyst in resurgence', 13 June 2010, http://lankagazette.com/topstories/hambantota-the-catalyst-in-resurgence/ (accessed 23 September 2010).

63 Routesonline, 'Hambantota International – Sri Lanka's second international airport', 3 October 2011, www.routesonline.com/news/36/the-hub/127528/world-routes-2011-hambantota-international-sri-lankas-second-international-airport/

64 Shirajiv Sirimane, 'Mattala int'l airport on track', *Sunday Observer*, 15 January 2012, www.sundayobserver.lk/2012/01/15/fea04.asp

65 Indika Sri Aravinda, 'Free landing at Mahinda's airport', *Sunday Leader*, 25 March 2012, www.thesundayleader.lk/2012/03/25/free-landing-at-mahindas-airport/

66 Kelly Her, 'Gateway to the world', *Taiwan Review*, 5 January 2011, http://taiwanreview.nat.gov.tw/fp.asp?xItem=159403andctNode=1446

67 Loa Iok-sin, 'Ancestors asked to protect land', *Taipei Times*, 12 August 2011, www.taipeitimes.com/News/taiwan/archives/2011/08/12/2003510564

68 Lee I-chia, 'Villagers lodge protest over land expropriation', *Taipei Times*, 8 October 2011, http://www.taipeitimes.com/News/taiwan/archives/2011/10/08/2003515229

69 Her, 'Gateway to the world'.

70 Chan Shun-kuei, 'Aerotropolis could be simply pie in the sky', *Taipei Times,* 26 September 2012, www.taipeitimes.com/News/editorials/archives/2012/09/26/2003543672

71 Denver Airport, Press kit 2012, p. 5, http://business.flydenver.com/info/news/documents/pressKit.pdf (accessed 6 February 2012).

72 Alex Coxon, 'Thinking big', *Global Airport Cities,* Issue 2, Vol. 5, pp. 15–17, www.globalairportcities.com/page.cfm/Action=library/libID=1/listID=8/libEntryID=693

73 Carroll McCormick, 'High life', *Airport World*, 27 April 2012, www.airport-world.com/home/item/1546-high-life

74 Denver Airport, Press kit 2012, p. 18.

75 James Ott, 'For Denver Airport high oil prices cause rejoicing', *Aviation Week*, 2 March 2011, www.aviationweek.com/aw/blogs/commercial_aviation/ThingsWithWings/ (accessed 20 August2011).

76 David Wethe, 'D/FW looks down: airport officials hope drilling for natural gas will pump some extra revenue out of the ground', *Fort Worth Star-Telegram*, 26 December 2005, www.redorbit.com/news/technology/340442/dfw_looks_down_airport_officials_hope_drilling_for_natural_gas/ (accessed 5 January 2012),

77 Dallas/Fort Worth Airport, 'Chesapeake Energy Corporation taps first natural gas well at DFW International Airport', 22 May 2007, www.dfwairport.com/pv_obj_cache/pv_obj_id_F3C98283F69AD7D0C-16FAFEE2D91BB17017B0000/... (accessed 25 October 2010).

78 Wethe, 'D/FW looks down'.

79 Dallas/Fort Worth International Airport Oil and Gas Lease 15 August 2006, www.dallascityhall.com/committee_briefings/briefings0806/20060815_TEC_LeaseDFW.pdf

80 Nicole Nelson, 'Pick n' mix', *Global Airport Cities,* Winter 2007–08, p. 22, www.insightgrp.co.uk/global-airport-cities-2007-03.html (accessed 7 March 2011).

81 Mark Belko, 'County trying to strike gas under its airports', *Pittsburgh Post-Gazette,* 9 September 2008, www.post-gazette.com/pg/08253/910509-52.stm

82 Joe Osborne, 'Shale gas can pollute the air, too', *Pittsburgh Post-Gazette,* 1 November 2010, www.post-gazette.com/pg/10305/1099670-109.stm

83 AskChesapeake.com, 'Airport hopes in Marcellus Shale gain altitude from Chesapeake experience in the Barnett', 20 October 2010, www.askchesapeake.com/Barnett-Shale/Articles/Pages/article.aspx?Filter1Field=IDandFilter1Value=13

84 Joe Bates, 'Energy on tap', *Airport World,* 15 April 2011, www.airport-world.com/home/item/458-energy-on-tap

85 Chemungcounty, 'Airport hosts natural gas conference', 28 October 2010, www.chemungcounty.com/index.asp?pageID=105andnid=597andCatId=2

86 Julie H. Wilson, 'Flying high: airport revenue takes off with natural gas production', Marcellus Airport Conference presentation, 10 October 2010, www.askchesapeake.com/Barnett-Shale/News/Documents/Airport.pdf

87 Jack Z. Smith, 'DFW governments adjust to life after the Barnett Shale boom', *Star-Telegram,* 29 February 2012, www.star-telegram.com/2012/02/28/3770930/dfw-governments-adjust-to-life.html (accessed 17 August 2012).

88 Dan Vergano, 'Texas earthquakes may be linked to wells for gas mining', *USAToday,* 10 March 2010, www.usatoday.com/tech/science/2010-03-11-quakes11_ST_N.htm

89 Chemungcounty, 'Airport hosts natural gas conference'.

90 Ann B. Crook, 'Natural resources and revenue generation: natural gas', Presentation to ACI-NA Environmental Affairs Conference, 27 June 2011, www.aci-na.org/static/conferences/enviro%202011/Monday/Ann%20Crook_27%20JUN%2011%20ACI%20Environmental%20Affairs.pdf

91 Pressconnects.com, 'Lawsuit claims natural gas driller contaminated water in Big Flats', 14 February 2011, www.pressconnects.com/article/20110214/NEWS01/102140345/-1/7daysarchives/Lawsuit-claims-natural-gas-driller-contaminated-water-Big-Flats

92 Ryan Budnick, 'DIA looks at drilling oil wells at airport', Denver Channel, 9 February 2012, www.thedenverchannel.com/news/30420234/detail.html

93 Huffington Post, 'Denver International Airport may increase oil and gas exploration on property', 10 February 2012, www.huffingtonpost.com/2012/02/10/denver-airport-oil-and-gas-wells_n_1268844.html

94 Scott Gilbert, 'Energy companies eye Adams Shale formation may yield oil, gas', *Metronorth News*, 24 March 2011, www.great8newspapers.com/EditorialEExprint.LASSO?-token.editorialcall=219477.114125

95 Josh Fox, *Gasland*, 2010.

96 Nina Berman, 'Meet the families whose lives have been ruined by gas drilling', *Guardian*, 12 April 2011, www.guardian.co.uk/environment/2011/apr/12/families-gas-drilling

97 Johnny Williams, 'Talisman Energy donates housing unit to Bradford County Airport', thedailyyreview.com, 20 April 2012, http://thedailyreview.com/news/talisman-energy-donates-housing-unit-to-bradford-county-airport-1.1302723

98 Bradford Airport, 'Snapshot of the Bradford Regional Airport', www.bradfordairport.net/view/snapshot-of-the-bradford-regional-airport.aspx

99 Andy Sheehan, 'Bids open for airport drilling', CBSPittsburgh, 5 December 2012, http://pittsburgh.cbslocal.com/2012/12/05/bids-open-for-airport-drilling/

100 Tom Fontaine, 'Allegheny County may not receive funds from gas drilling', Pittsburghlive.com, 19 March 2011, www.pittsburghlive.com/x/pittsburghtrib/news/s_728176.html?_s_icmp=NetworkHeadlines (accessed 23 March 2011).

101 Don Hopey, 'Marcellus Shale gas drilling put under microscope', *Pittsburgh Post-Gazette*, 13 June 2010, www.post-gazette.com/pg/10164/1065304-455.stm

102 Rick Steelhammer, 'Yeager Airport may get $70,000 annually in gas drilling deal', *Charleston Gazette*, 30 September 2011, www.airportbusiness.com/web/online/Top-News-Headlines/Yeager-Airport-may-get-70-000-annually-in-gas-drilling-deal/1$47857 (accessed 24 October 2011).

12 How Aviation Keeps Growing

1 Reuters, 'Record number of planes grounded brings percentage of global fleet in storage close to 9/11 peak', 24 February

2009, www.reuters.com/article/pressRelease/idUS178613
+24-Feb-2009+BW20090224

2   BBC News, 'Iata says airlines suffered 'worst year' in 2009', 27
    January 2010, http://news.bbc.co.uk/1/hi/8482654.stm

3   ACI, 'ACI releases World Airport Traffic Report 2010 – strong
    traffic rebound demonstrates industry's resiliency', 1 August
    2011, www.aci.aero/News/Releases/Archives/2011/2011/08/01/
    ACI-releases-World-Airport-Traffic-Report-2010--Strong-traffic-
    rebound-demonstrates-industrys-resiliency

4   ACI, 'ACI Releases its 2011 World Airport Traffic Report: airport
    passenger traffic remains strong as cargo traffic weakens', 27 August
    2012,   www.aci.aero/News/Releases/Most-Recent/2012/08/27/
    ACI-Releases-its-2011-World-Airport-Traffic-Report-Airport-
    Passenger-Traffic-Remains-Strong-as-Cargo-Traffic-Weakens

5   ACI, 'ACI airport economics survey 2010'.

6   ACI, 'ACI airport economics survey 2010', 17 December 2010,
    www.airports.org/cda/aci_common/display/main/aci_content07_
    banners... (accessed 22 February 2011).

7   ACI, 'Announcing the Airport Council International Airport
    Economics Survey 2011', 12 January 2012, www.aci.aero/cda/
    aci_common/display/main/aci_content07_banners.jsp?zn=
    aciandcp=1-7-46^45815_725_2__ (accessed 18 January 2012).

8   Dominic Welling, 'Travel company launches "airport-only" holidays',
    Global Airport Cities, 5 February 2013, www.globalairportcities.
    com/page.cfm/Action=library/libID=1/listID=7/listID=7/
    libEntryID=922

9   IATA, *2012 Annual Review*, p. 6, www.iata.org/about/Documents/
    annual-review-2012.pdf

10 John D. Kasarda, 'Are rising jet fuel prices leading to the end of
    aviation?' 22 December 2010, http://aerotropolisconcepts.blogspot.
    com/

11 CAPA, 'Airline profitability prospects improve but profit
    margins remain anaemic', 18 October 2012, http://centre
    foraviation.com/analysis/airline-profitability-prospects-improve-
    but-profit-margins-remain-anaemic-85722

12 Airbus, *Delivering the Future: Market forecast 2011–2030*, p. 32, www.
    eads.com/dms/eads/int/en/investor-relations/documents/2011/
    Presentations/2011-2030_Airbus_full_book_delivering_the_future.
    pdf

13 IATA, *2012 Annual Review,* p. 6, www.iata.org/about/Documents/
    annual-review-2012.pdf

14 IATA, *2011 Annual Review*, p. 8, www.iata.org/pressroom/
    Documents/annual-report-2011.pdf

15 Shweta Jain, 'Emirates saves $1bn by hedging fuel costs', 24 January 2008, www.emirates247.com/eb247/companies-markets/emirates-saves-1bn-by-hedging-fuel-costs-2008-01-24-1.217333

16 Msnbc, 'Airlines hedge against soaring fuel costs', 30 June 2008, www.msnbc.msn.com/id/25419436/ns/business-us_business/t/airlines-hedge-against-soaring-fuel-costs/

17 Martin Rivers, 'Should airlines hedge their bets on fuel?', *Flightglobal*, 25 July 2012, www.flightglobal.com/news/articles/analysis-should-airlines-hedge-their-bets-on-fuel-374733/

18 IATA, *2012 Annual Review*, p. 11.

19 Lianna Brinded, 'Airlines hedge less than half of fuel costs against price rises', *International Business Times*, 8 May 2012, www.ibtimes.co.uk/articles/338386/20120508/airlines-aviation-mercatus-energy-risk-management-hedging.htm

20 Boeing, 'Current market outlook 2012–2031', 2012, www.boeing.com/commercial/cmo/pdf/Boeing_Current_Market_Outlook_2012.pdf; Airbus, *Navigating the Future: Global market forecast 2012–2031*, 2012, www.airbus.com/company/market/forecast/?eID=dam_frontend_pushanddocID=25773

21 Dr Christian N. Jardine, *Calculating the Environmental Impact of Aviation Emissions,* Environmental Change Institute, June 2005, www.climatecare.org/media/documents/pdf/aviation_emissions__offsets.pdf

22 Airbus, *Navigating the Future,* p. 19.

23 Jay Menon, 'India's commercial air transport sector beset by myriad problems', *Aviation Daily*, 18 February 2013, www.aviationweek.com/Article.aspx?id=/article-xml/avd_02_18_2013_p04-01-545015.xml

24 Tao Wang, 'Why China doesn't need more airports', *Guardian*, 3 April 2013, www.guardian.co.uk/environment/2013/apr/03/china-air-transport (accessed 5 May 2013).

25 Hans-Martin Niemeier, *Expanding Airport Capacity under Constraints in Large Urban Areas: The German experience,* International Transport Forum/OECD, 2013, p. 11, www.internationaltransportforum.org/jtrc/DiscussionPapers/DP201304.pdf

26 HACAN, 'Short-haul flights: still clogging up Heathrow's runways', April 2013, www.hacan.org.uk/resources/reports/short.haul.flights.still.clogging.up.heathrows.runways.pdf (accessed 3 May 2013).

27 Airport Watch, www.airportwatch.org.uk/; Aviation Justice, http://aviationjustice.org/

28 Plane Stupid, www.planestupid.com

29 John Stewart, 'A sea of protest across Europe', HACAN, October 2012, www.hacan.org.uk/resources/reports/a.sea.of.protest.across.europe.pdf

Index